WRITING A SUCCESSFUL
TV SERIES

WRITING A SUCCESSFUL TV SERIES
How to Pitch and Develop Projects for Television and Online Streaming
With the Story-Type Method® Volume 3
By Emmanuel Oberg

Copyright © 2023 by Emmanuel Oberg. All rights reserved.
No part of this publication may be reproduced or stored in a retrieval system, distributed or transmitted in any form or by any means electronic, mechanical, audio, visual or otherwise without prior written permission of the copyright owner, except in the case of brief quotations embodied in critical reviews and certain other non-commercial uses permitted by copyright law. Nor can it be circulated in any form of binding or cover other than that in which it is published and without similar conditions including this condition being imposed on the subsequent purchaser.

Screenplay Unlimited, The Story-Type Method and The Structurator are registered trademarks of Screenplay Unlimited Ltd.

ISBN: 978-0-9954981-8-1 (e-book), 978-0-9954981-9-8 (paperback), 978-1-7394647-0-7 (hardcover with colour interior), 978-1-7394647-1-4 (hardcover with B&W interior)

By the same author in the Story-Type Method Series
Volume 1: *Screenwriting Unchained*
Volume 2: *The Screenwriter's Troubleshooter*

See **If You Want to Find Out More...** at the end of this book to **access free content and receive a discount on our interactive online courses**

The Story-Type Method® Series Editor: Naomi Telford
Author photo by Barbara Leatham Photography — Cover by JD Smith Design

Writing a Successful TV Series by Emmanuel Oberg – 1st ed.
Published in Great Britain in 2023 by

10, Orange Street, Haymarket, London WC2H 7DQ United Kingdom
Read more at www.screenplayunlimited.com

Emmanuel Oberg

WRITING A SUCCESSFUL TV SERIES

How to Pitch and Develop Projects For Television and Online Streaming

With **The STORY-TYPE METHOD**®

Contents

Introduction   11

How to Make the Most of This Book   15
A Quick Overview: The Three Dimensions of Screenwriting   18
   Story Format: The Visible Side of the Story Iceberg   19
   Story Structure: The Underlying Design   20
   Managing Information   21
   Understanding Story-Types   21
   The Dramatic 3-Act Structure   22
   The Three Dimensions of Screenwriting   27
   Feature Film Example: *Tootsie*   31
   TV Series Example: *Breaking Bad*   32
   A New Approach to Story Structure   34
   The Story-Type Method   37
   How to Develop Stronger Screenplays   41
   Reminder   42

1 Trends, Series Types and Conventional Series Design   43
   First Up   43
   1.1 Trends   44
      Commercials Don't Rule Content Anymore
      (and Thoughts on Series for Streaming)   44
      Fewer Episodes per Season and Higher Budget   46
      More Originality and Diversity   47
      Faster Pace   47
      Shorter Episodes   48
      More Non-English Language Series   48
      New Players   49
   1.2 Series Types   51
      Format   51
      Procedural (or Closed-Ended Series)   52
      Serial (or Open-Ended Series)   54
      Serial-Procedural Hybrid   55

Sitcom	56
Mini-Series (or Limited Series)	57
Anthology Series	58
Mini-Series Series (or Anthological Limited Series)	58
Web Series	59
Film Franchise	60
1.3 Conventional Series Design	61
When Commercial Breaks Dictate Story Format	62
Storylines: Where Format Meets Structure	69
Story Design 1: Defining the Storylines	70
Story Design 2: Breaking Each Storyline	71
Story Design 3: Story Weaving a One-Hour Episode	76
Let's Be More Dramatic	79
Cliffhangers	84
Teaser, Recap and Coming Next	87
Worst Point	88
What Lies Beneath	88
1.4 Hands-On: What's Your Type? (Part 1)	90
2 Underlying Series Design	**93**
First Up	93
2.1 Underlying Story Structure	94
Story Structure in Series	95
Fractal Aspect of Story Structure in Series	98
2.2 How to Identify Your Story-Type in Series	99
2.3 Use of Maslow in Series	104
Target Audience	106
Story-Type	109
Genre	113
2.4 Managing Information in Series	116
Surprise, Mystery, Dramatic Irony, Suspense	117
Using Dramatic Irony to Generate Suspense or Comedy	118
Using Surprise to Raise the Stakes or Generate Comedy	119
Using Mystery to Raise Tantalising Questions	119
Making Sure That Mystery Doesn't Kill Suspense or Prevent Identification	119
Using Managing Information to Create Cliffhangers	123
Examples	125
Stranger Things	126
Friends	129

2.5 Case Study: *Stranger Things*	131
Format, Series Type, Story Type, Genre and M-Factor	132
Season Design	133
Defining the Storylines in *Stranger Things*	136
Breaking the Storylines in *Stranger Things*	138
Identifying the Dramatic Design of Each Storyline	138
Breaking Down Each Storyline Into Dramatic Sequences	142
Dramatic 3-Act Structure in Joyce's Storyline	142
Breaking Down Dramatic Act 2 in Joyce's Storyline	144
Overall Notes	146
Story Weaving in *Stranger Things*	149
Identifying the Main Storylines at Episode Level	149
Managing Focus	150
Checking Causality	151
Handling Dramatic Sequences	151
Teasing with Cliffhangers	153
Developing Relationships	153
Final Thoughts	154
2.6 Hands-On: What's Your Type? (Part 2)	155
3 Project Development	**157**
First Up	157
3.1 Creating an Irresistible Bible	160
Overarching Questions and Aims	161
Pilot Commission or Straight to Series Bible?	162
Have You Nailed Your Format?	162
Are You Thinking Global From the Get-Go?	164
Is Your Story Engine Firing on All Cylinders?	165
From Cerebral to Emotional: Where Do You Set the Dial?	166
Are You Striking the Right Balance Between Mystery and Suspense?	167
Examples	169
From Procedural to Serial: How Much Mythology in Your Series?	170
Characters in Series: How Are They Different?	171
Are You Overplanning or Boxing Yourself In?	173
Series Design	175
Franchise, Series Type and Story-Type	175
Set-Up and Story World	178

World Building	180
Genre	181
Concept	182
Maslow	183
Theme	183
Character Design	184
Plot	185
Bible Components	187
Series Title	188
Series Logline	189
Series Overview (or One-Sheet)	189
Character Breakdowns	190
Story World	191
Pilot Story	191
Arc of the First Season (and Possibly More)	192
Arc of the Series	193
Tone, Genre and Style	193
Episode Loglines or Synopses	194
Package	194
Pitch Deck	195
3.2 Writing a Compelling Pilot / First Episode	196
Goals for the Pilot	197
Premise or Midstream Pilot?	200
The Premise	201
Pilot Components	202
Opening Image	203
Teaser or 3-Minute Hook	204
10-Minute Hook	205
Complications	206
End-of-Episode Hook	207
3.3 Case Study: *Killing Eve*	208
3.4 Hands-On: Pilot Checklist	212
Conclusion and Next Steps	**215**
Story-Type Method Glossary	**219**
Recommended Reading and Watching	**259**
If You Want to Find Out More...	**261**

"Welcome to the real world. It sucks. You're gonna love it."
—Monica Geller, *Friends*

Introduction

I love TV series. Like novels, they allow storytellers to explore more complex storylines and characters yet, like feature films, they rely on visual storytelling.

TV development also tends to give more creative control to writers and producers than directors, which from a writer's point of view is quite an attractive proposition.

For many, series have become a medium just as exciting as feature films. Today, the stigma sometimes attached to TV — many used to look down on television or streaming compared to cinema — has gone and countless A-List writers, directors and actors previously associated only with feature films have successfully embraced a TV series career.

The border between television and cinema is much more porous than it was a few decades ago, when you had to choose one or the other early on and that initial choice often defined the rest of your career.

TV and especially streaming have become a coveted medium, and there has never been a better time to break into the business. Although the streamers' spending spree of the early 2020s is definitely over, everyone is still looking for good stories.

However, series are technically and creatively more challenging to develop than feature films, so whether you come from a film background or not, it's essential to master some aspects of storytelling and script development specific to this medium in order to break into the series business successfully.

I have over twenty-five years of experience in the Film and TV script development process, having been involved as a screenwriter, development exec, story editor and creative consultant, working with major studios and broadcasters (Warner Bros, Working Title, Universal, Film4, StudioCanal) as well as independent producers. Over the last five years, I've designed a popular online course and live workshop on series development that complements this book.

Writing a Successful TV Series is not a theoretical essay for academics or critics but a practical guide for Film and TV creatives. Its main purpose is to resolve one problem and answer one question: How to get a TV series project picked up and made and how to reach a wide audience *without* limiting creative freedom.

It was written to help you identify design issues in your series and address them as early as possible in the development process. It should also help you find the best way to present and sell your concepts, increase the chances of getting your projects made and reach a wide audience at home and abroad, whether they're written in the English language or not.

It's intended for anyone involved creatively in developing TV series projects, including writers, directors, producers, story editors, creators, showrunners — regardless of their experience level. The more experienced, the more you should get out of this book. It should also be a perfect match for experienced film creatives wanting to branch out into TV series, or for experienced TV creatives who wish to look at their craft from a new perspective and possibly add a few instruments to their toolbox.

In this book, we'll dive into how successful series are *designed*, which is entirely different from the way they are superficially *formatted* (and I'm not talking about script format here but story format).

Nearly every book about series writing insists on shaping an episode using some variation of an artificial format in two, three, four or five logistical acts, with or without a teaser, and claims that this format is needed to "structure" an episode. However, none of them explain how series are actually designed underneath (at series, season and episode level), which is a key factor to their success.

Understanding the crucial difference between the *dramatic design* of series, seasons, storylines, episodes or scenes and the *logistical format* used by most in the industry to describe series episode "structure" will transform your approach to TV series development, irrespective of your level of experience.

It will give you more creative freedom because you'll be liberated from unnecessary constraints, yet you'll also be able to create stronger concepts and design better series, while still delivering the requested format for each show.

We'll also discuss how different types of series or series types (procedural, serial, sitcom, limited, anthology etc.) require different design approaches, and how choosing the right type of story or story-type (plot-led, character-led, theme-led or exception) at series, season and episode level can make or break your project.

Choosing the wrong combination of series type and story-type is the root cause of many series failures, whether at concept stage, during the first season or afterwards. Quite a few series run out of steam because their creator didn't realise that, by choosing a given story-type for the first season, they had boxed themselves in, preventing a viable season two, even when the first season has been a major success.

We'll discuss how managing information — dramatic irony, surprise, mystery, suspense — adds an essential dimension to series writing. Mastering this third dimension of screenwriting — the first two being managing conflict and character evolution — is going to dramatically increase the quality of your series design as well as their ability to attract and retain their intended audience, globally.

We'll explore the way in which Maslow's Hierarchy of Needs is running the show and how we can use it to understand how non-English language series such as *Squid Game*, *Occupied* or *Money Heist* (*La Casa de Papel*) became global hits.

Overall, we'll detail the flexible yet powerful tools and techniques needed to conquer this popular medium, focusing particularly on **getting your series commissioned**. We'll discuss the most efficient strategies for pitching your series, creating an irresistible bible / pitch deck, a compelling pilot, unforgettable characters and addictive storylines, all essential aspects of project development. We'll look at case studies for successful pilots / first episodes such as *Stranger Things* and *Killing Eve*, while drawing examples from many more hit shows.

Finally, if you'd like to go further in **applying these concepts to your projects at season level**, you'll have the opportunity to join a companion course and descend even deeper into extensive case studies. We'll look into detailed scene breakdowns, strands maps and storylines at episode and season level to study the actual design of successful series such as *Stranger Things*, *Sex Education*, *Big Little Lies* and *Occupied*, as well as exceptions such as *Happy Valley*, *Fleabag* and *Mr Robot*.

No other book or online course offers such a detailed analysis of so many different shows, and how they are designed at series, season, storyline and episode level. This in-depth reverse-engineering will reveal how successful series are actually designed by masters of this medium, so that you can design your own and, hopefully, reach similar success.

Right, let's dive into it, starting with how to make the most of this book.

How to Make the Most of This Book

Although you can absolutely read this book and get a lot out of it without any preparation, a significant part of *Writing a Successful TV Series* explores how we can apply the Story-Type Method to series writing specifically.

Preparation

Option 1 (for perfectionists): If you aren't familiar with this new approach to screenwriting, I invite you to read the first volume in the series, Screenwriting Unchained or take the Advanced Script Development online course (www.screenplayunlimited.com/online-courses/) *before* going through this book, to familiarise yourself with the advanced tools and techniques that can be used with any kind of screenwriting, including series.

This is how the *Story-Type Method* series of books is designed: Any volume can be read independently, but they all build on the concepts, tools and techniques detailed in the first volume / main online course, which introduces the method itself and explores the toolbox.

Option 2 (for those short on time or money): I understand that you might not want to splurge on another volume or invest in an online course when you've just purchased this book, so if you're willing to compromise a little, you'll find a link to download a free sampler of *Screenwriting Unchained* (first seventy pages) at the end of this book in If You Want to Find Out More... The sampler includes the introduction and the first chapter, providing an overview of the method up to and including the section on Maslow, with many info-graphs and examples. You'll also find an extra 10% discount off the *Advanced Development* online course, should you decide to go that route after reading the sampler.

Option 3 (for those in a hurry): Finally, for those who don't have the time to read the free sampler, I've included in this book a twenty-page introduction to the method, written from a slightly different perspective. This crash-course comes from a free online presentation called *The Three Dimensions of Screenwriting* that you can also watch (with animated info-graphs) at www.screenplayunlimited.com/3d-of-screenwriting/registration or explore as a mini-course at www.screenplayunlimited.com/courses/the-three-dimensions-of-screenwriting/.

You'll find this quick overview just after this section — it should be a great help to anyone new to the method. However, if you find it too intense, please consider one of the other two options for preparation, as I have a lot more time there to introduce concepts and develop them. If you're already familiar with my approach, feel free to skip this overview and go directly to the first chapter.

Reference Tools

Although I'll define some of the concepts detailed in *Screenwriting Unchained* in this book, I'll inevitably use terms that you might not be familiar with if you haven't read the first volume.

To overcome this hurdle, besides the inclusion of the Three Dimensions of Screenwriting section at the beginning, I've added a Story-Type Method Glossary at the end of this book, with definitions of the most important concepts, as well as references to chapters where they are discussed in more detail, both in this book and in other volumes.

Case Studies

I suggest you watch the first season — or at least the first episode — of *Stranger Things* and *Killing Eve*, as we'll use them for our main case studies at the end of chapters 2 and 3.

The companion online course includes further case studies. I'm able to go into more detail in these as, compared to the written page, videos are a more effective way to go through colour-coded storylines, episodes and strands maps.

If you haven't done so already, I also recommend that you watch the first season of *Sex Education*, *Big Little Lies* and *Occupied* (the other main case studies in the companion course) as I draw many examples from these series in this book.

I'll occasionally refer to these detailed case studies and to the companion course to remind you that this resource is available to further your understanding and provide additional help with the development of your projects.

Please look at the <u>If You Want to Find Out More...</u> section at the end of this book for more information on how to access free content and how to receive an additional discount for the online courses, including the TV Series add-on.

Right. Enough preamble. Time to begin our TV series journey!

A Quick Overview: The Three Dimensions of Screenwriting

As explained in the previous section, feel free to skip this quick overview and go directly to Chapter 1 (Trends, Series Type and Conventional Series Format) if you're already familiar with the *Story-Type Method* **and don't feel the need for a refresher.**

Before I start to explain what I call the three dimensions of screenwriting, I'd like to clarify how this approach is radically different from anything you already know about screenwriting and script development and why understanding this difference is key to getting unstuck and becoming more successful.

So, let's start with a simple question. What if screenwriting was like an iceberg and great storytellers were masters of story structure — the submerged, invisible side — but most screenwriting gurus were only talking about the visible part: the theories, formulas, the paradigms often used to discuss screenwriting?

Ever since Syd Field started talking about a 3-Act structure a few decades ago, newer approaches have tried to go beyond this simplistic approach by adding more acts or steps, becoming even more prescriptive, instead of looking at what was wrong in the approach itself, which is the fact that it's logistical — based on pages or minutes — rather than dramatic.

Three, four, five acts, eight sequences, fifteen beats, twenty-two steps... You name it. The visible part is about story *format*. It tells you how to cut your story into smaller, more manageable parts in a prescriptive way, which only leads to more predictable stories. It's not about story *structure*.

Making this crucial distinction is the first step towards resolving your script development problems. So let's dig deeper and explain **the difference between story structure and story format:**

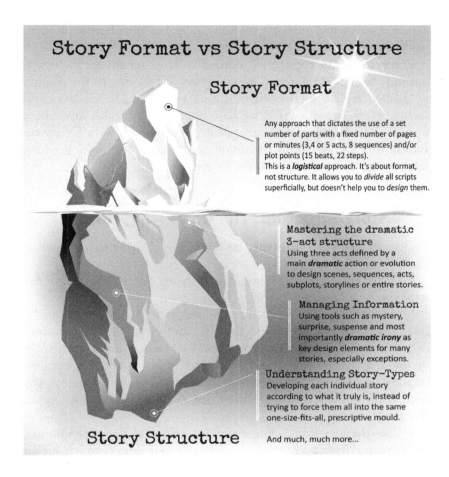

Story Format: The Visible Side of the Story Iceberg

Let's start with **story format**, the visible side of the story iceberg.

"Story format" is the term we'll use to describe any superficial approach that dictates the use of a set number of parts with a fixed number of pages or minutes — so again, it could be 3, 4, 5 acts, 8 sequences and/or plot points, such as 15 beats, 22 steps, and so on.

This is what I call a logistical approach. It's about format, not structure. It allows you to *divide* all scripts superficially, but it doesn't help you to *design* the story from a structural point of view. This approach is rooted in the past and really has no place in modern storytelling.

For example, in theatre, we needed to have act breaks to replace burning candles regularly, so we had plays in five acts. In the cinema, we had to replace reels of films during projection, so we had eight sequences. In broadcast TV, we have commercial breaks, so we have four or five acts for a one-hour episode, or seven acts for a TV movie. But all this is gone. With streaming, for example, we no longer have commercial breaks (except on the lowest tiers).

Story Structure: The Underlying Design

So, let's look at **story structure** now, which is the part that almost no one talks about.

Weirdly enough, what's going to help us go beyond the 3-Act structure *is* the 3-Act structure.

I'm talking about mastering the *dramatic* 3-Act structure. So instead of a vague beginning, middle, and end, we will use three dramatic acts to design our story: before, during, and after a main dramatic action or evolution. This approach is very flexible because, unlike logistical acts, dramatic acts can be as short or as long as you need them to be, for each specific story. We'll expand on this crucial difference shortly.

Unlike the logistical 3-Act structure, defined in pages or minutes, the dramatic 3-Act structure also has a fractal aspect, which means that you can use it to design not only the whole story, but also its parts: scenes, sequences, acts, subplots, storylines, episodes and seasons.

And so, mastering the dramatic 3-Act structure is simply going to revolutionise your approach to script development because suddenly you have a tool that you can use to develop any dramatic story, from a simple scene to a ten-season serial with fifteen different storylines.

It will not only help you to clarify the way you design any story, it will also help you to improve your scene writing, to write and design action sequences, or to deal with complex, multi-stranded and non-linear storytelling often found in TV series. More on this to come.

Managing Information

Another crucial part of story structure is **managing information**: Using tools such as mystery, surprise, suspense, and most importantly, dramatic irony as key design elements for many stories, especially exceptions.

We're going to talk more about managing information soon, but let me just define these terms quickly. **Mystery** is when you give enough information to the audience for them to become aware that there is something they don't know; **surprise** is when you suddenly reveal information that they didn't expect; **suspense** can only happen when the audience is aware of a danger, whether it's physical or psychological; and **dramatic irony** is when you give information to the audience, but keep that information from at least one character (the "victim" of the dramatic irony).

As you can see, all these tools have one thing in common: They are about how much or how little the audience knows in the story.

Mastering *managing information* is crucial because it will help you not only to create more subtle, more complex and more emotionally powerful stories, it will also help you to handle most exceptions — stories that don't fit into any of the main story-types, which leads us to the next point.

Understanding Story-Types

Finally, **understanding story-types** is another essential aspect of story structure: designing each individual story according to its true nature, instead of trying to force all stories into the same one-size-fits-all, prescriptive mould.

Very briefly, I've identified three main types of story, or story-types: **plot-led**, when the protagonist struggles primarily with an external problem (antagonistic characters or nature); **character-led**, when the protagonist fights primarily an internal problem and needs to change; and **theme-led**, when the main problem in the story lies in society.

This is crucial because depending on its type, you're going to design and write your story differently. Identify the right story-type for your project — or how to best handle it as a hybrid or an exception — and its dramatic engine will fire on all cylinders. Fail to identify your story-type — or how it works as a hybrid or exception — and your story engine will break.

These key aspects of story structure — mastering the dramatic 3-Act structure, managing information, understanding story-types — are part of what's going to help you make the difference between story format and story structure. We'll talk about these briefly in this overview, but for a full explanation, please look at the first and second options for preparation in How to Make the Most of This Book.

So, what does this mean for screenplay development? The reason scripts get stuck is often because those involved in the development process use tools that only tackle the visible part: **story format**. To improve the underlying design, to get stronger screenplays, we have to use structural tools. We have to master the invisible part: **story structure**.

This is what's going to help you get to a draft that's not just different, but stronger.

The Dramatic 3-Act Structure

As we said, one of the key parts of story structure is the **dramatic 3-Act structure**, so let's take a bit more time to explore what it is and how it can help you design your story.

As soon as the audience understands "Who wants what and why?" in a story, a sequence or a scene, we define what we call a main dramatic action, and we can use that to divide the story, the sequence or the scene in three dramatic acts.

Dramatic Acts vs *Logistical* Acts

The *Dramatic* 3-Act Structure

The *Logistical* 3-Act Structure

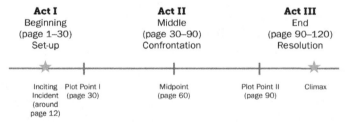

Copyright © Emmanuel Oberg. All Rights Reserved

The first dramatic act is everything that happens before the dramatic action, before we understand who the protagonist is, what they want, what their motivation is and what stands in their way. It's usually fairly short — say five to fifteen minutes in a feature film or a one-hour episode — but it has no set length.

Dramatic Act 2 shows the main dramatic action itself, so the protagonist trying to reach a conscious goal and facing obstacles.

And **dramatic Act 3** shows the consequences of this dramatic action, after we give an answer to what we call the dramatic question, the question that sustains the interest of the audience over most of the story: Will the protagonist reach their goal? Will they get what they want? Once you answer that question, the audience loses interest, so dramatic Act 3 tends to be very short, often just a few minutes in a feature film.

So we have three dramatic acts in a classically structured story because we have before, during, and after the main dramatic action. Nothing to do with page numbers or minutes and everything to do with how the audience understands and experiences the story.

This flexible approach leads you to focus on what matters from a *story design* point of view, on what allows the audience to get emotionally involved rather than on simply ticking boxes to force every story into a logistical format defined by a rigid formula.

What we've called character-led stories are a bit more complex than this, but they follow the same pattern. If what's primarily at stake in the story is defined by what the character *needs* rather than what the character *wants*, we also have three dramatic acts: before, during, and after a main dramatic *evolution*.

In this case, the protagonist is primarily facing an internal obstacle and is unaware of the goal they need to reach. The dramatic question becomes whether they'll find a way to change, to move on or to resolve their internal problem.

So, what does all of this allow you to achieve? Well, once you understand how the dramatic 3-Act structure works, you can apply it to everything.

If you want to, you can use it to design the whole story, irrespective of the number of logistical acts, whether it's three, four, five, or seven acts. For example, a Shakespeare play in five logistical acts, such as *Hamlet*, is designed in three dramatic acts. A one-hour TV episode, formatted in four or five logistical acts, is usually designed in three dramatic acts as well, especially if it's a procedural.

But does this mean you end up with a vast, shapeless second act? Not at all, because as we'll see in the next info-graph, the beauty of the dramatic 3-Act structure is that you can also use it to design parts of the story: dramatic acts, sequences, scenes, storylines, and subplots. This is what we call the fractal aspect of the dramatic 3-Act structure.

The *Fractal* Aspect of Structure

The *Dramatic* 3-Act Structure

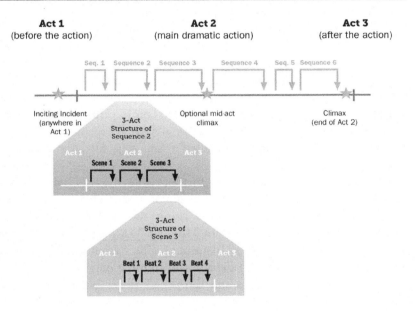

As you can see in this info-graph, you can use the fractal aspect of the dramatic 3-Act structure to divide a dramatic Act 2 that takes up most of a classically designed feature film or series episode into **dramatic sequences** (six in this example, but it could be fewer or more).

Each of these dramatic sequences — as shown for Sequence 2 above — can be designed in three dramatic acts, like a mini-movie. Usually, each dramatic sequence explores a subgoal: a different but connected way for the protagonist to try to reach their goal.

Most scenes in a sequence can also be designed in three dramatic acts, with a clear protagonist and goal at scene level, as illustrated with Scene 3 of Sequence 2 in this info-graph.

You can also use this fractal aspect of the dramatic 3-Act structure to design meta stories such as a film franchise, or seasons, storylines and even an entire TV series. For example, the whole of the original *Bourne* trilogy is designed in three dramatic acts, with a main dramatic question over Bourne's past and his ability to remember it. The five seasons of *Breaking Bad* are also designed in three dramatic acts, shaped around Walter White's evolution.

This aspect of the dramatic 3-Act structure is especially useful if you're developing exceptions, multi-stranded narratives or TV series because you can apply it at any story level.

If you take only one thing out of this quick overview, make it this: Mistaking story format for story structure is the root of the vast majority of story design problems. Understanding this can be a game changer in the way you handle script development. Mastering the dramatic 3-Act structure constitutes a key step towards achieving this.

Unfortunately, we can't dive further into the dramatic 3-Act structure and the difference between *dramatic* acts and *logistical* acts, but if you'd like to find out more about this and register for the online presentation mentioned in How to Make the Most of This Book, you'll get access to a 14-minute video from the Advanced Development course where I explain this in more detail.

Of course, story structure and screenplay development aren't just about the dramatic 3-Act structure, which is only one essential aspect of it.

So let's look at managing information now, the second key aspect of story structure in the "story iceberg". A good way to visualise this is through what I call **the three dimensions of screenwriting**.

The first two dimensions are directly connected to the dramatic 3-Act structure and to a main dramatic action or evolution, but the third dimension adds an essential layer that is almost never taught or discussed, yet can make or break your story.

The Three Dimensions of Screenwriting

For me, when you design a story, everything starts with character. Let's keep it simple for now and put aside multi-stranded narratives or TV series with many storylines and different protagonists. Let's say that we're talking about a single protagonist in a feature film or a TV movie.

Your **character** is the centre of your story, and if we don't care about your character, you don't have a story. We don't need to like them *conceptually*, as in sympathy — liking who they are and rooting for what they're trying to achieve — but we need to feel for them, as in empathy: understanding their conflicts, desires, and motivation so we can identify with them *emotionally*.

This involves everything that is static about the character, including their backstory, what happens before the story starts. But this is just **a point** in the following diagram, no dimension yet:

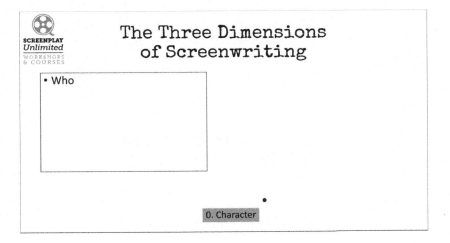

The first dimension, as shown in the next diagram, comes when you define a main dramatic *action*. A conscious want or goal for the protagonist. For example, if the story is plot-led, if the protagonist fights primarily an antagonist character or antagonistic forces — so if the main problem is located outside of the protagonist — the conscious want of the protagonist and what stands in the way often defines the plot. So you've defined a **line of action**. That's the first dimension of screenwriting:

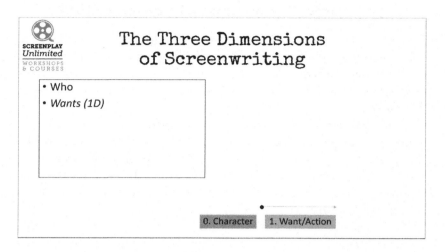

The second dimension, as shown in the next diagram, comes when you add a main dramatic *evolution*. If the story is character-led, if the protagonist fights primarily against themselves, if the main problem is located inside the protagonist, then their unconscious need to change — and how they themselves get in the way — is what defines the backbone of the story. Let's add this **line of evolution** to our diagram:

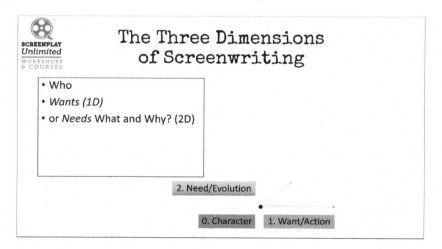

Note that this dramatic evolution could also be a need for the protagonist of a plot-led story to *grow* (to become stronger in order to reach their goal), rather than to *change* (if there is no need to change because there is nothing wrong in them / the main problem is external). So it could be the character-led element in a plot-led story, which means that this second dimension is present in most modern stories, whether they are plot-led or character-led.

So first you create the character, the story is a point. Then with the first dimension, you give them purpose with a clear dramatic action and the story becomes a line. With the second dimension, with a dramatic evolution, the character gets depth, and all of this is what I call **managing conflict**, based around "Who *wants* or *needs* what and why?":

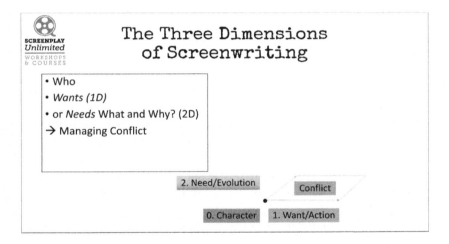

However, as we can see in the diagram above, the story remains two-dimensional: it's flat, it's a plane. There is still a missing dimension, which is related to the audience and how they experience the story as it unfolds.

The third dimension — by far the least discussed yet often the most important — is what I call **managing information**, based around "Who knows what when?" and the tools that can be used to handle this (mystery, surprise, dramatic irony, suspense). When we add managing information to the diagram, you can see that the story becomes **three-dimensional**:

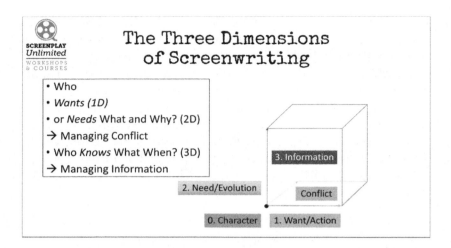

The story isn't flat anymore because although the audience is still following the same dramatic action or evolution, you're now playing with the audience's point of view as well: How much do they know as the story unfolds? Do they know less than some of the characters? Do they know more? Where does everyone stand on the vertical dimension (what we'll call the information ladder): audience, protagonist, antagonist, other characters, writer(s)? This is a whole new layer of storytelling that has a huge impact on the audience's emotional involvement and their ability to identify with the protagonist.

This third dimension — managing information — is the blind spot of most screenwriting theories because they focus on story *format*, which is how to cut any story into more manageable chunks of pages or minutes, and not story *structure*, which is how to design a moving, entertaining and meaningful story irrespective of its superficial format.

This is another key element of story design that complements the dramatic 3-Act structure. Mastering it constitutes a crucial step towards getting stronger screenplays.

Let's see how it works with a couple of examples. I've chosen well-known but fairly old titles to minimise the chances of spoilers.

Feature Film Example: *Tootsie*

First, let's look at a classic feature film, *Tootsie*.

We'll start with the **character**. Michael Dorsey, the protagonist, is a talented but unemployable actor. No one wants to hire him because he's too difficult to work with. That's just a point. No dimension yet.

The first dimension comes when you define the main dramatic action, a conscious want or goal for the protagonist. In *Tootsie*, Michael wants to make enough money — $8,000 — to produce a play for him to star in. And taking a female role in a sitcom is just a subgoal, a way for him to reach this main goal.

Funnily enough, no one remembers that part of the film because no one really cares about it. It's not what's at stake in the story. It's only what launches the story, what creates the main situation, and gives an initial dramatic drive to the story by defining "Who wants what and why?"

The second dimension comes when you add a main dramatic evolution, when you give the protagonist an unconscious need to change. In *Tootsie*, Michael needs to change because he doesn't understand women or what it means to be a woman. He's an incomplete human being and in order to find love, he needs to change. This gives him depth and makes him a more interesting character.

Now we know "Who needs what and why?", but the story is still flat. We have a three-dimensional character in a two-dimensional story. We've defined how to manage conflict in the story, but the storytelling remains flat.

The third dimension comes with the way you manage information and how you decide "Who knows what and when?" in the story. In *Tootsie*, there isn't much mystery, there are a few surprises, but the whole story is designed around a main dramatic irony: We know that Michael Dorsey is a man pretending to be a woman but most characters in the film don't.

This is what generates most of the conflict, most of the humour, most of the tension and most of the gags in the story. This main dramatic irony is what makes *Tootsie* a high-concept comedy and gives a third dimension to the story.

If you don't understand the importance of managing information in story structure, if you don't master the third dimension of screenwriting, learn how it works and how to use it in your projects, well, you have no way to understand the structure of *Tootsie*, which has nothing to do with the number of acts, sequences, beats, or steps. More importantly, you have no way to design a successful exception, which is what *Tootsie* is.

TV Series Example: *Breaking Bad*

Let's take a more recent example in a TV series this time and look at the five seasons of *Breaking Bad*, starting with the **character**.

Walter White, the protagonist, is a chemistry teacher who has to work two jobs to make ends meet. That's just a point, no dimensions yet.

The first dimension comes when you define the main dramatic action: a conscious want or goal for the protagonist. In *Breaking Bad*, the story starts with an intense teaser flashback that in fact buys the writer some time to introduce the protagonist, because the story needs a longer than usual set-up in the first episode.

However, fairly quickly, Walter White finds out that he has late-stage lung cancer. His goal is now to find a way to pay for his medical bills and provide financial security for his family before he dies, because his wife is expecting a baby and they're raising a disabled teenage son. So we've defined "Who wants what and why?"

The second dimension comes when you add a main dramatic evolution, giving the protagonist an unconscious need to change. In *Breaking Bad*, we quickly realise that Walter White is deluded. He's convinced that he's becoming a criminal to help his family, but in reality, he's doing it for himself, to heal his bruised ego.

His pride is what leads him to refuse an offer to pay for his medical bills from his former business partners early on. Instead, he starts to cook meth with a former student. Later, his pride also leads him to tell Hank — his brother-in-law and a DEA agent — that he hasn't found the real mastermind, leading to the investigation being reopened when Walter could have got away with it, had he said nothing.

Walter White believes that he's protecting his family, but he's in fact destroying it. And although there are strong antagonists in the story, in many ways, he's his own nemesis. He needs to realise this.

He will come to this realisation towards the end of the series, bringing a tragic but satisfying ending to his dramatic evolution, which shows his fascinating transformation from Mr. Chips to Scarface.

This second dimension gives him depth and makes him a more interesting character. And now we know "Who needs what and why?" but the story is still flat: We have a three-dimensional character in a two-dimensional story.

The third dimension comes with the way you manage information and how you decide "Who knows what when?" in the story.

In *Breaking Bad*, there isn't much mystery, there are quite a few surprises, but the whole story over the five seasons is designed around a main dramatic irony: We know that Walter White isn't just a science teacher, but is also cooking meth and killing people — mostly criminals at first, but later some innocent people too — and most of the characters around him don't know this.

His wife, his son, his sister and brother-in-law, the head teacher and his colleagues or students don't know that there are two Walter Whites: a loving father/husband, and an increasingly ruthless criminal. It's like a secret identity in a superhero movie, just inverted for the anti-hero that he has become.

This is what generates most of the conflict, most of the suspense, most of the tension in the story. And this main dramatic irony is what makes *Breaking Bad* a high-concept crime thriller. It elevates it above the average TV series drama and brings a third dimension to the story. If you don't understand dramatic irony and the importance of managing information, you're missing a large part of the story structure in *Breaking Bad*.

Of course, *Breaking Bad* episodes are superficially formatted in four logistical acts with a short teaser, and many will tell you that the whole series is designed in five "Shakespearian" acts, but dramatically the series is designed in three dramatic acts around Walter's evolution, as are many sequences, episodes, and storylines. It also relies heavily on a main dramatic irony throughout.

Like all great storytellers, Vince Gilligan, consciously or not, masters the screenwriting tools that make a difference when designing a story, even if few screenwriting theories mention them and even fewer explore their structural aspect in detail.

I've chosen two examples based primarily on dramatic irony for simplicity, clarity and impact, but it's not the only aspect of managing information. Some stories, like *Se7en* or *Squid Game*, rely more on mystery. Others like *Sleuth* or *The Hangover* play more with surprise. What matters is that you know how to handle these tools in order to deliver the emotional impact you're after as a storyteller and give a third dimension to your screenplays.

A New Approach to Story Structure

Managing information — the third dimension of screenwriting — is a crucial part of story structure because as we've seen, it allows us to generate suspense and tension in a thriller, to generate humour in a comedy, emotion in a drama, and most importantly, it helps us to handle most hybrids and exceptions, stories that are neither plot-led, character-led or theme-led.

We've not defined these terms properly yet, so you might think that a story is plot-led when the plot is most important, is character-led when the characters are most important and is theme-led when the theme is important. But the truth is that all great stories have a strong plot, strong characters, and a strong theme.

Let's look at the third key aspect of structure mentioned in the "story iceberg" and put all this together now.

I've defined **a new approach to story structure** called the *Story-Type Method*, which allows us to handle each story differently depending on its story-type. So let's see what this is all about and how it can help you during the development of your film and TV projects, starting with defining this new approach.

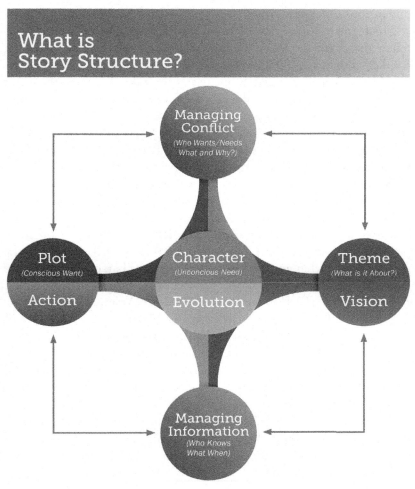

For me, the three main elements of story structure are character — always at the centre — plot and theme. These are closely connected to managing conflict, which is the well-known aspect of story structure related to **"Who wants or needs what and why?"** but they're equally connected to managing information, which is the less well-known aspect of structure related to **"Who knows what and**

when?" that we've just explored when we discussed the three dimensions of screenwriting.

Most great stories flex all of their dramatic muscles, working as much on character as on plot or theme, as well as on managing conflict and managing information, because all of this is structure. The key is knowing what is primarily at stake. So does the main problem in the story lie in the character, in the plot or in the theme? Then designing the story accordingly so that the story engine fires on all cylinders.

If you obsess about the plot or the plot-led aspect of structure, you might miss the most fundamental part of your structure in what we're going to call a character-led or a theme-led story.

If you're trying to force a protagonist to change because you've been told that the protagonist is the character who changes most, you might be doing a disservice to your plot-led story, because if the main problem lies outside the protagonist, there is no real reason for the protagonist to change, and often it's another character or even the antagonist who changes most, for example, Billy's father in *Billy Elliot*, Negan in *The Walking Dead* or Rebecca Welton in *Ted Lasso*.

Similarly, if you try to analyse stories like *Tootsie, Breaking Bad, Back to the Future, Happy Valley, Fleabag, Psycho, Mr. Robot, Amadeus, The Lives of Others, The Departed* or *Avatar* purely from a managing conflict point of view, you are missing a large part of their structure because they're built primarily on the way they manage information, using what we've called the third dimension of screenwriting.

As you can see, the 3-Act structure — even the dramatic one — doesn't even appear on this diagram. It might be one of the most efficient tools for generating and managing conflict, or creating and maintaining a strong identification link between the protagonist and the audience, but it's optional. You can also use other tools like dramatic irony to generate conflict and create identification in your story.

So this diagram applies to every story, but each story-type — plot-led, character-led, or theme-led — will use the dramatic 3-Act structure in a significantly different way.

The Story-Type Method

Let's see how we can clarify this with what I call **the *Story-Type* *Method*,** which makes it ten times easier than you think:

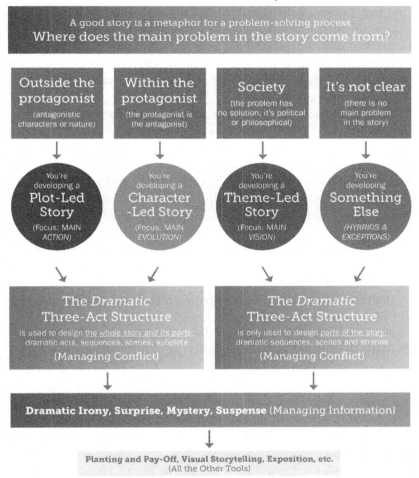

I tried to find the simplest way to define a good story for a film or a TV series, and for me it's simply that **a good story is a metaphor for a problem-solving process.**

So, ask yourself a simple question: Where does the main problem in the story come from? Can you identify that in your narrative?

If this main problem in your story comes from outside the protagonist, from antagonistic characters or nature, it means that **you're developing a plot-led story**. In this case, the focus is the main dramatic *action*, which means you're going to use the dramatic 3-Act structure to design the whole story, but also its parts: dramatic acts, sequences, scenes, subplots, and so on. This is what we've called managing conflict.

You're also going to use dramatic irony, surprise, mystery, suspense — which is what we've called managing information, the third dimension of screenwriting.

Now, if the main problem in your story is located within the protagonist, so if the protagonist is the antagonist, if they're primarily fighting against themselves, it means that **you're developing a character-led story**, and the focus in this case is the main dramatic *evolution*. That's the backbone of your story.

You're still going to use the dramatic 3-Act structure to design the whole story and its parts, you're still going to use managing information.

For both plot-led and character-led stories, we're also going to use other tools, which are planting and payoff, visual storytelling, exposition, and so on.

The most important difference between the two approaches is that in a plot-led story, the focus is the main dramatic *action*: "Who *wants* what and why?" In a character-led story, the focus is the main dramatic *evolution*: "Who *needs* what and why?" As a result, you're going to design the story differently, because you'll know that what's really at stake in the story isn't what the character *wants* but what the character *needs*.

For example, very often the protagonist of a character-led story ends up giving up on what they *want* (their conscious goal) in order to get what they *need* (their unconscious goal). This might feel like a downer in a plot-led story, but it can be the key to a satisfying ending in a character-led story, for example in *Silver Linings Playbook* or *Two Days, One Night*.

You'll also know that you won't need an antagonist because the protagonist *is* the antagonist in a character-led story. Most of the time, you'll need a *catalyst* character instead, a character who pushes the protagonist to change, who might look like an antagonist on the conscious goal but is actually a co-protagonist on the unconscious need: they *help* the protagonist to change, like Tiffany in *Silver Linings Playbook* or Maeve in *Sex Education*. See the <u>Story-Type Method Glossary</u> for more details on each of these terms if you're not familiar with them.

Now, where things start to change even more is **when you can identify the main problem as lying in society**. In this case, the problem often has no solution. It's political, it's philosophical or it's spiritual. And this means that **you're developing a theme-led story**, where the focus is the main vision of the storyteller.

Usually, this means that you're dealing with a multi-stranded narrative: different storylines connected to the same theme, with no clear protagonist. You don't have a single protagonist overall. Instead, you have a different protagonist in each of the storylines.

With a theme-led story, you won't be able to use the dramatic 3-Act structure at story level because there is no before, during and after a main dramatic action or evolution, but you'll still be able to use it to design each of the storylines.

So each of the storylines will have its own protagonist and each of the storylines can be plot-led or character-led, and you can design them accordingly, which is crucial for TV series and multi-stranded narratives.

Of course, when you're dealing with a theme-led story, you can still use dramatic irony and all the tools related to managing information.

When it's not clear, when you can't identify a main problem in the story — either because there is no main problem or because you have more than one and you're struggling to identify which is the main one — it's often because you're developing something else.

You're developing an exception or a hybrid. A hybrid being a story where you are actually going from one story-type to the other, so for example, your story might start as character-led and become plot-led (as in *Edge of Tomorrow*), or it could start as plot-led and become character-led (as in *Breaking Bad*), or it could be an exception: There is no clear story-type that applies to your story.

And that's fine. You can still use the dramatic 3-Act structure to design parts of the story — dramatic sequences, scenes and strands — and you'll definitely use managing information, because that's usually how you handle an exception.

Often, it's a main dramatic irony that will shape your story, as in *Tootsie* or *Breaking Bad* for example. Or you'll have a flashback structure, as in *The Secret in Their Eyes* or *Mr. Robot*. You will have some form of unclassical structure that is going to lead you to use all these tools, but in a slightly different way.

The *Story-Type Method*, for me, is the missing element. Although I coined it and defined it, I didn't invent it. I just looked at how successful feature films and TV series were actually designed, even when they were not conventionally structured. That's how I came up with this approach.

Mistaking story structure for story format might just be what's been preventing you from getting stronger drafts of your projects. To sum this up, let's see how we can apply the *Story-Type Method* in development so that you feel less frustrated or stuck.

How to Develop Stronger Screenplays

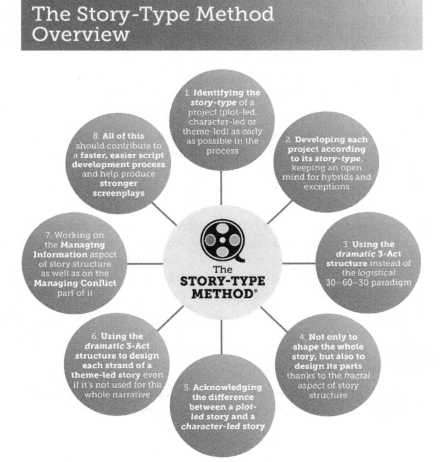

So how can you use this approach to get a new draft that's *stronger* and not just *different*?

1. As early as possible in the process, **identify the story-type of your project** — is it plot-led, character-led, or theme-led?

2. **Develop each project according to its story-type**. Of course, keep an open mind for hybrids or exceptions, which you'll find a way to handle specifically, often through managing information.

3. **Use the dramatic 3-Act structure** instead of the logistical 30-60-30 paradigm (or 25-50-25 percent of whatever the length of your script is). So, instead of using a *logistical* approach to story structure, you're going to use the *dramatic* 3-Act structure.

4. **Not only to shape the whole story, but also to design its parts**, thanks to the fractal aspect of story structure: seasons, episodes, storylines or strands, as well as dramatic acts, sequences and scenes.

5. **Acknowledge the difference between a plot-led story and a character-led story**: Is what's truly at stake the main dramatic *action* (what the protagonist *wants*) or the main dramatic *evolution* (what the protagonist *needs*)? Clarifying this will help you to craft a satisfying ending.

6. When you're dealing with a theme-led story, **use the dramatic 3-Act structure to design each of the storylines**. Even when the dramatic 3-Act structure can't be used to design the entire story, you can still use it to design its parts, for example, its strands or its storylines in a multi-stranded narrative or in a TV series.

7. **Work on the managing information aspect of story structure, as well as on the managing conflict part of it**, using tools such as mystery, surprise, suspense and dramatic irony to add a third dimension to your storytelling.

8. All of this, ideally, should contribute to a **faster, easier script development process** and help you produce stronger screenplays.

Reminder

As explained in How to Make the Most of This Book, this brief overview of the *Story-Type Method* doesn't fully replace reading *Screenwriting Unchained* — the first volume in the series — or following the Advanced Development workshop or course but, along with the Story-Type Method Glossary that you'll find at the end of this book, it should provide a decent snapshot of the approach and help you follow as we build on these foundations.

1 Trends, Series Types and Conventional Series Design

First Up

In this first chapter, after discussing **current trends**, we'll look at **series types** — defining the main types of series: serial, procedural, limited, anthological, etc.

Then we'll look into **conventional series design**. This superficial approach is mostly about a logistical format, each act being based on a set number of pages or minutes. The most common format for a one-hour episode in a modern series is probably the so-called "5-act structure", with or without a teaser.

Although it's only moderately useful when designing original series, it's important to understand this approach because it still shapes most of the discussions around series development, especially in the Anglo-Saxon world.

So this first chapter might not be the sexiest in the book, but the idea is to lay out the fundamentals first, before we can go on to more exciting stuff.

1.1 Trends

Let's start with a tiny bit of history, to put things into context before we explore the main trends in series development.

Developing a Series: Trends

What are the main trends in global TV development?
- Commercial breaks don't rule content anymore
- Fewer episodes per season
- Higher budgets per episode and overall
- More originality and diversity
- Faster pace
- Shorter episodes
- More non-English-language series
- New players (Apple TV+, Disney+, Paramount+ etc.)

Commercials Don't Rule Content Anymore (and Thoughts on Series for Streaming)

For me, a major difference between how series are written today and the way they were ten or fifteen years ago is that, thanks to premium channels and online streaming, series aren't primarily conceived to sell ad breaks anymore, which has a huge impact on the nature of stories that can be told.

When a series was broadcast by one of two or three channels in each country, it needed to reach the widest possible audience because shows were financed primarily by advertisement.

In fact, shows were often ways for broadcasters to bring "eyeballs" to the advertisers.

Patrick Le Lay, former head of TF1 in France, famously said that his channel was selling "available human brain time" to advertisers. The shows were designed to entertain the audience so that they would be receptive to the commercials.

The larger the audience a show could seduce, the higher the price for the commercial time slots. This has been the basis for TV series programming around the world for decades: attract as many people as possible from a specific demographic so that commercials can be sold at the highest possible price.

Premium channels (such as HBO or Showtime in the U.S. or Canal+ in Europe) disrupted this by using a new financing model: the revenue coming from subscription, not from advertisement. This ad-free programming paved the way for more focused content, as it was no longer necessary to seduce the widest possible audience — only the audience ready to pay for the subscription. The larger, the better, but this model could be profitable outside mainstream programming.

Online streaming pushed this subscription model further by breaking the notion of scheduled programming and lowering the cost. There was no allocated time or place to watch a show. Anyone could watch anything, anytime, anywhere, on any device.

Now able to raise finance from a world-wide audience, streamers had the budget and the freedom to create more original shows, and of course this tapped into the younger generations' desire to consume content on their own devices, in their bedrooms, rather than on a television in the living room.

This is how shows like *Transparent* or *Life in Pieces* were made possible, and why non-English language shows such as *Occupied*, *Money Heist*, *Lupin* or *Squid Game* were able to find a global audience. The commercials-free model has directly impacted the kind of content that can be created, and the evolution is still on-going.

It should be noted that over the last couple of years, Netflix and other streamers — Hulu, Disney+, Paramount+, HBO Max — have started to offer a low-cost tier with non-skippable ads to combat the post-pandemic drop in subscriptions and reduce churn. So we now have around four to five minutes of commercials per hour, both before and during content, in these ad-based offers.

Others such as Paramount's Pluto TV or Fox's Tubi have gone further and follow the FAST model (Free Ad-Supported Streaming Television): no subscription fee and funded solely by advertising.

From a story design point of view, it doesn't really matter, but it looks like an ad-break logistical format might become more prevalent with streaming content in the years to come, because of this recent evolution. Whatever happens, as long as you make the distinction between logistical format and dramatic structure — which we'll discuss at length soon — you'll be fine.

The downside of this abundance in the number of cable, satellite, TV channels and streaming services available in any country is that every show is competing not with three or five others in the same programming slot, but with three to five hundred available anytime, anywhere.

This means that in order to stand a chance of success, shows have to grab the audience right away and keep them hooked. It's never been easier to find the right show for you, but it's also never been easier to leave if you get bored.

These two extremes define the opportunities and the challenges of modern series design.

Fewer Episodes per Season and Higher Budget

A season used to be around twenty-two weekly episodes of sixty minutes, it's now down to six to ten episodes on average on streaming and premium channels, which gives a higher budget per episode and makes it harder for networks to compete.

A series like *Game of Thrones* was almost unimaginable on TV a few decades back. The overall budget for series has been on the rise globally over the last decade, opening the door to many genres besides the standard sitcoms, drama, soap operas and law, medical and cop procedurals: Sci-fi, action/adventure, fantasy and more can be made convincingly today, with decent budgets, on TV or streaming.

However, while streamers seem to be evolving towards a tent-pole model with a few prestigious, high-budget series such as Amazon's adaptation of *The Lord of the Rings*, they are also reducing expenses and cutting the overall number of shows made. Streamers and studios are realising that high budget doesn't mean high profitability. Low budget isn't a dirty word anymore, which is fantastic news for storytellers. A great story doesn't have to cost much to produce and can reach a wide audience, making a show super profitable.

This is the current opportunity for series makers looking to break into the business: If you're not one of the few successful showrunners and teams working on one of the tent-pole projects, the new entry point is for high-concept, mid-to-low budget, crossover or mainstream series with global potential. Exactly what we're talking about in this book.

More Originality and Diversity

Another positive aspect of streaming and premium channels over the last decade was that they have been open to experimental shows as long as they could cross borders (*Fleabag, Transparent, Life in Pieces*).

Netflix has always been more mainstream, but they still select some edgier shows, especially non-English language series (*Money Heist, Occupied, Squid Game, Lupin* etc) that are designed in such a way that they can reach a global audience.

However, the laudable diversity of recent years might be abating. Streamers and studios have been more cautious recently. The needle for content seems to be moving from niche back towards mainstream.

No matter how trends come and go, as long as your story engine is firing on all cylinders, originality remains a great way to break in. So keep reading, because that's what we're going to be working on!

Faster Pace

Whether due to a shorter attention span or not, everything has been compressed. If you watch a show from the 90s, it often feels unbearably slow. Nowadays, set-up and exposition are reduced to the absolute minimum. Overall, shows tend to have a much faster pace, especially plot-led procedurals or mini-series.

Inciting incidents in a procedural — the incident that starts the main dramatic action in the episode — that used to happen around minute 10 or 12 in a one-hour episode, are now moved to minute 5 or 6 if not earlier.

Character-led series can be slower from a pace point of view, but they often compensate for this with outrageous, weird or quirky content that grabs attention in a different way. A show will be fascinating due to the content, theme or relationships explored instead of being gripping because of pace and tension.

In any case, the aim is the same: grabbing our attention quickly so that we can't stop watching.

Shorter Episodes

Episodes are not only "faster", they are getting shorter. Sixty minutes becomes forty-five — as with *Money Heist*, when Netflix reformatted the original Spanish show initially broadcast as 60-minute episodes — and thirty minutes becomes fifteen… We've even seen experimental mini-formats designed to accommodate the mobile phone generation and its short attention span.

This, along with the disappearance of ads, makes it even more important to understand the difference between *dramatic* and *logistical* acts. The former can deal with any story length as well as its parts, thanks to its fractal aspect. The latter needs to be "redefined" every time the episode length or the number of commercial breaks changes. We'll look into this later in the chapter.

More Non-English Language Series

Streaming offers a fantastic opportunity for non-English language series.

For example, Netflix keeps increasing the development of non-English language programming, both scripted and non-scripted. This long-term trend was confirmed as early as 2019 at Content London by Kelly Luegenbiehl (Vice President of Global Franchises at Netflix London), mentioning series such as *The Rain* (Denmark) or *Dark* (Germany). She also reported that 50% of Netflix subscribers watched non-English language content, up from 30% a couple of years before. So there is a strong demand for good stories in any language. Shows like *Lupin* or *Squid Game* have since confirmed this trend.

This evolution is particularly interesting if your aim is to write series that are not in the English language, and if you plan to use the dramatic language and visual storytelling to cross borders.

Recent years have proven that just because a series is not in the English language, it doesn't mean it can't reach a global audience.

For me, the goal has always been to make local stories that travel well abroad, stories that are strongly rooted in wherever they originate from but, because of the way they're told and designed, can reach a wide audience abroad, irrespective of their budget. Streaming offers a wonderful opportunity to achieve this, if that's something you aspire to.

New Players

After the disruption caused by premium cable channels (such as HBO) a few decades ago, online streaming has completely changed the Film and TV industry over the last ten years, a transformation that the pandemic both accentuated and accelerated. As a result, the industry is still in a constant state of flux.

After the pioneers such as Netflix, Amazon or Hulu (owned by NBCUniversal and Disney), new players continue to make the future unpredictable: Disney+ and Apple TV+ were successfully launched at the end of 2019 while Quibi (10-minute "quick bites" service on mobile phone for Millennials created by Jeffrey Katzenberg and Meg Whitman), launched in April 2020, met with limited success and was gone by the end of that year.

Since then, Amazon has bought MGM, gaining access to their huge film catalogue while Netflix has added a few gaming studios to their portfolio, and purchased a decommissioned army base in New Jersey to turn it into a production studio, joining the one it already owned in Albuquerque.

Apart from Sony/Columbia who have a deal with Netflix, every single major has launched their streaming offer: Warner launched HBO Max and Discovery+, Paramount launched Paramount+ (it had also absorbed Showtime, previously owned by CBS), while Universal already owned Hulu (jointly with Disney) and Fox owns Tubi.

So there are clearly many shifts continually taking place and that's unlikely to stop any time soon, making any "state of the industry" paper — including this one — outdated as soon as it's written. What's especially unpredictable is which player(s) will dominate the market a few years from now.

However, what's fairly certain is that the need for quality content will keep rising, that content will be more and more varied and that good stories will still need to be told. ChatGPT might be able to throw out tele-novella episodes at a disturbing pace, but it can't write *Big Little Lies*, *Breaking Bad*, *Sex Education* or *Fleabag*.

As long as you're aiming for high-end TV, all these channels still need to be fed. The future is unknown, but one thing is sure: It's going to be an exciting time for the storytellers of the 21st century!

These were the latest trends... Now let's discuss the main elements that characterise a series.

1.2 Series Types

We're going to discuss each of the elements that characterise a series in detail, but as an introduction let's just quickly list them:

Developing a Series: Different Types

Here are the main elements that characterise a series:
- Format, then the series type:
- Procedural vs Serial
- Serial-Procedural Hybrid
- Sitcom (single or multi-cam)
- Mini-Series (or Limited Series)
- Anthology Series
- Mini Series Series (or Anthological Limited Series)
- Web Series
- Film Franchise

Format

The generally understood meaning of format simply defines the length and broad genre of the episodes in a series.

The two main historical formats for TV series are the one-hour drama and the half-hour comedy.

In the U.S. the one-hour drama is 42 minutes if distributed on an ad-supported network, 56 minutes if distributed on a premium network (no commercial breaks) and anything between 45 and 75 minutes on streaming (usually without any commercial breaks, but that's changing). In Europe, the length can vary but 50-52 minutes is a fairly common length.

The half-hour comedy is usually around 22 minutes long, plus ads and can be single cam or multi-cam. We'll discuss this further in the section on sitcoms.

More recently, we've also seen one-hour dramedies such as *Orange Is the New Black* and half-hour dramedies (*Transparent, Fleabag, After Life*). So the line between longer drama and shorter comedy is becoming blurred.

"Format" can also have a second meaning, which is the underlying concept or the underlying rights to the adaptation of a foreign series or IP. For example, in order to adapt *The Office* or *The Bridge* in the U.S., studios bought the format from the UK or Danish rights holders.

Finally, "format" can also mean a TV series bible as a selling tool, a pitching document or proposal written before the series is commissioned. In that case, the term "bible" itself refers to the document recording key creative information about the show once it's in production. We'll discuss these biblical nuances further in Chapter 3.

For now, let's talk about different types of series, starting with procedurals, historically the first series type.

Procedural (or Closed-Ended Series)

Definition: A problem is introduced, investigated and solved within a closed-ended, self-contained episode. Exceptionally, a complex case can run over a few episodes, but that's the exception, not the rule.

They tend to be police, law, crime or medical. They come from four of the most common genres in the TV series history: cop shows, medical shows, legal shows and private investigator shows. While the latter was mostly dead, it has seen a revival over recent years, starting with the *Magnum P.I.* reboot, which opened in 2018. This high-profile example was axed after its fifth season, but other private investigator procedurals have been launched in the last few years, signalling a possible comeback.

Structure: Each episode is plot-led (the main problem or "A" Story is the case that the protagonist tries to solve) and tends to be one-hour long. Ongoing character arcs, subplots and themes are secondary. This structure is fairly straightforward, which makes procedurals simpler to design than serials, for example. Each episode is like a mini-feature film lasting under an hour.

Main advantages: Besides the fact that they are easier to structure, episodes can be watched in any order, so it doesn't matter if you miss one. We'll explore this in detail later, but the main problem in the story usually sits very low on Maslow's pyramid — it tends to be about survival, about protection — and that means that it has the widest potential audience, which is why networks love procedurals: They need to reach a very wide audience to make the show happen, and a main problem at the bottom of Maslow almost guarantees that. Please see "Maslow's Hierarchy of Needs" in the Story-Type Method Glossary at the end of the book if you're not familiar with the use of Maslow in the *Story-Type Method*.

Main downsides: There is little room for character development, though that's changing. There is a trend towards more serial elements being introduced in procedurals, especially in character-led subplots or storylines. Procedurals are not as binge-inducing as serials, so they're not always sought by streamers, especially the younger part of the audience. Finally, procedurals can lack sophistication, unless they integrate a soap element, a serialised element.

Examples: *CSI, Law and Order, House M.D., Luther, Magnum P.I., ER*

Exceptions: Procedurals (live action or animation) for children. Procedurals tend to be around one-hour long, except of course when they are made for a young audience. Children's procedurals are usually shorter — as short as three to five minutes — due to the limited attention span of their target audience. They tend to be about relationships, friendships, family, esteem, and values or education, so the main problem lies higher in Maslow. Slapstick works very well for the youngest audience — the acceptable level of danger, threat or violence goes up as the age goes up. It's important to find the right balance depending on the age of the target audience.

Examples: *Avatar: The Last Airbender, Pingu, Puffin Rock, Charlie and Lola, Dino Dana, Octonauts*

Serial (or Open-Ended Series)

Definition: In serials, storylines are serialised over many open-ended episodes and seasons, until a finale.

They tend to include a "soap" element — serialised storylines about relationships (family, friendship and/or sexual). The number of episodes is, in theory, infinite.

Serials are currently the predominant form of modern TV series, and one that requires a significantly different structural design to feature films, simply because of the number of storylines and the fact that they span over many episodes. While a procedural episode is built almost like a mini plot-led movie, serials have a more complex design. We'll look at this later in the chapter.

Structure: Serials can be plot-led, character-led or theme-led at series and season level. Of course, you can have hybrids or exceptions too. However, most episodes tend to be plot-led. It's not a rule, you can have theme-led or character-led episodes, but even when you have a series that is theme-led or a character-led overall, each episode will usually have a main plot that is plot-led. We'll discuss this in more detail soon.

Serials are built around a story world and a mythology that allows them to develop the story over many seasons, each of which includes 6 to 24 episodes, more frequently 8 to 22.

Episodes tend to be 22 to 60 minutes long. Usually, 22-30 minutes for comedies, 45-60 minutes for drama.

The last episode of a season ("finale") can sometimes be longer, up to 90 minutes.

Main advantages: Serials are designed to hook the audience so that they have to watch the next episode and all the episodes in the right order, for the story to make sense. They often explore complex or challenging characters and themes, so they tend to be more sophisticated than procedurals.

Main downside: It can be difficult to find the right balance between complexity and clarity: Because you have so many storylines to manage, it's quite easy for writers and/or the audience to get lost between them.

Examples: *Game of Thrones, The Walking Dead, Occupied, Sex Education, Mad Men, Homeland, Succession, The Last of Us, Westworld, Deadwood, Breaking Bad, Downton Abbey, Lupin,* etc.

Serial-Procedural Hybrid

Serial-Procedural hybrids can be varied in design, but they often alternate a procedural episode (with a closed-ended case) and a "mythology" episode that develops an overall arc over the series (character relationships, thematic arc, investigation). Usually, the procedural element focuses on the plot, while the mythology element focuses on the characters and their relationships or an ongoing investigation.

Examples: *The X-Files, Dexter, Lost*

Serial-Procedural hybrids can also handle a procedural element over a season instead of an episode. This means they have room to explore more complex "cases", while still keeping a procedural element. These more complex cases can be a slow-burn mystery — a whodunit, a howdunit or a whydunit — and often a new antagonist is picked every season. This might be a variation of the same antagonist stemming from the same meta-antagonist.

Handling a procedural element over a season also allows for the development of stronger storylines and deeper relationships between the characters.

Examples: *The Wire, Broadchurch, Stranger Things, 24, Wednesday, Squid Game*

Finally, Serial-Procedural hybrids can be just that, a serial with a strong procedural element, or a procedural with a serial element so strong that it makes it difficult not to watch episodes chronologically, because you'd miss too much of the ongoing story development, both regarding character relationships and plot.

Examples: *Sex Education, Grey's Anatomy*

Let's look briefly at two examples:

Broadchurch focuses on the resolution of the Danny Latimer murder case in the first season, with the investigation led by Ellie Miller (Olivia Coleman) and Alec Hardy (David Tennant). Season 2 focuses on bringing the murderer to trial and Hardy being haunted by a previous case. Season 3 focuses on the rape of a local woman at a birthday party and the attempts of the Latimer family to move on from Danny's murder.

The five seasons of *The Wire* all take place in Baltimore — which gives the series some thematic unity — but focus on a different aspect of the city's administration: Season 1 is about the drug problem fuelled by the Barksdale organisation and its effects on the urban poor; Season 2 is about the blue-collar urban working class in the city port; Season 3 comes back to the Barksdale organisation but focuses on the city's political scene; Season 4 on the school system and the mayoral race; Season 5 on the media and media consumption. Although some of the characters return, each season brings a new set of characters as well.

Sitcom

Definition: A situation comedy, usually one of two main types.

30-minute Multi-camera Sitcom: A sitcom that uses a laugh track, usually shot in a studio, two to three main locations, a few exteriors, three gags per page, sometimes in front of a live audience (*How I Met Your Mother*, *Friends*, *The Big Bang Theory*, *Mrs Brown's Boys*). Each episode returns to the starting point and there is little to no character evolution. It's comfortable and easy. It's just a set of characters that you enjoy spending time with, until they almost become part of your family — if you like the series, of course.

30-minute Single-Camera Sitcom: (*The Office*, *Curb Your Enthusiasm*, *Veep*, *Brooklyn Nine-Nine*). This is a comedy shot like a movie. More exteriors but still little character evolution, which is a characteristic of a "pure" sitcom.

Structure: Like procedurals, sitcoms tend to have a fairly simple design: An A-Story that shapes most of the episode and a couple of subplots (B and C stories). Main plots and subplots tend to be resolved within an episode, except when there are some storylines that span over the whole series (like the Ross/Rachel relationship in *Friends* or the Jim/Pam relationship in *The Office*).

Each episode usually starts with a short teaser or intro and ends with a kicker or outro.

True sitcoms are based on characters that are flawed (uptight, jealous, lazy, etc.) We know they're flawed but we don't want them to change: It's their flaws that make us laugh. The minute they start changing, the sitcom is over because one of the main sources of comedy in the story is taken away.

This is one of the unwritten rules of sitcoms: characters don't change, and that's just fine. What needs to be designed, on the other hand, are characters that are interesting and strong enough for us to want to watch them again and again.

Some series use a 30-minute format yet they're not a sitcom. For example, dramedies such as *Transparent* or *Fleabag* that tend to be more realistic, more raw, less comfortable and where character arcs tend to be stronger. Their structure is less simplistic and closed-ended than the more traditional sitcoms.

Mini-Series (or Limited Series)

Note: Mini-series or limited series are also called "serials" in the UK and a few other places. Let's put this aside to avoid confusion.

Definition: A mini-series or a limited series has a fixed number of episodes (more than one and less than thirteen, usually four to eight) and tells one story with a beginning, middle and end in a single season. The distinction between mini-series and limited series is blurred as the terms are often inter-changeable and many people use one or the other, meaning the same thing. When a distinction is made, it's usually that a mini-series is closer to a few episodes of feature-length (two or three episodes of ninety minutes to three hours each), while a limited series is usually six to eight episodes of one hour.

Structure: Technically, a mini-series or a limited series is not as challenging as a serial because it doesn't run over many seasons and often has fewer storylines. Although some are more complex than others, they can be a bit like a long feature film, only with room for more characters and more character development. If you're moving from feature film to TV series, the easiest first step is probably to write or develop a mini-series.

Like a feature film or a serial, overall, a mini-series or limited series can be plot-led, character-led, theme-led or a hybrid/exception.

Each episode is usually forty-five to sixty minutes long, without a specific story-type, although there is often a main plot and a few subplots in each episode. There can be more subplots if the series is theme-led (as in the first season of *Big Little Lies*, which was originally designed as a limited series), or if it's a disaster story where most of the storylines are plot-led and show various co-protagonists trying to deal with the same event (*Chernobyl*).

Examples: *Bodyguard, The Night Manager, Chernobyl, The Queen's Gambit, Mare of Easttown, Unbelievable*

Anthology Series

Definition: An Anthology series brings a new world and set of characters in each episode. In the past, series such as *Twilight Zone* or *Alfred Hitchcock Presents* were anthologies. *Black Mirror* is a more recent example. Episodes tend to be around one hour long, but they can be half an hour too, in any genre. Episodes usually share the same theme and/or the same genre. This is what joins them in the same anthology, rather than being random stories.

Structure: The episodes in an anthology series tend to be plot-led because there isn't much time for character development, but some episodes can be character-led or have a strong character-led element. Note that it's already difficult to design a character-led story in one hour and a half or two hours in a feature film. So in a one-hour episode it's doable, but tricky.

Examples: *Twilight Zone, Alfred Hitchcock Presents, Black Mirror*

Mini-Series Series (or Anthological Limited Series)

Definition: It sounds complex but it's quite simple. To create a mini-series series or anthological limited series, you take a limited series (closed-ended stories at season level), and you make a series of them. This is a fairly recent evolution, each mini-series bringing a new set of characters and story world in each season, but each mini-series being linked thematically or by genre to the others.

Structure: Identical to mini-series or limited series, you just have more than one that are only related to each other through genre or theme.

This is an attractive proposition, especially for feature film writers branching out to series, because you can write closed-ended stories with a beginning, middle and end at season level — which feels like familiar territory from a structural point of view — yet you can keep the title, genre, brand and franchise to help market the next season without having to start over. It's almost like developing separate feature films, except the stories are longer, thematically linked and share the same title.

True Detective is an example, though not a consistently successful one, because despite a glorious first season (designed as a limited series), the following two seasons failed in comparison.

In some ways, *The Wire* could be seen as an anthological limited series: Each season explores a significantly different aspect of the story world and brings a new set of characters. But because some elements remain (the main location, Baltimore; some of the characters), it falls more into the serial-procedural hybrid type.

Examples: *True Detective, Fargo, American Horror Stories*

Web Series

Definition: A web series is a short form narrative video series, usually low or no budget, often used as a calling card to sell longer-form series. There is no fixed length, but episodes (sometimes called webisodes) tend to be anything between three and ten minutes, on average five to six minutes for a comedy and seven to nine minutes for a drama. The stories usually revolve around either one character, the presenter of the show — maybe two characters if it's a duo — or a high concept situation. They are often based on a simple set-up, repeated every time.

Web series are quite interesting when you want to test an idea or provide a proof of concept, especially if you don't have a track record. It's a valid option if your series doesn't require a significant budget or a well-known cast.

Sometimes it can be a trap to make a web series if it's not designed as such, or if it's not a really low budget series, simply because it's almost impossible to deliver for no budget something that needs a budget. So it can be a great calling card, as long as it's for the right project.

Examples: *We Are Savvy, Single by Thirty, Awkward Black Girl* by Issa Rae (who went on to make *Insecure*).

Film Franchise

Although we won't explore this in detail, a film franchise is quite similar to a TV series. *James Bond, Indiana Jones, Fast & Furious, Rambo, John Wick* and *Mission Impossible* are plot-led procedurals, each instalment following a well-defined franchise.

The Marvel Cinematic Universe movies are a mix between an anthology series (individual superhero instalments, for example with origin stories) and serial-procedural hybrids if we consider each feature film as one season (*The Avengers*).

Just as TV series have evolved towards serials, so have film franchises. Therefore, many of the concepts, tools and principles described in the following sections also apply to film franchises in many ways, especially regarding story-types and the use of Maslow's Hierarchy of Needs (more on this later). So, if you're developing a film franchise, this book should be helpful.

1.3 Conventional Series Design

I'd like to talk now about what I call conventional series design, where the number of commercial breaks determines the logistical story format of each episode.

For example, in a half-hour sitcom episode (22 minutes plus ads), we have three logistical acts because there are two commercial breaks. Scripts tend to be around 25-30 pages long, so each logistical act is around ten pages long. Each episode usually starts with a short teaser or intro and ends with a kicker or outro. That's the logistical format of a sitcom / comedy episode.

Let's take another example. Each hour-long drama episode lasts around 48-52 minutes plus ads, and the scripts are 50-60 pages long. In these, three ad breaks means four logistical acts. Four ad breaks means five logistical acts, and so on. The duration of each logistical act depends on the number of ad breaks, but usually they are also about ten to fifteen pages long. That's the logistical format of a one-hour long episode.

The number and duration of these acts are completely arbitrary as they are only dictated by the number of ad breaks. This approach is logistical, not dramatic.

As explained in <u>A Quick Overview: The Three Dimensions of Screenwriting</u>, by "logistical" I mean based on a set number of minutes or pages — dictated by the length of candles in a theatre, by the footage of a film reel in cinema or here by the number of ad breaks — and not on dramatic events, principles or elements.

Talented writers, consciously or not, use a dramatic structure underneath this logistical format, more specifically they use the fractal aspect of story structure and the dramatic 3-Act structure.

This fractal aspect, which means that each part can be designed in the same way as the whole, is an essential element of series design because it allows writers to design each storyline individually before they weave them together.

As we'll start hopping between the logistical format and the dramatic structure underneath in the next two sections, I'll highlight the parts that focus on the **dramatic structure,** just as I have done in this paragraph.

This should allow you to see more clearly when we're discussing the superficial format often used in conventional series design and when we're talking about the actual story structure lying underneath.

It should give you an insight into the tools used by the masters of the craft, both consciously and unconsciously.

When Commercial Breaks Dictate Story Format

Let's begin with the origin and evolution of the logistical format.

In a one-hour drama, convention started with four logistical acts of around fifteen minutes each, with twelve minutes of content per act and three minutes of commercial breaks. This led to the historical "4-Act structure" for TV series episodes.

When advertising revenues went down, networks decided to add more commercial breaks to compensate, and that led to five or six logistical acts, with or without a teaser, which meant up to six or even seven short acts for TV movies or 90-minute episodes.

In order to deliver this new 5-Act format, sometimes Act I in the historical 4-Act format is cut in two to make five acts, sometimes it's Act IV that's cut into two shorter acts, leading to five acts as well. Sometimes, logistical Act I is called Teaser, sometimes you have a proper teaser and then four to five acts.

Confused? Don't worry, none of this really matters. Just remember that this logistical approach is simply dictated by the number of commercial breaks (usually three to five per one-hour episode), which means that you need the screenplay to be formatted accordingly.

When there are three to five commercial breaks per episode, you have to take this into account while writing because you need cliffhangers to make sure the audience comes back to the show after each ad break.

I'm sure that by now all this is just about as clear as mud, so let's try to visualise this.

Picture a string of sausages. Can you see it? Great. Now, imagine that this sausage string is your episode.

The logistical approach is just about defining how many sausages you want in the string.

The number of sausages (logistical acts) defines the length of each sausage, but it doesn't say anything about the ingredients, what's going to be in the sausage or how to cook it. It just tells you how many sausages you have in the string and whether you want a bit more spice at the beginning of each sausage (teasers) or at the end of each sausage (cliffhangers).

This really is story *format*. It's a simplistic way to approach series design. We have to define this because, again, that's the established, conventional language used in series development.

No one can ever agree on whether an episode should have four, five or six acts, because without commercial breaks, there is no reason to have logistical acts. Nevertheless, people still tend to discuss series design in terms of logistical acts, which is why it's important to clarify the way these work.

We, however, are going to spend a lot more time on story *structure*: defining the ingredients and how to cook them, because that's what's going to define whether the sausage tastes good or not, and whether your audience will want to watch your episodes or not.

Of course, you can think about *structure* (the sausage ingredients, the best way to cook them) and still present them to the broadcaster or to the buyer in the requested *format* (how many sausages, how long they should be) so that they can sell their commercials if need be.

Now I'm going to use a slightly more sophisticated way than a sausage string to explain these two layers in an episode and illustrate the difference between the logistical and the dramatic approach:

Dramatic Acts vs *Logistical* Acts (One-Hour Drama With Teaser)

The *Dramatic* 3-Act Structure

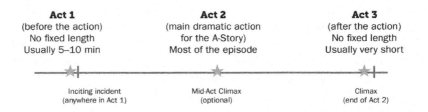

The *Logistical* 5-Act Structure (Teaser)

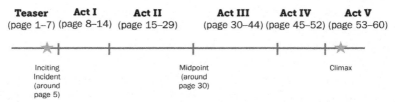

Copyright © Emmanuel Oberg. All Rights Reserved

Let's start with the **logistical approach** at the bottom of this diagram. Here, we're using the *logistical* 5-Act "structure" with a teaser for a one-hour episode, which is the most common logistical format used to discuss TV series today. To make it simpler, let's imagine it's a closed-ended procedural with a clear A-Story (the main plot of the episode, more on this in the next section on storylines).

Logistical units are defined according to an arbitrary number of pages or minutes — one page per minute, roughly. We have a teaser, which is one to seven pages; a first logistical act, from page 8 to 14; Act II, from page 15 to 29; Act III, from page 30 to 44; Act IV, from page 45 to 52; and Act V, from page 53 to 60.

You tend to have an inciting incident around minute five — it used to be around minute 10 or 12 — and a dramatic climax towards the end of the story, somewhere in logistical Act V.

As you can see, this has very little to do with dramatic structure. It's cut into chunks of similar length, because we try to spread the ad breaks evenly over the episode. If you look more closely, you see that the first 25% is made of the teaser and Act I and the last 25% is made of Act IV and Act V. There is a very simple reason for that: many writers used to favour the logistical 4-Act structure when they only had three commercial breaks. This means that underneath this 5-Act structure in the diagram, you can see a 4-Act structure, with act breaks at the end of logistical Act I, logistical Act II and logistical Act III.

This is why the 5-Act structure with a teaser is so popular. It's because writers can design episodes using the 4-Act logistical structure they are familiar with and then split two acts more or less equally into two mini-acts to give the buyer what they want, which is five commercial breaks instead of three.

So this is the logistical approach, when you use a logistical 5-Act structure with a teaser.

Let's move to the **dramatic approach**. If we look at the top half of the diagram, it shows the *dramatic* 3-Act structure of that same episode. Each episode often has a dramatic 3-Act structure that follows the 3-Act structure of the A-story (before, during and after the main dramatic action in the storyline), especially in a procedural.

Even in serials you have a first dramatic act, which is what happens before the inciting incident in the episode, then you have a dramatic Act 2 that takes up most of the episode and shows the main dramatic action. It doesn't have to be the whole length, but it's definitely longer than any other logistical acts and then you usually have a very short dramatic Act 3, which shows the consequences of the main dramatic action.

To divide this long dramatic Act 2 into more manageable units, we'll use dramatic sequences instead of logistical acts (more on this in the next section).

As shown in the diagram, we can also have an optional mid-act climax if the protagonist's goal on the A-Story changes at some point during dramatic Act 2.

This is how talented showrunners and writers shape a narrative, often unconsciously. Even when they discuss structure from a logistical perspective, underneath that they instinctively design their storylines and especially the A-Story using a dramatic 3-Act structure. They set up a main problem, they explore it over most of the episode and they resolve it by the end of the episode.

It's really pointless to argue about the number of sausages, or their size. When you're thinking story design and story structure, you want to focus on how each *dramatic* element of the story is designed.

Usually it's using a dramatic 3-Act structure at scene, sequence, storyline and episode level — a protagonist trying to reach a goal and either succeeding or failing.

But story elements can also be designed using a main dramatic irony. For example, you can design a sequence or a storyline around a dramatic irony that's set up, exploited and resolved at sequence or storyline level.

Either way, you identify seasons, episodes, storylines, sequences, scenes, and then you work on all these elements using the fractal aspect of the *dramatic* 3-Act structure. We'll soon see how this works in more detail.

The *logistical* 5-Act structure tells you how to *format* an episode, but it doesn't help you to *design* a season, an episode or a storyline in a way that is linked to how an audience engages with it emotionally and intellectually.

Now, let's take a closer look at the way in which acts are broken down using the logistical approach. For simplicity, we'll be using the historical 4-Act format for a one-hour drama episode, with three commercial breaks.

Logistical 4-Act Format of a 1-Hour Drama Episode (3 commercial breaks)

Scenes	1	2	3	4	5	6	Act length	Ad Breaks	TOTAL
Act I / Teaser	Opening					Inciting TP/CH	12 min.	3 min.	15 min.
Act II						Reversal TP/CH	12 min.	3 min.	15 min.
Act III						All Is Lost TP/CH	12 min.	3 min.	15 min.
Act IV						Ending TP/CH	12 min.	3 min.	15 min.
TOTAL							48 min.	12 min.	60 min.

TP = Turning Point
CH = Cliffhanger

For each logistical act, we have six scenes. In this conventional approach, each scene is around two minutes long, so if we take logistical Act I, including the teaser, we have an opening scene and then, by the end of the six scenes, we have a 12-minute act, a 3-minute commercial break and a total of fifteen minutes. This will be the same for each logistical act.

At the end of each of these 12-minute logistical acts, we have a turning point or a cliffhanger (unresolved conflict or key piece of information), the idea being to ensure that the audience returns to the show after the commercial break.

The first turning point / cliffhanger is often the inciting event that launches the dramatic action of the A-Story. Of course, it doesn't have to be in Scene 6, but it tends to be within this first logistical act. We then have a reversal at the midpoint, which is another turning point / cliffhanger, usually an obstacle or a surprise.

Then at the end of Act III, you have a formulaic "All Is Lost" turning point, which is when everything looks dark and depressing for the protagonist, again with a new cliffhanger.

At the end of Act IV, you won't have a cliffhanger or turning point if it's a closed-ended procedural, but if it's a serial or a limited series for example you would have one to tease the next episode or season.

This is the original, historical 4-Act logistical format. If you need more commercial breaks, you split Act I and/or Act IV into two mini-acts and presto! You get additional commercial breaks. Don't forget the cliffhanger / turning point at the end of each new act, to make sure that the audience comes back to the show after each ad break.

If you're not familiar with these logistical acts and would like to practice spotting them, you can easily identify ad breaks in produced shows. Even when they are removed due to the absence of commercials — for example when the series is released on streaming or physical media — there is still a fade to black at the end of each logistical act. This is very visible in network shows such as *The Walking Dead* or *Lost*.

Overall, this approach is quite formulaic, but writers who come from feature films and who are used to the simplistic Syd Field or Robert McKee approach feel at home, because it's really mini-Syd Field: Each of the four logistical acts is roughly 25% of the total duration of the episode. So instead of 30-30-30-30 (logistical 3-Act structure with a midpoint according to Syd Field in a two-hour feature film), here you have 15-15-15-15, which is exactly the same approach, just on a smaller scale.

It's purely logistical. It doesn't tell you much about the actual episode *structure*, it only helps you to deliver the requested *format*, because you'll need cliffhangers if you have commercial breaks.

But as commercial breaks have mostly disappeared with streaming and premium channels, we can focus on more effective, less predictable, less formatted storytelling.

This has already started to happen, and most writers and showrunners developing for streaming or premium channels have reverted to a 3-Act or a 4-Act logistical "structure" to format their episodes, even if they end up delivering them in five acts afterwards.

They will work on the episodes in three or four logistical acts depending on what they prefer to use — it's the personal choice of the showrunner or the writer — and before delivery, they will cut them down into the number of required logistical acts.

From a story design point of view, most of the focus is on the beginning (to hook the audience into the series / episode) and the ending (to make it compelling for the audience to watch the next episode / season). That's why we still need teasers and cliffhangers but can safely forget about the four-to-six logistical act format, unless we're writing for a network with commercial breaks.

Whether a new episode "structure" will arise out of the recent requirement from streamers to include ads on their low-cost tiers (or FAST channels) remains to be seen, but whatever materialises, it would still be another *logistical* format.

As we go on exploring this logistical approach in conventional series design, we'll also look at how we can go beyond this and follow a more dramatic approach, as this plays an even more significant part in the next section.

Storylines: Where Format Meets Structure

Now, let's talk about storylines because that's where story design starts — including, if they're talented and successful, for showrunners and writers who consciously use a logistical approach to format their story.

For sitcom or drama, in each episode, convention requires at least two storylines, called A-Story and B-Story (or A-Plot and B-Plot) and then optional ones: C, D, etc. The A-Story defines the main plot (the main problem explored in the episode). The other ones are subplots.

You can have as many subplots as you want, major ones and minor ones, especially in serials. But in sitcoms and procedurals, you tend to have one main plot and a couple of subplots at most.

Some will take up more space and will be more important than others, but you're unlikely to handle more than four or five storylines in each episode, even if there are more than that at season or series level.

Usually, you'll end a logistical act on the A or B story, not on a C or D story.

From a dramatic point of view, we can introduce, develop and resolve these storylines in one episode — for example in a procedural or a sitcom. We can also weave them over many episodes or seasons, as in a serial or a limited series.

In the latter case, the main plot, the A-Story in an episode, can also become a subplot in the next episode, and this can rotate through the series, one storyline becoming the main focus for an episode, a few episodes or a season. So, in *Game of Thrones*, we might focus primarily on the Stark storyline in one episode but on the Targaryen storyline in the next.

Usually, only the A and B stories need to be designed in three dramatic acts. The other storylines can be designed in three acts if they are as important, but they can also be made up of just a few beats (three to five) that show a simple evolution. In this case, they are called runners.

Another option might be to split your A-Story between sub-A-Stories (A1, A2, A3, A4) if all the protagonists share the same goal. It might look like the main dramatic action is split into different storylines, in different locations, but the co-protagonists are trying to reach the same goal, so it's actually the same storyline, the same A-Story. This is how *Stranger Things* is designed.

The key thing is to start by identifying your A-Story — when there is one — over each season. Is there a storyline driving the design of the season?

Then, go down a level and identify the A-Story for each episode. As we said, it's not always going to be the A-Story that you've identified at season level. Sometimes, a B or C-Story at season level will become the A-Story for a specific episode.

Series design starts with storylines. I call the first stage of this process Story Design 1, which is when we define the storylines at episode level (also called "Mapping the Strands" in the *Story-Type Method*).

Story Design 1: Defining the Storylines

Here's what happens if we split our hypothetical one-hour episode into one main plot and two subplots.

From a logistical point of view, it remains very formulaic: If you follow the conventional 4-Act logistical paradigm, then your A-Story takes around 50% of the episode, which means it has fourteen to fifteen scenes, each about two minutes long. That's about thirty minutes in a one-hour episode.

The B-Story is about a third of the overall length, so about nine to ten scenes, around twenty minutes. The C story is whatever remains, four to five scenes, so eight to ten minutes.

This means that overall, you have about thirty scenes and the total will be anything between fifty-four and sixty minutes:

Storylines (Strands)

Approx.	%	Scenes	Length
A-Story	50%	14 to 15	28 to 30 min
B-Story	33%	9 to 10	18 to 20 min
C-Story	17%	4 to 5	8 to 10 min
TOTAL	100%	27 to 30	54 to 60 min

This gives you a rough idea of what you can do in a procedural, if you want to follow the formula as it's been used over the years, especially for network procedural design.

Now let's see how we can reconcile logistical format and dramatic structure in the same episode, which requires a degree of mental agility.

We'll start with Story design 2, which is when we break each storyline (also called "Sequencing the Strands" in the *Story-Type Method*).

Story Design 2: Breaking Each Storyline

Logistically, the A-Story defines the main plot of each episode. It's about half an hour long. "Breaking" a storyline in logistical terms simply means dividing it into scenes of about two minutes long.

In this example, as we said, the B-Story is about 18 minutes long, and the C-Story is about eight minutes long.

This is what our hypothetical one-hour episode would look like, according to the logistical approach:

Dramatic A-Story	1	2	3	4	5	6	7	8	9	10	11	12	13	14	28 min
Dramatic B-Story	1	2	3	4	5	6	7	8	9						18 min
Dramatic C-Story	1	2	3	4											08 min
TOTAL															54 min

Again, no indication of any structural element. This is just a matter of time management — dividing each storyline into an arbitrary number of 2-minute scenes, according to the formulaic length of the A, B and C-Story. Breaking a storyline this way is purely logistical.

To focus on a more dramatic approach, once you've defined your storylines in Stage 1, take each of the main storylines and try to identify whether it's designed around a main dramatic action or evolution. If it is, you'll be able to identify a 3-Act structure at storyline level: before, during and after the main dramatic action or evolution within each storyline.

Again, you don't have to follow any of the prescriptive elements from the logistical approach regarding the length of each storyline, or how many you should have, especially in a serial or limited series.

Then, in each storyline, try to identify what triggers the main dramatic action (inciting incident, the event that triggers the protagonist's goal) and what concludes the main dramatic action (climax, where you give an answer to the dramatic question: "Will the protagonist of the storyline reach their goal or not?"). This will give you the dramatic 3-Act structure of each storyline: before, during and after a main dramatic action or evolution. Note that the A-Story tends to be plot-led in most episodes, even if the series is character-led or theme-led at season or series level.

So, for example, if the A-Story in a procedural is about resolving a crime, the inciting incident could be when the crime is committed. The protagonist of the storyline is the detective in charge of the case. Their goal is to resolve the case. The storyline concludes when they arrest the criminal. This defines a main dramatic action at episode level.

Now that you have mapped your main storylines and have identified whether they are plot-led or character-led, you need to sequence them, to divide them into dramatic units instead of simply breaking them into an arbitrary number of two-minute scenes.

To do so, within each storyline, try to identify dramatic sequences — groups of dramatic scenes exploring the same subgoal. A subgoal is often a way for the protagonist to reach their goal. This means using the fractal aspect of story structure to break our storylines in the way that we would break the dramatic Act 2 of a feature film, as shown in this diagram:

The *Fractal* Aspect of Structure

Sequencing the Strands / Storylines

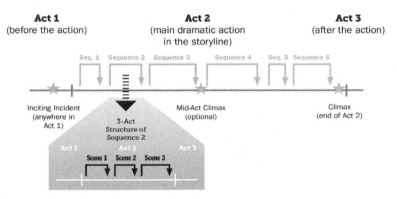

For example, in our crime procedural, the first half of the A-Story in the episode (identifying the criminal) could be split into three dramatic sequences: a first one about gathering DNA evidence, a second one about getting information from a key witness and a third one about investigating a cold case possibly related to this new crime.

Similarly, each sequence can be divided into dramatic scenes designed around a clear protagonist and goal at scene level, connected by a sub-subgoal (ways for the protagonist to reach the subgoal).

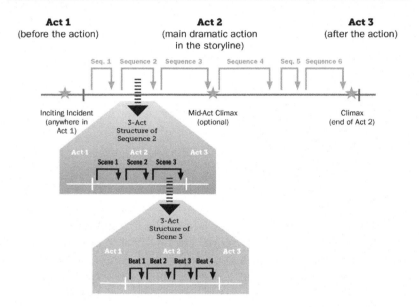

In our criminal procedural example, the second dramatic sequence about getting information from a key witness could be made of three dramatic scenes: a first scene about identifying the witness, a second one about locating them, and a third one about getting them to talk. The protagonist of each scene isn't necessarily the protagonist of the sequence or episode.

As a rule of thumb, the more storylines in your episode, the fewer dramatic sequences in each storyline. So, in a one-hour plot-led procedural with a strong A-Story and a couple of minor subplots, the main storyline could have four to six dramatic sequences. However, in a theme-led serial episode where you handle up to five equally important storylines, you might only have room for one dramatic sequence per storyline in each episode.

In total, you have room for about five dramatic sequences per one-hour episode, whether you develop them chronologically in the A-Story or simultaneously in five different storylines woven together.

It can be useful to think about structural tools such as a mid-act climax to design some storylines further, for example when you can't handle the same dramatic goal over the whole episode. This can be a lot more useful than a midpoint (logistical middle of the episode). We'll see what this dramatic design can look like in the next infograph, along with the logistical format.

Overall, using the fractal aspect of the dramatic 3-Act structure will allow you to keep working at a dramatic level, making sure that each scene moves the main dramatic action at storyline level forward, instead of simply looking at scenes from a time management perspective. You'll also know what's at stake in each scene, sequence, storyline and episode, which will increase the dramatic drive and pace in the writing, as well as the audience's emotional involvement in the narrative.

This dramatic approach might also allow you to raise the stakes or increase tension or suspense. For example, instead of "identifying the criminal", which sounds quite pedestrian, you could design the first half of the A-Story around "saving the next victim". Suddenly, you have a much more exciting dramatic action, as the stakes are higher — preventing a future crime instead of resolving a past one. Identifying the criminal might just be a consequence of this first dramatic action, instead of taking up half the episode. This is how you can shift the balance from cerebral (mystery about the criminal's identity) to emotional (saving the life of their next victim).

This method ("Mapping the Strands" for Story Design 1, "Sequencing the Strands" for Story Design 2 and "Weaving the Strands" for the upcoming Story Design 3) is defined in great detail in *Screenwriting Unchained* (the book or the <u>Advanced Script Development course</u>) and really helps when developing series. We'll also see how it works at episode level in the case study of *<u>Stranger Things</u>* at the end of Chapter 2.

Once we've defined (or mapped) and broken (or sequenced) these storylines, we're going to weave them so that we end up with a coherent episode rather than three separate storylines. This is done in both the logistical and the dramatic approach, though not in the same way. I call this Story Design 3.

Story Design 3: Story Weaving a One-Hour Episode

Let's see what our hypothetical episode looks like when we compare logistical and dramatic elements to see how format can meet structure:

Storylines: Where Format Meets Structure

WRITING A SUCCESSFUL TV SERIES
How to Pitch and Develop Projects for Television and Online Streaming
With The STORY-TYPE METHOD

Story Design 3: Story Weaving of a One-Hour Episode

Logistical Format	Act I					(CH) Act II					(CH) Act III					(CH) Act IV				
Scenes	1	2	3	4	5	1	2	3	4	5	1	2	3	4	5	1	2	3	4	
Scenes	1	2	3	4	5	6	7	8	9	10	11	12	13	14
Dramatic A-Story	X		BA2					MAC				Climax BA3		
Dramatic B-Story				X	BA2						Climax		BA3	
Dramatic C-Story						Act 2								
Dramatic Structure:	Act 1 I.E.					Act 2					MAC					Act 3			

Logistical Format:
Act I, II, III, IV = Beginning of Logistical Act (4-Act structure in this example)
(CH) = Potential Cliffhanger (before a commercial break)

Dramatic Structure:
Act 1, 2, 3 = Beginning of Dramatic Acts (3-Act structure following the A-Story)
I.E. = Inciting Event for the episode
X = Inciting Event for each storyline
BA2 = Beginning of Dramatic Act 2 for each storyline
BA3 = Beginning of Dramatic Act 3 for each storyline
MAC = Optional mid-act climax for the episode

SCREENPLAY Unlimited
WORKSHOPS & COURSES

Emmanuel Oberg

The logistical format sits at the top, in orange: Act I, Act II, Act III and Act IV mark the beginning of each logistical act, with a cliffhanger (CH) at the end of each act, before a commercial break.

At the bottom, you'll find the dramatic 3-Act structure in the same episode, outlined in blue: Act 1, Act 2 and Act 3 show the beginning of each dramatic act, following the 3-Act structure of the A-Story, with an optional mid-act climax (MAC).

In each storyline, X marks the inciting incident, BA2 the Beginning of Act 2 and BA3 the Beginning of Act 3.

So let's see how the different storylines are designed, sequenced, and woven in a one-hour episode using the dramatic 3-Act structure.

The green line shows the dramatic A-Story, so the main inciting incident takes place in green Scene 2 in this example. This is when dramatic Act 2 begins because the protagonist of the main plot, of the A-Story, starts to try to reach their goal and the audience understands what it is. The A-Story defines the main action in this episode.

It's usually a good idea to start the A-Story first, as it will help the audience to understand that it's the main dramatic action — what's primarily at stake in the episode.

The inciting incident triggers the protagonist's goal for that storyline in that episode, so the audience starts to wonder "Will the protagonist reach their goal or not?" This is the dramatic question, explored over the entirety of dramatic Act 2, and so most of the episode. By the end of the episode in that storyline, you give an answer to this question during the climax (green Scene 11 in this example).

At this point, the protagonist of the A-Story enters dramatic Act 3, which also starts dramatic Act 3 of the whole episode, as the main dramatic action is over. This is why the dramatic acts in an episode usually follow the dramatic acts of the A-Story.

So, for this hypothetical episode, dramatic Act 1 lasts until the A-Story starts, because it's the most important dramatic action in the episode. Then dramatic Act 2 starts when the protagonist of this storyline starts to act and when we understand what their goal is.

Dramatic Act 3 starts when this dramatic action is resolved. Of course, because there are other storylines, their respective dramatic acts will start at different times. In this example, dramatic Act 3 for the episode starts around green Scene 12.

Let's have a quick look at the other storylines. The B-Story is shown here in orange. All these are just examples in a hypothetical episode. I'm not saying that in all B-Stories, the inciting incident should always be in orange Scene 2. It's just an example showing how you can look for a dramatic structure underneath the logistical format. So the B-Story starts a bit later than the A-Story, the inciting incident for the B-Story only happens Scene 2 in the storyline, around minute 10 of the episode. The beginning of Act 2 in the B-Story is orange Scene 3 and dramatic Act 3 for the B-Story is the last orange scene.

The C-Story is much shorter, with just one dramatic act per scene. It could also be a runner, with just a few beats and no clear dramatic action.

Of course, you can have two or more storylines that meet in the same scene. In that case, you'll have two or more colours in the same scene. I didn't show that in this example to make the graph easier to read, but that's not the reality of what happens in an actual episode. We'll see this in the case study of *Stranger Things* at the end of Chapter 2.

Note that this logistical approach is based on scenes lasting two minutes, one of the many reasons why it's outdated, even if it's still taught in TV screenwriting classes around the world.

Today, most scenes would be around a minute long. A few scenes might be longer, maybe up to three or four minutes if it's an important scene, occasionally more, for example if it's a climax.

In modern series and especially in serials and limited series, we'll be mapping, sequencing and weaving storylines following the dramatic approach highlighted in this section. None of the prescriptive logistical milestones apply, except maybe in the simplest procedurals.

Modern serials or limited series commissioned by a streamer or a premium channel don't have clear logistical acts or cliffhangers arriving like clockwork every twelve pages or fifteen minutes, because they don't have commercial breaks. So the storytelling is much more fluid, more organic, and scenes are significantly shorter.

Let's Be More Dramatic

Let's stay with storylines for a moment because they form an essential part of series design and let's look at them from a dramatic approach, beyond episode level. This is especially relevant for serials and limited series, as most procedurals or sitcoms feature closed-ended episodes and only include minor ongoing storylines.

Storylines can span over many episodes and seasons — especially in theme-led serials like *Game of Thrones*, *Occupied* or *Succession* but also in plot-led ones such as *The Walking Dead*.

No matter how long they last, each storyline tends to be designed in three dramatic acts, divided into dramatic sequences.

Any one storyline can be plot-led, character-led or a hybrid — which starts as plot-led, becomes character-led or the opposite — so it's crucial to identify the main problem and what's at stake in each storyline. This will help you to create dramatic tension in each of the storylines, which is the best way to engage your audience. The A-Story is the most important dramatic action in the story and the B and C stories and so on are just less important dramatic actions, either in the season or in the episode, depending on which level you're looking at.

All this will help you to keep the audience engaged. A storyline will "lose the plot" when its protagonist starts to do something that has nothing to do with what the audience perceives as being their overall conscious goal or unconscious need. The protagonist's goal or need can evolve, but it should always be clear for the audience.

So, to keep the audience engaged over time, it's crucial that you keep track of what's at stake in each storyline at series, season, episode, sequence and even scene level. It's like an advanced form of plate spinning: you need to keep track of where each plate is, when you last "revived" it, and make sure that no single plate loses too much momentum. If even a single plate falls, the magic is broken, and you've lost your audience.

In series design, the only way to achieve this is to master the fractal aspect of the dramatic 3-Act structure and use it — consciously or not — to map, sequence and weave your storylines.

Storylines should also be connected to each other so that there is causality in the story — what happens in one storyline impacts on the others and stems from what happened before in the other storylines as well.

All this becomes clearer when you start looking at case studies of actual series. We're going to see how it's done in a plot-led series with the case study of *Stranger Things*, at the end of Chapter 2.

To give you an idea of what it looks like and to help you process the information in this section without having to wait until the end of Chapter 2, here is the A-Story in the first season of *Sex Education*, from the detailed case study in the companion course. It reveals the dramatic structure of Otis Milburn's storyline, and shows how eight dramatic sequences are mapped into eight episodes. Each sequence ends with a realisation or a step towards Otis' evolution, as it's a character-led series.

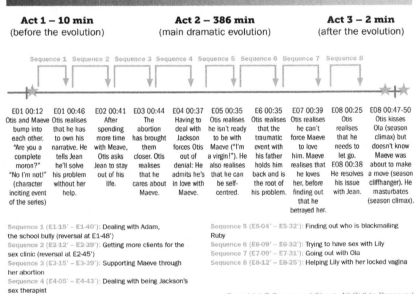

We can also produce a scene breakdown to see how the storylines are mapped, sequenced and woven over an entire season, tracking the A, B, C and D-Story in each episode. For example, here is the strands map of Episode 1 of *Occupied*.

[Note: If you'd like to download all the strands maps in landscape and in colour, please see If You Want to Find Out More... to access the bonus content for this book.]:

Storylines: Where Format Meets Structure 83

WRITING A SUCCESSFUL TV SERIES
How to Pitch and Develop Projects for Television and Online Streaming
With The STORY-TYPE METHOD

Structure (Theme-Led Series)

SCREENPLAY Unlimited
WORKSHOPS & COURSES

Strands Map for the First Episode of *Occupied* (45 minutes)

Storyline/Minute	1	2	3	4	5-6	7-10	11-12	13-14	15	16	17-19	20	23-24	25	27	29	30-31	32	32-35	36	37	38	39	40	41	42	43	44	TOTAL (Ep. 1)
A. Norway Prime Minister Jesper Berg	TFB							X											SX / FB	C						CH1		EC	22 min.
B. Bodyguard Hans Martin Djupnik and his wife Hilde									BA2		S1		MAC		S1		C					BA3					CH2	EC	19 min.
C. Journalist Thomas Eriksen								X															C			CH1		EC	14 min.
D. Restaurant owner Bente Norum, Eriksen's wife								X																			CH1		6 min.
E. Wenche Arnesen, Djupvik's boss at the PST									X											C	BA3						CH1	EC	11 min.
																													72 min.

At Season Level:
SX = Season Inciting Event

At Episode Level:
TFB = Teaser Flashback
X = Inciting Incident of the strand / storyline
C = Climax of the strand / storyline
MAC = Mid-Act Climax of the strand / storyline
BA2 = Beginning of dramatic Act 2
BA3 = Beginning of dramatic Act 3

A-Story: A + B + E (Djupnik trying to rescue Berg, Berg and the government trying to resolve the crisis)
B-Story: C (Eriksen trying to investigate Berg's abduction)
C-Story: D (Bente trying to keep her business going)

Episode Cliffhanger 1: Berg announces Russian "cooperation" on TV, Eriksen is appaled, Bente seems fine with it
Episode Cliffhanger 2: Djupvik worries about the safety of his family and the future of his country

Emmanuel Oberg

You might want to do something similar for your own project or your favourite series to map, sequence and weave the storylines at season level. It takes a fair bit of time, but it's a great way to learn, apply and master the concepts we're discussing in this book.

To sum it up, **from a story format point of view**, we have to identify the needs of the broadcaster and deliver a visible format: You're expected to make it clear in the script where the logistical act breaks are, because that's where the broadcaster will put the commercial breaks. If there are ad breaks in your show, you need to show logistical act breaks in the script. That's their primary function.

So you first identify the needs of the broadcaster, then you deliver a visible format that fits the expected number of commercial breaks, usually two to six. This means that we often have to use cliffhangers — unresolved conflict at the end of each logistical act — to make sure that the audience returns to the show after each ad break.

But **from a story design point of view**, and especially with ad-free premium channels and streaming, these logistical formats become mostly irrelevant.

Many writers use them because they're familiar and make sense to them. There's nothing wrong with using logistical act breaks consciously if it helps you to break a one-hour episode into more manageable units of ten to fifteen minutes. If that's the way you work, that's absolutely fine, as long as you're aware that this is not the underlying design. The underlying design uses dramatic *structure* — particularly its fractal aspect — not logistical *format*.

We've started to see how this underlying design works in this section on storylines and we'll explore this in more detail in Chapter 2 — especially in the case study of <u>Stranger Things</u>, as mentioned earlier — but for now please bear with me while we look at a few more elements often found in the conventional, logistical approach.

Cliffhangers

First, I'd like to spend a bit more time on cliffhangers, because although they stem from the need for commercial breaks, they are still very useful when it comes to breaking the linearity or predictability of a story, even when there are no commercial breaks.

With ad-free streaming and premium channels, we don't need a cliffhanger every twelve pages or fifteen minutes because we don't have commercial breaks, but we can still use them. They remain relevant, especially if we don't use them in a formulaic way.

A cliffhanger is simply an unresolved conflict: Before you move to a different storyline, before a commercial break, before the end of the episode, at the end of a season, you leave one or more characters in a difficult situation, and/or you give the audience a key piece of information. This can be achieved through *managing conflict* — for example you introduce a new obstacle, show that the antagonist has become stronger or cut away from a scene or sequence before or during its climax — or through *managing information* — you set up, exploit or resolve a mystery or a dramatic irony, you reveal a surprise to leave the audience wanting more.

Either way, whether you use managing conflict or managing information, the audience needs an answer because a question has been raised. It's like opening a parenthesis. The audience can't bear the idea of not seeing it closed at some point. They have to go on or come back to the show. It's very efficient as long as it's not done in an artificial or predictable way.

As we said, cliffhangers at the end of a logistical act have become less relevant but they still make sense when leaving a storyline — so that the audience wants to get back to it — and at the end of the episode or the end of the season, so that the audience wants to watch the next one.

You'll find a great example of a cliffhanger at the end of the pilot of *Transparent*. **Please watch it now, or skip the end of this section if you mind spoilers.**

For those of you who haven't watched *Transparent* and don't mind spoilers, let's quickly summarise what happens in the episode. A father invites his children for dinner and clearly struggles to say something important to them, so they wonder if he's dying of cancer or something, but he ends up telling them that he's selling the family house. After dinner, he makes a phone call to a friend or lover. We find out that he's transgender but couldn't bring himself to come out to his children as planned during dinner.

The mystery, at that point, is resolved for the audience with a surprise that sets up a dramatic irony. We had a mystery because during the dinner, like the children, we didn't know what was wrong.

When we realise, after the children have left, that the father is transgender, it's a resolution of that mystery. It's also a surprise because we were not expecting it, and it sets up a strong dramatic irony: Now we know that the father is transgender, but his children don't.

Towards the end of the episode, his married daughter asks a female friend, that she's just got back in touch with, to give her opinion on the selling potential of the father's house, while he is away. They start to make out in the house, which is a dramatic irony the father is now a victim of.

At the end of the episode, when the father returns to the house, these two dramatic ironies are resolved — the daughter sees her father dressed as a woman, and he sees her making out with a girl friend — and that's the cliffhanger of the first episode of *Transparent*.

It's a powerful ending because you really want to know what's going to happen next. You've seen the shock for both parties when they find out what they didn't know about each other. We want to know how the daughter is going to react to this information that she has about her father. We want to know how the father is going to react after finding his daughter in this situation, especially given the fact that she's married. We also want to know how, when and if the other children will find out about their father, now that one daughter knows, but the other siblings still don't.

As you can see, this isn't achieved through managing conflict: there is no obstacle, fight or argument between the characters. It's done in a much more subtle way, purely through managing information, using mystery, surprise and dramatic irony to generate suspense and tension.

All these questions at the end of the pilot were an effective way to leave the audience wanting to know what's going to happen next, which is really what an end of episode cliffhanger is about — raising questions that the audience has to see answered.

It's a classic example of an end-of-episode cliffhanger. As mentioned earlier, the pilot for *Transparent* was produced by Amazon along with pilots for other series and they then asked their audience to decide which series should get made.

The pilot of *Transparent* clearly worked because the audience voted for it and Amazon commissioned the first season. If you haven't seen *Transparent*, try to watch at least the first episode, it's well written, with a tantalising ending.

Teaser, Recap and Coming Next

A few more elements that are mostly logistical: *teaser*, *recaps* and *coming next*. I don't know about you, but I tend to skip *recaps* — what happened in previous episodes — and I always skip *coming next* — what happens in the next episode. I don't need to be told what happened when I've just watched an episode and I hate being told what's going to happen in the next one.

It makes more sense when you have a week between episodes, to remind the audience what happened previously and to tease them with what's going to happen next week, because it will be a whole week before they have a chance to follow and we want to make sure they show up. But with binge watching and every episode in a season available to stream from day one, it's become mostly irrelevant.

Teasers can be justified if they serve a dramatic purpose, especially a teaser flashback in a first episode. Whenever you have a first dramatic act that is too long, when you need more than ten minutes to set up the story world, introduce the characters and so on, a teaser flashback can be a great option: Starting the episode a little further into the story, at a very conflictual moment, so that you grab the attention of the audience within the first few minutes and quickly set the genre and tone. Then, you go back and take the time to introduce your characters, which is what you'll see in the first episodes of *Breaking Bad*, *The Queen's Gambit*, *The Walking Dead* or *Occupied*.

If you use a teaser just to have a short opening sequence before the credits, if it doesn't serve a dramatic purpose — for example introducing the theme or setting up a mystery or a dramatic irony — if it's not part of your franchise — as, for example, the teaser at the beginning of each episode of *Sex Education*, which explores the theme and sets the procedural aspect of each episode — it's just pointless. So, if you have a teaser, make the most of it, otherwise, nothing is mandatory. Teasers, especially teaser flashbacks at the beginning of a pilot, can feel cliché today if used in a non-imaginative way, because it's been done so many times.

Worst Point

Depending on the show's genre, there are many other prescriptive elements in the logistical approach to TV series writing. These are prescriptive plot points that some showrunners or writers might use.

One of them is the "Worst Point", which is the equivalent of "All Is Lost" in the feature film formulaic paradigm. About three quarters into the story, your protagonist has to reach the lowest point… Sure, that's possible, but why should it happen in every story at minute 45 if it's a one-hour episode? Personally, I don't see any reason to do this in such a formulaic and predictable way, especially if there are no commercial breaks. If we don't have to follow a logistical format, I don't see why we should see the same event happen at a specific moment in every story.

Of course, you can integrate these logistical plot points, if anyone insists on them, whether it's the showrunner or the broadcaster, but a series will be successful despite these formulaic crutches, not because of them. And it can definitely be successful without them. So, if you plan to develop series for streaming, set this aside and enjoy that freedom while you can, because that's one of the things that streaming and premium channels have given us: freedom from commercial breaks, hence from logistical constraints.

What Lies Beneath

We need to know about all these conventional elements, because again, this is the established language in the TV series industry, pretty much worldwide.

This logistical approach isn't always used in Europe, but elsewhere — especially in the U.S. — any discussion about TV series "structure" tends to be about logistical acts, specific plot points and turning points, teasers, cliffhangers and so on. That's fine. It's useful to understand this superficial approach in order to interpret feedback or follow a discussion without being confused.

As we said, this approach is mostly based on logistical *format* rather than on story *structure*, and the main reason for this is to give the illusion that there is a formula that can be followed and repeated. It's very reassuring, especially when you have a limited amount of time to churn out dozens of episodes.

If you think about it, when writers work on a newly commissioned series or a renewed season, they usually have a very short amount of time to write each episode. Sometimes a writer might have as little as one week to write a full episode. So these logistical way-points can be useful to break a story in a superficial way, following an industrial recipe.

From that point of view, just as Syd Field or Blake Snyder can be useful if you want to break down your two-hour feature film into logistical units, this conventional, logistical approach can help.

Talented writers simply integrate these logistical and artificial constraints. Even when they consciously follow a logistical approach to format their episodes, unconsciously they use more flexible, more powerful tools to structure their series and make them original, fresh and addictive.

I'm not suggesting you should entirely forget about these logistical elements. You should know about them because it's the primary language you're going to use in the foreseeable future to discuss series development and there are legitimate situations where you're expected to deliver a specific format depending on the number of ad breaks in the show. That's why we have spent a significant amount of time detailing them.

Just remember they don't have much to do with story structure and series design.

In the next chapter, we'll explore further the underlying series design and detail the structure that lies under the superficial format, besides the part on storylines that we introduced in this chapter. We'll illustrate how this works with the case study of *Stranger Things*. If, by the end of Chapter 2, you still feel the need for more details on mapping, sequencing and weaving storylines at episode and season level, I invite you to read about possible options in Conclusion and Next Steps at the end of this book.

1.4 Hands-On: What's Your Type? (Part 1)

I'd like to suggest a few questions that you might want to ask yourself at this stage, thinking about your project. To start with, we're going to tackle two questions related to conventional series design — and we'll leave those regarding the underlying series design until the end of the next chapter. These first questions should be fairly easy to answer and will help you to clarify the type of project you're working on.

What is the series format of your project?
Namely, the broad genre — whether it's comedy or drama — the number of episodes per season and the length of each episode.

This is a great opportunity for you to think about the best way to tell your story. Look at the number of episodes and the total amount of time that you've chosen for your series: Have you found the right length for your story? Could it be shorter, or would it benefit from being longer?

Sometimes you don't have a choice. You're just filling a programming slot and the number of episodes is set. Depending on the country, you might have other specific constraints as well: some countries rarely have seasons longer than six to eight episodes, others have much longer seasons. However, if you have more freedom, it can be a good idea to question your initial choice.

For example, writers often give too much time for their story to unfold, making it feel slow. In some genres, it can be perfectly fine to have an elongated story, but in others it's not ideal. Sometimes, going from ten to eight episodes, or from eight to six, or even just cutting one episode can have a positive impact on the pace of your series (not to mention the budget).

So, if you're developing a series that could benefit from a faster pace, just open that door for a moment. You might end up with exactly the same number of episodes, but you might also realise that you can condense the story so that it fits in fewer episodes without losing anything, while gaining pace and tension.

You could also ask yourself if you're starting the story too early. Try to identify when things get truly exciting in your series. Is it from the first episode, ideally early in the first episode, but certainly no later than the end of it?

Or does it get interesting by the end of Episode 3? If that's the case, should you condense the first three episodes into one so that you get to that exciting point by the end of this new first episode? Or should you go even further and simply cut Episode 1 and 2 and start with Episode 3?

Let's look at *Stranger Things* Season 2. One of the great aspects of the first season was how quickly and efficiently it started. Season 2 has a much weaker start, because it takes two or three episodes to get the main action started and it uses mystery a lot more than dramatic irony. If *Stranger Things* had started with Season 2 — which is obviously ridiculous because it couldn't have, but just hypothetically — they'd probably have been in trouble, or they might have attracted a different audience.

So that's one of the elements that you want to have in mind regarding your series. Do you have the right number of episodes, are they the right length and are you starting your story too early? It's rarely a problem for a story to start too late (too quickly), but starting the story too early or too slowly is a common flaw in many series projects.

What is the series type of your project?

Serial, procedural, hybrid, anthology, sitcom… This is going to help you understand the product you're selling, but it's also going to help you to identify the design, the story engine you need for your series. If you're developing a procedural, the story engine for the series — but also for each episode — is going to be quite different from the engine that drives a serial or a limited series.

For example, with a **classic procedural** such as *CSI*, you have a closed-ended plot-led 3-Act structure at episode level, maybe a soap element in a couple of character-led ongoing storylines, but no overall goal at season or series level, except a very generic one (to catch criminals). In a series such as *Grey's Anatomy*, you might have more of a serialised element.

With a **sitcom**, you have a main plot and a couple of subplots per episode, all closed-ended, with a few ongoing character-led storylines.

With a **limited series**, you'll most likely have a dramatic 3-Act structure at season level, with a main dramatic action or evolution if the series is plot-led or character-led. The series could be multi-stranded but plot-led, like *Chernobyl* or it could be character-led, like *Mare of Easttown*. You might not have a clear 3-Act structure at episode level, or when there is one it won't necessarily follow episode breaks, i.e. you might have a 3-Act structure that defines the A-Story in each episode, but it might not start, unfold and end within the same episode. For example, the A-Story in Episode 3 might have started at the end of Episode 2 or it could draw to a conclusion at the beginning of Episode 4. This is one of the reasons why it's so important to make the distinction between logistical and dramatic acts.

With a **serial**, as in *The Walking Dead*, you might have an overall 3-Act structure at series level, a different — but connected one — at season level and another 3-Act structure at episode and storyline level. This is similar to the structure for limited series that we looked at previously. You might also have a procedural element in a character-led serial, as in each episode of *Sex Education*.

And so on… As you can see, identifying your series type is the first step towards series design. We'll expand on this in the hands-on at the end of the next chapter, once we've discussed series design further.

2 Underlying Series Design

First Up

Now we're getting into more exciting territory, because this second chapter focuses fully on the **underlying series design**. It's all about achieving a strong emotional identification for the audience.

We covered some of this creative process in the first two sections of <u>1.3 Conventional Series Design</u>, especially when we talked about storylines and how this is where the actual story design starts in series.

So we're going to talk now about the fractal aspect of story structure in a series, how we can use Maslow's Hierarchy of Needs to widen our potential audience, and how managing information is often what makes or breaks a series. Then we'll see how all this plays out in a case study. It's time to update your story structure software to the 21st century... Enjoy the upgrade!

2.1 Underlying Story Structure

We now have a clearer idea about the conventional approach with its superficial format used to slice episodes, like sausages, according to the number of commercial breaks.

We've also started to see how we can follow a more dramatic approach when working on storylines, both at episode and season level, so now let's move on from storylines to look at the overall series design and structure.

This design is achieved through the tools and principles used — consciously or not — by writers, creators and showrunners, even when they apply a superficial, logistical format at episode level.

When showrunners talk about the way they break storylines and design episodes, 99% of them mention one of the logistical formats that we've discussed. It could be three, four, five, six, sometimes seven logical acts. They tend to discuss structure and design in logistical ways. That's fine. They work that way and when they're talented they produce fantastic shows using that approach consciously. Unconsciously though, they use the tools we've started to explain in Storylines: Where Format Meets Structure and the principles we're going to discuss now at season and series level.

Mastering these tools is key to designing a successful series, creating an irresistible bible and writing compelling pilots and episodes.

Let's take a bit of time to go through this dramatic approach. Some of this is going to look familiar if you've done the Advanced Script Development course or read *Screenwriting Unchained*, its free sampler or A Quick Overview: The Three Dimensions of Screenwriting as I'll be using some of the same info-graphs, but most of the content will be new because we're going to explore these elements specifically from the point of view of series design and writing. If you're not familiar with the method, it will be really helpful to catch up at this point. Please look at How to Make the Most of This Book to find out how to do this.

Story Structure in Series

Let's start with my definition of structure, as a combination of different elements: plot, character and theme, and most importantly, managing conflict and managing information.

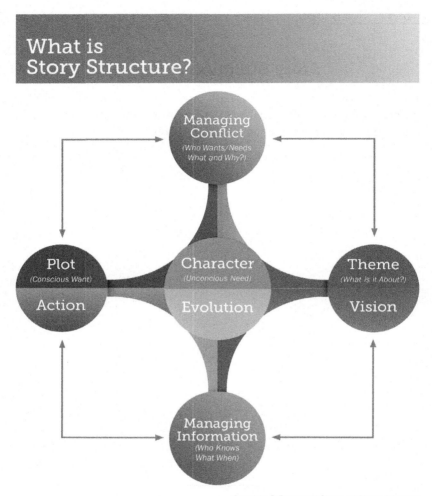

Managing Conflict (Who wants or needs what and why?) defines a main action or a main evolution in order to increase the emotional identification of the audience and help them focus their interest in the story. **Managing Information** (Who knows what and when?) helps us to break linearity and predictability in a story and to enhance both the intellectual and emotional involvement of the audience in the storytelling process.

In a series, as mentioned earlier, most procedurals and sitcoms are plot-led at episode level, for both their A and B-Story. They possibly include a couple of character-led subplots that run over a few episodes or a few seasons.

But of course, great series have strong characters and a strong theme, irrespective of the plot. A series tends to be successful if the audience falls in love with the characters and wants to see them again and again.

It's really all about characters, which is why — just like feature films — character is always at the centre of structure. We need to like the characters if we're going to come back to the same series and watch it, episode after episode. Some series are plot-led, some are theme-led, but all of them have strong characters, not just character-led ones.

Hybrids and serials tend to have a strong theme-led element, a multi-stranded element, and so different storylines within each episode and within each season. The A-Story over an episode will not necessarily be the same in the next one: The A-Story over one episode might become a B-story in the next episode. A subplot in one episode could become the main plot in the next one.

Some episodes in hybrids and serials might not have a very clear A-Story — one storyline that is clearly more important than the others and that defines the 3-Act structure of the episode. As mentioned earlier, you could have different A-Stories that are all connected to the main goal, in which case you have A1, A2, A3, A4 — a single A-Story split between different characters trying to resolve the same problem. You see this in *Stranger Things* or *Chernobyl*, for example.

What you really want to avoid is the situation where we don't know what's at stake in any given episode. As long as you define that clearly, as long as we know what's primarily at stake in each episode, you're free to achieve this any way you see fit.

You also want to make sure that the audience understands the connection between the different storylines. When you have more than one storyline, they must be connected in some way, usually through the theme (when the series is theme-led, like *Game of Thrones* or *Succession*) or through the plot (when it's plot-led, like *The Walking Dead* or *Chernobyl*). Otherwise, the audience loses focus and the story can easily become boring.

Fractal Aspect of Story Structure in Series

In order to design a successful series, you have to put aside the superficial episode format and look instead at the fractal use of story structure: How each storyline is designed, how they're connected and, most importantly, do they raise interesting questions, with strong stakes? This is what will engage the audience emotionally.

What's at stake in a story is defined by what happens if the protagonist fails to reach their goal (or fails to change if the series is character-led).

Once you're clear about that, you can start breaking down the storylines into dramatic sequences and weaving them with surprises, mystery and dramatic irony. This is how managing conflict and managing information becomes part of structure.

You design each storyline by clarifying whether they are structured around a main dramatic action or evolution, as we've seen in the previous chapter, but you also use managing information to create mystery and surprise — for example in cliffhangers to make sure that we want to watch the next episode or the next season.

So, the goal is to create compelling characters that we care about and events that keep us wanting to know what's going to happen next. That's really the main objective of story structure and story design: get the audience in a situation where they want to know what's going to happen next. That's what you want to achieve, and following an artificial format is not going to help you reach that.

We'll explore how to achieve this in the rest of the chapter and end with a case study to illustrate how it all works.

2.2 How to Identify Your Story-Type in Series

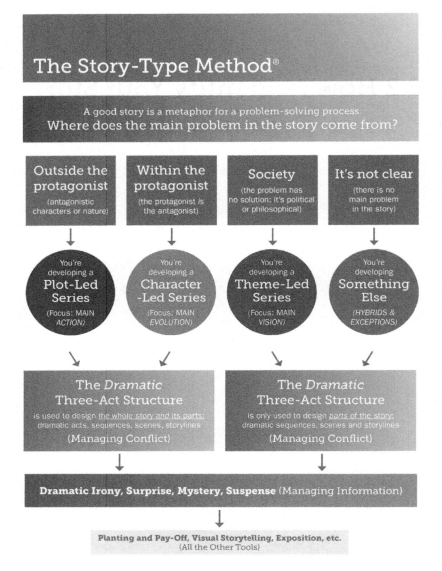

Let's revisit the familiar info-graph above to see how we can determine the story-type of a series, so that we can define the best way to develop it.

We start with the idea that a good story is a metaphor for a problem-solving process. So, let's ask ourselves: Where does the main problem in the story come from, at season level?

If the main problem comes from outside the protagonist, you're most likely developing a plot-led series, in which case the focus is the *main dramatic action*. Think of series such as *Stranger Things or The Walking Dead.*

And in that case, we use the dramatic 3-Act structure to design the whole series, most probably the whole season, but also its parts, whether it's episodes, dramatic acts, sequences, scenes, and so on, and that's what we call managing conflict.

We also use managing information — dramatic irony, surprise, mystery, suspense. These elements can be used irrespective of the story-type of your project, along with less structural tools such as planting and pay-off, visual storytelling, exposition and so on.

If the main problem lies within the protagonist, so the protagonist *is* the antagonist, you're most likely developing a character-led series and the focus is the *main evolution* of the character. This means that most likely at season level, possibly at series level, the backbone of the series is the evolution of your protagonist.

It's less likely to be the evolution of a group of characters sharing the same need, but either way this main dramatic evolution will shape the dramatic backbone of your season. Think of series such as *Sex Education or After Life.*

In that case, we'll still be using the dramatic 3-Act structure because we'll have one main dramatic *evolution* defining three dramatic acts, but we'll also use it to design parts, whether it's episodes, storylines, sequences, scenes, and so on through managing conflict. As with a plot-led series, we'll also use managing information and all the other tools.

If the main problem lies in society, or in the story world more generally — often it doesn't have a solution and might be political or philosophical — you'll have many storylines and no clear protagonist overall. You're most likely developing a theme-led series and the focus is the main *vision* of the creator. Think of series such as *Big Little Lies* or *Succession.*

In that case, you can't use the dramatic 3-Act structure to design the whole season as there is no main dramatic action or evolution, but you can still use it to design parts of the story. For example, you could use it to design each episode as plot-led. And of course, you can also use it to design storylines, dramatic sequences and so on, as we've seen in the previous chapter.

When you develop a feature film, it's fairly easy to identify if your story is theme-led, because it tends to be multi-stranded, with each strand connected to the same theme. When a feature is multi-stranded and we have no clear protagonist, we're usually dealing with a theme-led story.

With series, especially serials and limited series, it's more difficult, because most of them are multi-stranded anyway. To identify whether your multi-stranded series is theme-led or not, one of the easiest ways is to go back to the other two story-types and to see if you have one main dramatic action or one main dramatic evolution that actually shapes the story, at least at season level. This will give you a strong indication that despite the fact that it's multi-stranded, it's not theme-led. If you have a clear protagonist and one main dramatic action or one main dramatic evolution, your series is unlikely to be theme-led. You're most probably dealing with a plot-led or a character-led series.

Another element that can give you a hint: When you look at the storylines, do all the protagonists in each storyline have the same goal, and are all the dramatic actions in each of the storylines triggered by the same inciting incident? Very often, when the same inciting incident triggers the same goal in different storylines, it tends to be a plot-led series, even if it's multi-stranded.

Chernobyl, for example, looks like it's theme-led — and in a way it is because there is a problem in society: the oppressive Russian state and the way they cover up information.

But if you think about it, all the different storylines share the same inciting event and most of them are plot-led: Each protagonist in each of the storylines has a main conscious goal, which is related to the main problem (dealing with the aftermath of the accident in the nuclear power plant). Which is why, despite the fact that it's multi-stranded, *Chernobyl* is actually plot-led, like many disaster series.

When it's not clear, when you're struggling to identify a main problem in your series, it might be because you have more than one problem and it's difficult to decide which is the main one — especially if they aren't connected to the same theme, which would point to a theme-led series. It might be because you have no main problem, so you can't identify one at all. Or it could be using non-linear storytelling and hopping between different time frames or time loops.

If this sounds like your project, you're probably developing something else, a hybrid — a series that combines two or more story-types — or an exception — a series with no clear story-type. Think of series such as *Happy Valley*, *Mr. Robot*, *Fleabag*, *Russian Doll* or the first season of *True Detective*.

In this case, you won't use the dramatic 3-Act structure to design the whole series or the whole season, because it's an exception or a hybrid, but you might still use it to design parts of it. And you'll often use managing information as the main structural tool. So managing information will likely be a key part of the way you design your story as a series — so that it works as an exception.

Otherwise, you might be dealing with an exception that doesn't work (yet), and you might want to consider if it would be beneficial for your series to rely more clearly on one of the main story-types, or how you can make it work as a hybrid or an exception, which usually involves looking at the way you manage information.

I'm aware that it becomes trickier to assess your story-type when you're dealing with series. They are significantly more complex to develop and analyse than feature films. I hope this is starting to help though.

If you need more guidance in this area and you've already read <u>A Quick Overview: The Three Dimensions of Screenwriting</u> at the beginning of this book, you might want to try the interactive story tool on the website, which has been designed to help you identify your story-type. Please see <u>If You Want to Find Out More...</u> at the end of this book for more details.

In any case, looking at how we can use Maslow in series should help further, so let's discuss this next.

2.3 Use of Maslow in Series

When we talk about series design, Maslow is very much running the show. I find it especially relevant when thinking about the design of the whole series, but it remains useful at season and episode level.

Let's look at a few illustrations you may already be familiar with, this time specifically from a series design perspective, starting with the classic representation of Maslow's Hierarchy of Needs:

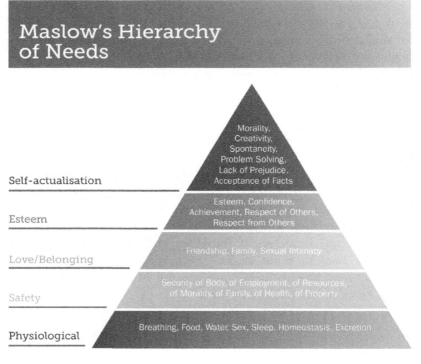

I'm going to go through the different levels quickly, as this is something I've already analysed in detail in *Screenwriting Unchained*, which many of you will have already read.

The lowest one, **physiological**, is the most universal and fundamental level that every human being can relate to. It's about survival, staying alive (or, as far as sex is concerned, keeping the species alive).

The next level, **safety**, is also universal: security of body, employment, resources, morality, family, health, and so on. Most human beings can relate to that too: It's about protecting your loved ones and keeping a roof over their heads.

Love/Belonging sits in the middle of the pyramid. It's about friendship, family and sexual intimacy. You need to be a bit more "evolved" to relate to this level (and have your lower needs satisfied to be able to focus on it, according to Maslow).

Just above that, we have **esteem**: esteem, confidence, achievement, respect of others and from others.

And, finally, **self-actualisation**, which is the highest (and most abstract) level: morality, creativity, problem solving, lack of prejudice, acceptance of fact. I won't get into the sixth level of Maslow — a late addition about intrinsic values such as truth, fairness and justice — because it's less relevant to storytelling.

Now let's see how we can use Maslow's Hierarchy of Needs during the development of a series in relation to its potential audience, story-type and genre.

Target Audience

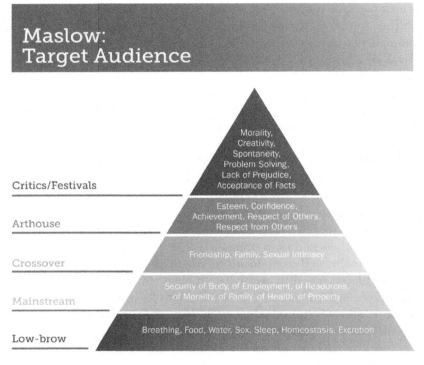

Part of knowing your potential audience is looking at the main problem in your series and positioning it on Maslow's pyramid. This will give you a first indication. Then look at the main problem inside each of the storylines and see if you're expanding or reducing your potential audience. Obviously, it's not a rule. It's just to get you thinking.

It's not a formula either, because it's more fluid than that. But it should help you assess your potential audience, depending on where the main problem lies in your series and in each of the storylines.

Usually, if you think about the main problem, the lower in the pyramid, the larger the potential audience, simply because more people can relate to that problem. Typical examples are *The Walking Dead*, *Lost* or *Squid Game*, which are primarily about physiological and survival needs, so can potentially reach the widest possible audience, irrespective of the shooting language.

Similarly, the higher you go in the pyramid, the more you're at risk of shrinking your potential audience, because only some of the audience can relate to these higher levels.

The top level is the one which, taken in isolation, can reach the fewest people, so has the most limited audience.

Now of course, storylines are an important element of series design, so with series you should not only look at the main problem at series or season level, you should also look at the main problem in each storyline. You might find one main problem in the story located at the top, while other storylines explore problems lower in the pyramid, which would balance things out.

For example, if *Occupied* hadn't explored problems rooted much lower in Maslow's Hierarchy of Needs for many of its storylines, it's unlikely it would have met such commercial success. However, as it works on many levels, it is both emotionally satisfying and intellectually challenging.

Money Heist follows an inverted pattern. As a heist story with a hostage situation, it has a main problem firmly rooted in the first and second layer of Maslow, which suggests a wide potential audience as everyone can relate to these issues. But each storyline explores a problem about relationships, love/belonging, friendship, sexual intimacy, all the way up to morality. This vertical exploration of the pyramid helps to expand its potential audience too, by making the story more sophisticated.

Stranger Things is a supernatural horror thriller where a young boy and then a teenage girl have gone missing. Its main problem is firmly rooted at the bottom of the pyramid. It's all about safety / survival / protection of the family and this suggests in itself a wide potential audience, because pretty much everyone can relate to this layer of the pyramid, irrespective of their language or culture.

So this is where the main problem lies in *Stranger Things*, but each storyline explores problems located higher in Maslow's Hierarchy of Needs, all the way up to problem solving and acceptance of fact.

Hopper's goal, for example, is to find Will, like almost everyone else in the story, but he also has a need to move on from the death of his daughter, and the conflicts that he experiences in the story are going to help him do this. This is the character-led element of his storyline.

Having elements in the story located higher in the pyramid means that you can extend your audience to people who might not want a simple horror but are interested in relationships and strong themes. For example, in *Stranger Things*, the themes of trust, loss and friendship.

So you never take just one element in isolation. If you have a main problem rooted at the bottom of the pyramid, check if you have elements in the story located higher, to give it more substance and make it more complex. If you have a main problem lying at the top, can you try to widen your potential audience with elements and problems in each storyline rooted much lower in Maslow's pyramid?

Great stories tend to explore the pyramid vertically, finding material in almost every layer.

For example, *After Life* is about a man who has lost his wife to cancer and can't bear to live without her. The whole story is character-led, it's about his need to move on from the death of his beloved wife. This main problem lies at the top of the pyramid: It's all about acceptance of facts.

However, the protagonist is also suicidal, which means that there is a strong element of survival (as long as we care about the character). He's not necessarily likeable, but he experiences a lot of conflict, so we start to identify and empathise with him and want him to survive. We give him the goal to fail (not to kill himself), so that he gets to live the rest of his life, even if it's without his wife.

This part of the story takes us to the lower levels of Maslow and, adding to that, it's also a gross-out comedy. It's Ricky Gervais: You have a lot of humour, coming from lower layers in the pyramid, mainly food and sex — reliable sources of gross-out humour — that helps to significantly widen its potential audience.

Again, it's not a formula, but if your main problem in the story lies at the top, try to think: What could I use in the story to widen its potential audience? Dealing with a serious, sad or tragic problem doesn't prevent you from including story elements rooted lower in the pyramid.

Of course, if you're developing a tragedy, you might not want to introduce that much gross-out humour — though it could produce something quite interesting. The idea is that you can explore any problem, just try not to stay solely in one layer of the pyramid.

In feature films, unless you're developing a multi-stranded narrative, you tend to have one main plot and maybe a couple of subplots, while in series, you're usually dealing with many storylines. Identifying a main problem inside each storyline and where that problem is located on Maslow's pyramid is going to help you enhance the dramatic drive in your series and get a sense of your potential audience.

Story-Type

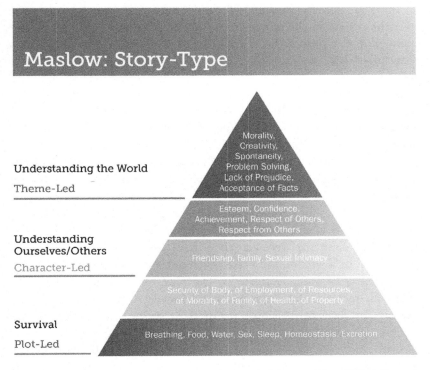

Let's see how we can use Maslow in series in relation to story-types.

The key thing to remember is that if your series is plot-led, your audience expects you to explore primarily a lower level; if it's character-led, you're expected to delve into the middle of the pyramid; and if it's theme-led, you'll often be exploring the top at series or season level, but you'll gain a lot by venturing into lower levels at episode or storyline level.

Let's see how we can develop this more precisely, depending on the series type.

Procedurals, especially cop shows and medical shows, series like *House M.D.*, *Luther*, *CSI* and so on tend to have a main problem that lies at the very bottom of the pyramid. A killer is on the run, and we have to catch them before they commit another murder. A patient needs help otherwise they'll die... These can potentially reach a very wide audience because their main problem is about survival. It's rooted at the bottom of Maslow's pyramid.

There are some character-led arcs in these procedurals, developed over the season or the whole series, but they tend to be subplots. The main plot, the procedural element in each episode, is usually about survival, even if there is also a problem-solving element sitting at the top.

Sitcoms tend to be plot-led at episode level and character-led with a permanent negative answer (characters don't change) at series level. They usually focus on the middle of Maslow's pyramid, as they are about relationships (family, friendship, sexual intimacy).

Of course you have exceptions. *Fleabag* is more character-led than a typical sitcom, but it still mostly explores the middle of Maslow's pyramid.

It gets a bit more complicated with **serials or limited series**, as always, but they tend to be either theme-led or to have a strong theme-led element, because they have more storylines than a procedural or a sitcom. I'm thinking about a proper theme-led series like *Game of Thrones*, *Succession* or *Occupied*. Serials can also be plot-led or character-led at series and season level. As a result, serials can exploit any level of Maslow's pyramid, at series, season or storyline level.

Both plot-led and character-led serials tend to be plot-led at episode level: There is usually a main plot that defines a main dramatic action in each episode, even if the series itself is character-led at season level.

Let's look at a few examples of serials or limited series:

The Night Manager is a plot-led limited series. It's about a British ex-soldier trying to stop a secret arms dealer, who also happens to have killed the protagonist's lover. The protagonist's life is at stake, because the antagonist is victim of a strong dramatic irony: He doesn't know the protagonist's true identity, but we do. So we fear the resolution of this dramatic irony, which is a classic and efficient way to generate suspense and tension in a thriller. We know that if the protagonist's cover is blown, he's probably going to get killed. We also fear for the lives of other characters who are suffering due to the antagonist's actions. The series is plot-led because the main problem — the antagonist — is external, even if there is a character-led subplot: the protagonist needs to move on from the death of his lover and his related guilt. So, the thriller element explores the lower part of the pyramid (survival), the love/relationship element explores the middle (sexual intimacy) and the guilt element explores the top (acceptance of facts).

Breaking Bad is completely different, because it's really about the evolution of the protagonist. Vince Gilligan described it himself as "A character who goes from Mr. Chips to Scarface". Walter White, the main protagonist of *Breaking Bad*, has many opportunities to get out over the seasons, but he doesn't because he's compelled to go on, until his wife helps him to realise that they have more money than they'll ever need. In terms of Maslow, the story is very much about 'achievement' and 'respect from others'. The main problem is his ego, his pride. It leads him to destroy the very thing he believes he's trying to protect: his family. Although we understand his motivation and root for him because of the conflict he experiences, after a few seasons we give him the unconscious goal to change, to realise that he's wrong.

Each episode of *Breaking Bad* is a beat towards that evolution. It's such an extreme evolution that it's fascinating to watch and constitutes the backbone of the series. As soon as we identify that the character needs to realise that he's going in the wrong direction, the series becomes character-led even if many episodes are plot-led and if most of the obstacles are external. This is because there is an almost permanent internal conflict / dilemma for the protagonist.

Even if we don't approve of Walter's objective, we understand his motivation, which is all about family and survival. And that's key when it comes to Maslow. Vince Gilligan rooted his protagonist's motivation in the 'security of family, of health' layer. This is one of the elements in *Breaking Bad* that contributed to widening its potential audience, despite the fact that the character was morally flawed and that the main problem (about esteem, respect from others) sat higher in the pyramid.

One last example, **Game of Thrones**. The separate strands remain unconnected for a long time. Each storyline has a different protagonist with a different goal and of course the main problem lies in the story world — which House will sit on the Iron Throne and rule over the other families? It's a theme-led series, the main theme being power and survival, which sits quite low on Maslow.

In *Game of Thrones*, each strand or storyline is designed as either plot-led or character-led — or occasionally as a hybrid, which is when the strand starts as plot-led and becomes character-led, or vice versa. Most of the strands are about survival, one way or the other, and often use sex or violence to reach as far down as possible in Maslow's pyramid. This is how the series is designed overall, which explains in many ways its mainstream appeal.

While there is no rule or formula in relation to Maslow (or anything else!), it can help to think about the story-type of your series, and make sure that you're exploring the levels in Maslow that your story suggests and that your audience expects. Otherwise, make sure that you have a good reason to defy these expectations (and that it doesn't make the budget unrealistic). This should help you to get it made and reach its intended audience.

Genre

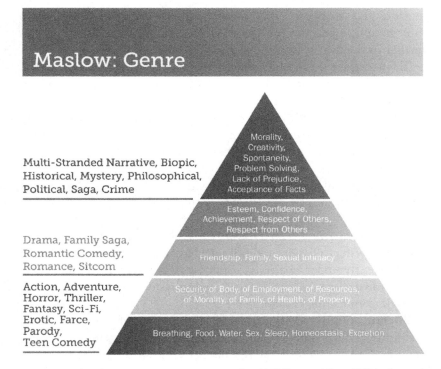

What can we say about Maslow regarding series genre?

Procedurals, especially cop shows and medical shows, tend to have a main problem lying at the bottom of Maslow and to explore the survival layer: a killer is on the run and we have to catch them, a patient is about to die and we try to save them. This is why they are usually plot-led and can reach a wide potential audience.

There's one thing to consider carefully if you're developing a procedural, or if you have a cop show, a private investigator show, any story where you're exploring a whodunit, a howdunit, a whydunit. If it's about a murder that has already been committed and if you create a mystery about who the killer is or how or why they did it, you are right at the top of Maslow. It's primarily intellectual, it's about problem-solving and, as such, it's not a thriller at all.

That's fine if that's what you want, but if you're after more than an intellectual puzzle, if you want an emotional involvement from the audience as well, make sure that you also explore lower layers in the pyramid, especially if you want to have a thrilling element or some tension and suspense. This usually comes from management of information, especially the use of dramatic irony. We'll discuss this further in the next section, Managing Information in Series.

To increase a thriller element, you might also want to ensure that someone's life is at stake, especially when the protagonist is investigating a murder that has already been committed. Maybe they're risking their life trying to catch the murderer, or the murderer might be about to strike again, in which case it's the next victim's life that's at stake. It could also be the protagonist's loved ones whose lives are in danger.

All this will allow you to explore lower levels in Maslow's pyramid, which is what you're expected to do with a thriller.

Some series have successfully combined mystery with thriller elements. *The Girl with the Dragon Tattoo* is a good example: There is a strong mystery element (whodunit), but the two main protagonists are frequently under threat, and they are also trying to protect other people's lives. In this way, having a main mystery overall doesn't hold us back from feeling suspense and tension.

Sitcom, family shows, drama and soaps are usually about relationships, friendship, family, sexual intimacy. For example, *Friends*, *How I Met Your Mother*, *The Big Bang Theory*, all these series tend to explore the middle rather than the bottom or the top of Maslow's pyramid.

Sitcoms, when they're successful, can reach a very wide audience, possibly larger than your typical drama, and that's because they use humour. While the main problem usually lies in the middle of the pyramid, they often reach lower with gags based around food, sex or excretion, which are universal sources of comedy. If you go low with gags, you can set the main problem as high as you want in the pyramid and still potentially reach a wide audience.

Serials can fall into any genre, so tend to explore a combination of layers. Some have a main problem at the top of the pyramid, but if they reach a wide audience, they will usually include storylines that explore lower layers.

Stranger Things, which is a supernatural horror thriller, has a main problem rooted at the bottom of the pyramid in the first season: 'Saving and rescuing Will and Barbara' for the main co-protagonists;

'escaping and surviving from Brenner and the Demogorgon' for Eleven. However, some aspects also involve mystery and problem-solving: What happened to Will Byers? What is the Creature and where does it come from? Who is Eleven and what happened to her?

So, make sure that you set a main problem in your series at the right level according to its genre, because this will help you to reach your intended audience. But remember that you can explore lower problems in other elements (storylines, gags) to widen your potential audience.

2.4 Managing Information in Series

In this brief discussion on Maslow, we've already seen how managing information can play a role in defining the genre (mystery or thriller), what's at stake (intellectual or emotional question) and which part of the pyramid a story explores, all of which have an impact on the potential audience.

Now we're going to discuss managing information further because it really is a crucial part of series design.

Get this right and it will bring you the keys to the kingdom. Underestimate the power and importance of managing information in series and you might be reducing your chances of developing a successful one.

Surprise, Mystery, Dramatic Irony, Suspense

Let's start with a quick recap on managing information. This is going to be brief because I'm aware that many of you will have read <u>Screenwriting Unchained</u> or done my <u>Advanced Script Development Course</u> or workshop, where I dive deep into the way this essential aspect of storytelling can be used in any form of screenwriting. At the very least, you've read <u>A Quick Overview: The Three Dimensions of Screenwriting</u> at the beginning of this book, which also brushes on this. In this section, I'd like to focus on how managing information applies specifically to TV series.

Developing a Series
Managing Information

Managing Information in series:
1. Using dramatic irony to generate suspense or comedy
2. Using surprise to raise the stakes or generate comedy
3. Using mystery to raise tantalising questions
4. Making sure that mystery doesn't kill suspense or prevent identification
5. Using managing information to create cliffhangers

In a story, each piece of information to be shared with the audience can be revealed or exploited as a dramatic irony, a surprise or a mystery, and the way in which we deliver information to the audience (what we'll call "managing information") can also be used to generate suspense. Let's briefly define these terms again before we go further.

Dramatic irony is when the audience is aware of information that at least one character on screen doesn't know about.

Surprise is when you suddenly reveal information to the audience that they are not expecting.

Mystery is when you give enough information to the audience so that they become aware that there is something they don't know. If you don't give that first little bit, they don't know they don't know, so there is no mystery. As soon as you give them that little bit of information, they know they don't know, which makes them start to wonder. That's how mystery works.

Suspense comes when the audience is aware of a danger. To create suspense, you give the audience information about where the danger lies and make no mystery about the reality of the threat.

Using Dramatic Irony to Generate Suspense or Comedy

One of the most common ways to create suspense is to use dramatic irony: You tell the audience about the danger, but you don't tell some of the characters. We then fear what's going to happen to the characters because they don't know about this threat.

You can also make the antagonist victim of a strong dramatic irony to generate suspense. For example, the protagonist is trapped by a serial killer, we know they're trying to escape but the antagonist doesn't. We're going to fear the consequences of the resolution: What's going to happen when — or if — the antagonist finds out. We know that at some point the antagonist will find out, because a dramatic irony needs to be resolved. That's a classic way to use dramatic irony to generate suspense or tension in a thriller or in drama.

Dramatic irony is also a powerful tool to generate comedy. It's used to create situation comedy and we'll see an example of that in the next section, with *Friends*.

Dramatic irony can also be used to create a classical misunderstanding — when two characters are victims of two different dramatic ironies and these two dramatic ironies feed into each other. This creates a misunderstanding, which generates comedy because we know what each character is thinking — and they're both wrong. These are just two examples of how you can use dramatic irony to generate suspense or comedy in a series.

Using Surprise to Raise the Stakes or Generate Comedy

As we experience a story, whether it's an episode or a season, we want the stakes to be raised at some point. We want to feel that things are getting worse, just to break the feeling that we might be in a status quo, a routine, which makes the story predictable.

To raise the stakes, you can introduce a new obstacle or you might make the antagonist stronger in some way. The idea is to give unexpected information that leads us to realise that something bad is going to get worse.

Surprise is also used a lot in comedy, because in comedy almost every gag is a surprise. When you set up a gag, you get the audience to think that something is going to happen, but when you pay it off, we get something else, that we weren't expecting, which makes us laugh.

So surprise works at many levels in a series, not just for cliffhangers and end-of-episode or end-of-season twists. It can be used to raise the stakes in a thriller as well as in every single gag in a comedy.

Using Mystery to Raise Tantalising Questions

This is a key part of series design because many series are slow-burn mysteries, for example *Broadchurch*, *The Returned (Les Revenants)*, *Fortitude* or even *The Mare of Easttown*. Each season can be built around one big mystery, meaning that as the season unfolds, you're going to give enough information so that we know there is something we don't know, but not enough for us to find out what it is, until the end.

As soon as you introduce mystery in a series, you start an intellectual process: We want to resolve that mystery. You might bring in surprises as well along the way, but your main engine will be mystery.

Making Sure That Mystery Doesn't Kill Suspense or Prevent Identification

When you design your series around a slow-burn mystery, you reveal information in layers like an onion — often using misdirection until you have a final reveal, a final surprise. This can help to keep your audience engaged, but it can also cause problems. It's important to make sure that mystery doesn't kill suspense or prevent identification.

How do you achieve that? Well, first of all, you don't use mystery alone, you use other tools as well. You try to balance the fact that yes, there are things we don't know, but we're privileged in other ways. Even if we like the mind game and the puzzle-solving, we never want to be the one who knows the least in the story.

So if you have a strong mystery in your series, try to bring in dramatic irony and surprise to balance out the amount of information that we don't have with information that we do (and ideally that some characters in the story don't have) to make us feel privileged rather than isolated.

While dramatic irony can work on its own in a series, I would really advise against using just mystery. The situation you want to avoid at any cost is when the protagonist knows more than the audience over a long period of time. We can identify and empathise with a protagonist who is trying to resolve a mystery as long as they don't know more than we do about it. When they do, as Holmes often does in *Sherlock*, we usually have a co-protagonist who doesn't — Watson — with whom we can identify more easily.

Naturally, your protagonist knows more about their own backstory than we do. This isn't a problem as long as it doesn't prevent us from understanding the protagonist's goal or motivation. There are many things protagonists know about their past that we don't need to know.

But when the protagonist's backstory is relevant to the present story — particularly to the main plot — you have to be cautious. If we're kept in the dark about something that impacts how they feel and the decisions they make, then we'll feel more and more alienated and distant.

Let's see how we can work around a potentially problematic mystery.

The first option is to make sure that the mystery over the protagonist's backstory doesn't last for too long. You can see an example of this approach in the first season of ***Happy Valley***, where the protagonist, Catherine Cawood, initially knows a lot more than we do about key elements of her backstory. However, we quickly catch up with her — and even get to know more than she does, as it's an open mystery (we'll talk more about this in the next section). So there can be elements we don't know about the protagonist, that are relevant to the story, as long as we catch up quickly, ideally early in the first episode. If you bridge that information gap between the protagonist and the audience in the first episode, it's usually fine.

When this isn't possible, an alternative is to make sure that your protagonist doesn't have the information either. So even if the mystery centres around their past, can you design the story so that the protagonist doesn't know about it or doesn't remember it? I know it's a cliché, but it's often used to avoid this potential identification problem.

The beginning of *The Walking Dead* is designed this way. After a short teaser flash-back that sets-up the genre (Zombie horror drama), we learn a little bit about the main protagonist, Rick Grimes, before he gets shot around minute ten. We then continue with a semi-cold start: Rick wakes up from a coma, in hospital. He has no idea what has happened to the world around him during his coma, so we catch up gradually, alongside him. We resolve the mystery with the protagonist, as the story unfolds. We never feel that he knows more than we do about important elements of his backstory and we avoid long expository scenes.

So you can give your protagonist amnesia as in *Bourne Identity*, make them miss key events as in *The Walking Dead*, or, as in *Sex Education*, use a repressed memory. Amnesia, coma or repressed memory are different ways to make sure that the protagonist doesn't know more than the audience about their relevant backstory. In this way, the protagonist doesn't stand above the audience on the information ladder over a long period of time, which would make identifying with them difficult, if not impossible.

This is unfortunately what happens in *Sharp Objects*, a psychological drama based on Gillian Flynn's debut novel, created by Marti Noxon. The protagonist, crime reporter Camille Preaker, has clearly experienced trauma in the past, but the storytellers don't share this information with us, which creates a mystery over the protagonist's backstory.

As a result, we can see that the protagonist is deeply unhappy, but we struggle to identify with her emotionally because we don't know why. It takes a long time before we have enough information to feel close to the protagonist, and by that time many in the audience might have given up.

There were some differences on the set about how much of the script ended up on screen, and the end result is a beautifully directed limited series with excellent acting, but a story that leaves many cold, mainly because of the way information is managed. Unless you're a fan of mystery, you simply don't know enough to truly care about the protagonist.

I'm not saying that you can never put the audience in a situation where they know less than the protagonist. I'm only saying that if you want the audience to be able to identify emotionally with the protagonist, you want to avoid a situation where the protagonist knows more than the audience over a long period of time.

What about a protagonist whose backstory we only reveal over the course of the series? The answer is "it depends", as always. If not knowing the information is not crucial to the main plot, if it's something that's in the background, if it is only indirectly connected to the main action, if it doesn't impact our understanding of the protagonist's motivation, emotions and decisions, then it's fine to keep that as a mystery. If it's a small thing compared to the story events, you can reveal it gradually. This is what happens in *The English*, the limited series created by Hugo Blick, with Emily Blunt. We learn about the protagonist's backstory fairly late, but it doesn't prevent us from being able to identify with her because we understand her main conflict early on.

If, on the other hand, the information kept from the audience is essential to the main plot, if the decisions and the emotions that your character experiences during the main action are connected to this knowledge that they have and that we don't have, it becomes tricky. You might be able to create a successful exception (such as *Fleabag*) and I'd love to watch it when it's done if you manage to pull it off, but it's going to be difficult.

The main reason is that you're asking us to identify with a character who is not sharing with us something that's crucial if we're to understand the way they behave and share their emotions. That creates a distance between the protagonist and the audience, and of course you don't want that. Unless you don't want the audience to be close to that character, which is rarely the case for a protagonist.

Having a mystery over a character who is not the main protagonist is entirely possible. Sometimes, we have a mystery over the backstory of a secondary character. They could be the main character — the most fascinating or the most interesting character in the story — but not the character you want the audience to identify with emotionally.

For example, Eleven in the first season of *Stranger Things* is not the protagonist. She might be the main character, she's definitely fascinating, she will be an occasional co-protagonist, but she isn't the main protagonist because she isn't the character who experiences the most conflict in the story, especially at the beginning.

So there is a strong mystery over Eleven's backstory, it's relevant to the main story, we don't necessarily understand all her emotions and all her decisions, but none of this is a problem because she's not the main protagonist. Her backstory — what happened to her before the beginning of *Stranger Things* — is revealed over the course of the first season, mostly visually through flashbacks. That's absolutely fine because not knowing her backstory doesn't prevent us from identifying with Will Byers' mother, brother and friends who, along with Hopper, are the main protagonists of the first season.

Using Managing Information to Create Cliffhangers

One last aspect of managing information in series: cliffhangers. When we create cliffhangers, we often use mystery, surprise or dramatic irony, so that the audience wants to go back to a storyline or to watch the next episode or the next season.

As explained in the first chapter, cliffhangers are an unresolved conflict. Writers often think of cliffhangers in terms of managing conflict, and so they will simply stop the episode before the end of the fight or the scene, or before the argument is over. This is fine, but managing information offers a more subtle way to create cliffhangers, by leaving the audience with information that they weren't expecting (whether it's a surprise or the set-up of a dramatic irony) or by setting a mystery and telling the audience something that makes it clear that they don't know something, so they want to find out what it is.

As we can see, mystery, surprise and dramatic irony can all be used to generate cliffhangers.

Overall, the way you manage information in series has a huge impact on your potential audience. If you rely primarily on mystery and keep raising questions without answering any, the audience will most likely shrink over time. You want to find the right balance between raising questions and answering them within an episode or a season. For example, by closing subgoals — whether they are victories or defeats — or by giving information to the audience, using surprise and dramatic irony.

Rather than having a main mystery over more than one season, it's often beneficial to resolve it and replace it with another at the end of each season. Of course, there are successful exceptions to this, such as *Lost*.

The end-of-season cliffhanger doesn't have to be a mystery. It could be a dramatic irony or any combination of managing information tools, allowing you to provide a satisfying ending to the season, while suggesting there is more to come. Either way, managing information often achieves that more successfully than managing conflict.

Examples

True Detective, *Broadchurch*, *The Killing*, *The Girl With the Dragon Tattoo*... We call these closed mysteries in TV series lingo. This just means that neither the protagonist nor the audience know what lies behind a mystery. It's closed, and the protagonist usually tries to resolve the mystery over the whole season (if a serial) or over each episode (in a procedural).

On the other hand, series like *Happy Valley* or *Columbo* — to take a classic example — are open mysteries. An open mystery is a misleading name, because it's actually when you have dramatic irony instead of mystery: the audience knows "who's done it", but not the protagonist. So the mystery is for the protagonist, not the audience. This is the case in *Columbo* at episode level (the audience knows who the murderer is from the start) or in the first season of *Happy Valley* (the audience knows who the antagonists are and what they are planning or doing while the protagonist doesn't). In these, the mystery for the audience is about how and when the protagonist will resolve the case (so how and when the dramatic irony will be resolved), not about the identity of the perpetrator.

This is a powerful and original way to manage information. When you use dramatic irony, it allows you to create more tension, more suspense, more emotional involvement for the audience because of what we know and what the protagonist doesn't.

In the first season of *Homeland*, we have a powerful combination of mystery and dramatic irony: We know that returning war prisoner Nicholas Brody is being spied on by secret service agent Carrie Mathison, which is a strong dramatic irony he is a victim of, but we don't know if Brody is a disturbed veteran or a converted terrorist, which creates a tantalising mystery.

Dramatic irony also works in comedy, to generate tension and humour. For example, the first season of *Ted Lasso* relies on a strong dramatic irony that causes most of the conflict in the story: Ted doesn't know that his boss — football club owner Rebecca Welton — hired him because of his lack of knowledge. She doesn't admire him or believe in his original approach; she wants to destroy the club in order to get revenge on her ex-husband. The audience knows this from the beginning, and that makes us feel a lot of conflict for Ted, as well as for Rebecca. Her growing dilemma as she gets to know and appreciate Ted makes her a complex, evolving antagonist. This strong dramatic irony and evolution is over by Season 2, which takes away a significant part of the story engine that defined the first season.

Understanding how to manage information is key to achieving the kind of involvement you intend to create in the audience.

If you want suspense, dramatic tension and emotional involvement, for example if you want your show to have a strong thriller element, you might want to use more dramatic irony to generate suspense, either by telling the audience but not some characters where the danger/threat comes from (*Stranger Things*), or by making the antagonist the victim of a dramatic irony, so that we fear the consequences of them finding out (*The Night Manager*).

If you're primarily after intellectual gratification, then you'll probably favour mystery and possibly surprise (*Broadchurch*, *Fortitude*, *Sharp Objects*).

Now we're going to look at two different examples in more detail. First, *Stranger Things*, which brilliantly combines mystery, surprise and dramatic irony to generate suspense. We'll focus on the set-up, the first eight minutes before the opening credits of the first episode. And then we'll look at *Friends*, to illustrate the use of dramatic irony and surprise to generate humour in a comedy, in this case a sitcom.

Stranger Things

Let's take a look at the way information is managed in the opening of ***Stranger Things***. It's quite an effective set-up, so it's interesting to analyse how it works. **If you haven't done so already, I suggest you watch the first episode, then come back to this analysis.**

We start with a very short teaser, about one and a half minutes. You can consider that the whole of the opening sequence — before the credits — is a teaser in itself, but this mini-teaser at the beginning of the sequence hooks the audience immediately.

When we see the scientist being killed by the Creature — lots of tension, suspense and conflict right away — of course it sets up a mystery: What's this Creature? What's happening in this lab? We know that there are things we don't know in relation to the lab and the Creature. It raises our intellectual curiosity. We want to know what's going to happen in the story because we're curious. That's the way mystery works: As soon as you set up a mystery, you open a bracket that the human mind will always want to close.

Mystery can be a very efficient hook, especially at the beginning of a story, but in this case the mini-teaser doesn't just create a mystery. It also sets up a dramatic irony because from that point on, we know that there is a threat. The Creature has just killed a scientist, so we know that there is danger lurking in the neighbourhood. And of course, we've understood that we're watching a horror thriller. We know that the Creature isn't going to spend the rest of the story in the lab. It's going to get out and cause mayhem in town.

So we've created mystery — the audience wants to know more about the lab and the Creature — but we've also set up a dramatic irony: the audience knows there is a danger and most of the characters in the story at this stage don't. That's how dramatic irony can be used to create suspense and tension.

This is achieved very quickly, in just a minute and a half. The next scene — the boys playing Dungeons & Dragons — would probably be too long if you hadn't had that teaser but the storytellers play on the fact that we know there is a *real* Demogorgon outside and the boys don't.

This scene introduces the young protagonists, and the writers start to exploit the dramatic irony. Of course, there is also a parallel between the Demogorgon in the game and the Demogorgon we've just seen in the lab.

Then Will cycles away with Dustin. As soon as Will is alone on that road, and as soon as we see the sign to Hawkins Lab, the dramatic irony kicks in again, because from that point on, we know that Will is getting closer to the threat that we've just seen.

When Will sees the silhouette on the road, it's a surprise for him, but it's not a surprise for us. It's the beginning of the direct exploitation of the dramatic irony: We're not surprised in the sense that we knew that the monster was around, but there's still an element of surprise because we didn't know exactly when and how the creature would appear.

So it's a mini-surprise, but really it's a partial resolution of the dramatic irony. As soon as Will sees the Creature, the dramatic irony he was a victim of — the fact that we knew there was a monster on the loose, and he didn't — is resolved for him, and that triggers his goal in the rest of the sequence, which is to try to escape the Creature. He runs back home and tries to find a way to escape, but he fails: The Demogorgon gets him. This is the climax of the sequence that shapes the second half of dramatic Act 1 in the first episode.

We're still in the first dramatic act of *Stranger Things*, but this eight-minute opening sequence, designed like a mini-movie, gives it a very tight structure.

It includes a dramatic sequence, mystery, surprise, as well as setting up, exploiting and partially resolving a strong dramatic irony. The climax of the sequence — Will's disappearance — is also the inciting incident for the whole season. This powerful combination makes it a very effective opening sequence.

The key thing here is the balance between mystery, dramatic irony and surprise.

In the first season of *Stranger Things*, we have a lot of mystery — everything related to Eleven, the lab and the Creature — but we also have a lot of dramatic irony — we know what happened to Will, we know that he's been taken by a creature that escaped from the lab and that Will is in real danger, which creates suspense.

For a long time, no one else knows that. This strikes the right balance between the amount of mystery and the amount of dramatic irony in the story. It provides both intellectual and emotional gratification.

The audience is much more willing to accept not knowing about something if on the other hand, they know more than some of the characters. They don't feel neglected the way they would if the writers had only used mystery.

The trick is to combine all the tools we can use to manage information, so that if there is a mystery, we have one or more dramatic ironies to balance it out and also some surprises along the way to break linearity and predictability. That way, we don't spend all our time waiting for a final reveal.

This was our thriller/horror example, where we had mystery to intrigue and puzzle, but also dramatic irony to generate suspense, tension and an emotional involvement for the audience.

Friends

Let's see how we can use dramatic irony and surprise to generate comedy. *Friends* remains a masterclass in managing information, despite some jokes that, taken out of context, might have aged poorly. The creators themselves, Martha Kauffman and David Crane, have acknowledged this and confirmed that they would write it differently today. Still, I'm a fan of *Friends*. Whether you like the show or not, try to watch at least the first season. The way they use dramatic irony and surprise to create comedy is second to none.

Usually in sitcoms we tend to have little mystery. Mystery is often a comedy killer, because it makes you think, and we rarely watch a sitcom to think.

Let's do a mini case study on Episode 14, Season 5, "The One Where Everyone Finds Out". **I suggest you watch the episode now if you haven't done so recently**. I'd like to focus on two different aspects:

First, the way the writers handle two storylines. There is a very clear A-Story and B-Story in this episode. Then, I'd like to look at how they use dramatic irony and surprise to generate comedy. This episode is all about resolving dramatic ironies in a hilarious way. That's why it's called "The One Where Everyone Finds Out".

Let's see briefly how the episode is designed. The B-Story is about Ross trying to get Ugly Naked Guy's apartment. The A-Story is the face-off between Chandler and Monica and Rachel and Phoebe, and as we said, it's entirely based on dramatic irony. We have the partial resolution of a dramatic irony when Phoebe finds out that Monica and Chandler are in a relationship, because we knew before her from previous episodes. This dramatic irony is not fully resolved and is exploited further because Ross still doesn't know.

This partial resolution — Phoebe knows — sets up a new dramatic irony, which is that Monica and Chandler don't know that Phoebe, Rachel and Joey know. Every time you resolve a dramatic irony, you can set up a new one and this keeps running over the whole episode, generating comedy.

For example, when Monica and Chandler find out that the others know, it's an opportunity for another reversal where the victim finds out, but the next victim doesn't know they've found out. This is a classic way to use dramatic irony in order to generate comedy in sitcoms.

It's usually a good idea to make sure that there is some sort of connection between the A-Story and the B-Story, so that it doesn't feel like you could take one out without affecting the other. Here, the B-Story is connected to the A-Story because Phoebe finds out about Monica and Chandler when she goes with Rachel and Ross to look at Ugly Naked Guy's apartment. Phoebe and Rachel then have to prevent Ross from finding out.

One last thing about this episode: When you have a running gag in comedy, especially when it's a gag that runs through the series — like the Ugly Naked Guy — this is also a form of dramatic irony.

It privileges the audience who know about Ugly Naked Guy. They feel included because they are in on the running joke. Yet someone who hasn't heard about Ugly Naked Guy will still find it funny, so won't feel excluded.

I hope these examples give a measure of how crucial managing information is when writing series, whether to generate suspense and tension, to design cliffhangers or to bring in gags and humour.

2.5 Case Study: *Stranger Things*

To illustrate how everything we've covered up to this point works at series and episode level, I'd like to go through a partial case study of the first season of *Stranger Things*. **Please watch it (or at the very least watch the first episode) before reading the rest of the section to avoid spoilers and make the most of the analysis.**

[**Note**: If you'd like to download the scene breakdown and the strands map of the first episode, please see If You Want to Find Out More... to access the bonus content for this book.]

The series probably doesn't need an introduction, but let's start with a quick overview from Wikipedia:

Stranger Things is an American science-fiction horror drama television series created by the Duffer Brothers, who also serve as showrunners and are executive producers along with Shawn Levy and Dan Cohen. Produced by Monkey Massacre Productions and Levy's 21 Laps Entertainment, the first season was released on Netflix on July 15, 2016. Its second, third, and fourth seasons followed in October 2017, July 2019, and May and July 2022, respectively. In February 2022, it was renewed for a fifth and final season.

Set in the 1980s, the series centers around the residents of the fictional small town of Hawkins, Indiana, as they are plagued by a hostile alternate dimension known as the Upside Down, after a nearby human experimentation facility opens a gateway between it and the normal world. The ensemble cast includes Winona Ryder, David Harbour, Finn Wolfhard, Millie Bobby Brown, Gaten Matarazzo, Caleb McLaughlin, Natalia Dyer, Charlie Heaton, Cara Buono, Matthew Modine, Noah Schnapp, Sadie Sink, Joe Keery, Dacre Montgomery, Sean Astin, Paul Reiser, Maya Hawke, Priah Ferguson and Brett Gelman.

The Duffer Brothers developed Stranger Things as a mix of investigative drama and supernatural elements portrayed with horror and childlike sensibilities, while infusing references to the pop culture of the 1980s. Several thematic and directorial elements were inspired by the works of Steven Spielberg, John Carpenter, David Lynch, Stephen King, Wes Craven and H. P. Lovecraft. They also took inspiration from experiments conducted during the Cold War and conspiracy theories involving secret government programs.

One of Netflix's flagship series, Stranger Things has attracted record viewership on the streaming platform. It has been critically acclaimed for its characterization, atmosphere, acting, soundtrack, directing, writing, and homages to 1980s films. It has received numerous nominations and awards. An animated spin-off series, developed by Eric Robles and produced by Flying Bark Productions, is in development.

Format, Series Type, Story Type, Genre and M-Factor

Regarding **format**, the first season of *Stranger Things* includes eight drama episodes of about fifty minutes each, for a total of just under four hundred minutes.

In terms of **series type**, it's a serial-procedural hybrid because it's a serial with a different main problem to solve in each season. The procedural element is at season level, instead of being at episode level, as it would be in a "pure" procedural.

In fact, *Stranger Things* explores a different facet of the same antagonist in each season: Dr. Brenner and the Demogorgon in Season 1; the Mind Flayer and its Demodogs in Season 2; the Mind Flayer again alongside the flayed humans as well as antagonistic humans in Season 3; and Vecna in Season 4.

All the non-human antagonists are connected to the initial breach opened by Eleven and are controlled by the Mind Flayer, who is the supra-antagonist of the series. However, in each season, the main problem at season level is resolved, even if the Mind Flayer remains lurking in the background.

When you're dealing with a serial-procedural hybrid, you try to find a satisfying ending for each season, so you provide some answers — for example, you answer the main dramatic question of the season — and, at the same time, you raise a few questions so that you tease the next season, often by managing information.

The **genre** is supernatural horror thriller and the **story-type** at series and episode level is plot-led: The antagonists (Demogorgon, Brenner and the lab) are all external to the protagonists.

We've already discussed *Stranger Things* in relation to Maslow in the target audience and genre sections of 2.3 Use of Maslow in Series, so we'll focus here on the **M-Factor** for the series. Please look up these terms in the Story-Type Method Glossary at the end of this book if you're not familiar with them.

The story-type, main problem and genre all lie at the bottom of the pyramid, which suggests the widest possible audience. This is one of the reasons why the Duffer Brothers were able to raise a relatively high budget for the first season of *Stranger Things*, despite the project being an original story.

The series primarily targets tweens and teenagers. The adults' storylines explore other parts of Maslow's pyramid, such as the middle (relationships) and the top (acceptance of facts). So it's a great design for a family show (12+ for the first season, 14+ for the later ones, though official age ratings go as high as 15 for all seasons).

All of these elements fit together, which leads me to give a high M-factor to *Stranger Things*.

Season Design

Let's see how the Duffer Brothers approached the design of the first season. They discuss this in their pitch bible, which you can find easily on the internet if you'd like to take a look.

They used a logistical approach to break down the story at season level into more manageable units of two or three episodes, leading to a 3-3-2 logistical 3-Act structure.

Even if the Duffer Brothers used this logistical approach consciously, it doesn't mean that, unconsciously, they didn't use all the tools we've been discussing. Here is how we could show the difference between logistical format and dramatic structure in *Stranger Things*:

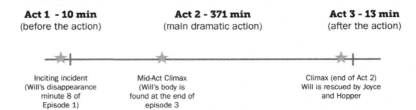

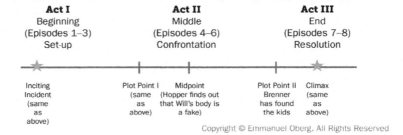

Logistical Format

Let's look at the Duffer Brothers' **logistical approach** first, shown at the bottom of the info-graph:

In their pitch bible, they talk about the first season in logistical terms, as would be expected: **Act I** (Beginning/Set-Up) Episodes 1 to 3; **Act II** (Middle/Confrontation) Episodes 4 to 6; and **Act III** (End/Resolution) Episodes 7 to 8.

The **inciting incident** is Will's disappearance minute 8 of Episode 1.

When Will's "body" is found at the end of Episode 3 (logistical Act I), it's clearly an important turning point for the Duffer Brothers (**Plot Point I**).

The **midpoint** is when Hopper finds out that Will's body is a fake.

The second turning point (**Plot Point II**) is when Brenner locates the kids, at the end of Episode 6 (Logistical Act II).

The **climax** is when Will is rescued by Joyce and Hopper, though you could argue that it's also when Eleven kills the Demogorgon.

Dramatic Structure

Let's look at the first season from a **dramatic approach** now (top half of the info-graph):

We'll start with the **inciting incident**, which is Will's disappearance, minute 8 of Episode 1. This is the same in both the logistical and the dramatic approach.

This event triggers the **main dramatic action**, which is the co-protagonists (Will's mother, brother and friends) looking for him and trying to rescue him.

It also raises the **main dramatic question** that remains open over the whole season, at least for the audience: Will they find a way to rescue him before it's too late?

Dramatic Act 1 includes the opening credits, and is about ten minutes long.

Dramatic Act 2 starts minute 11 of the first episode, when we see Joyce starting to look for her son. She's the first one to act, the others will soon join her and become co-protagonists.

In dramatic terms, **Plot Point I** (Will's body is found) is the climax of Episode 3, but it's also a mid-act climax at season level, because that's the point at which some of the protagonists stop looking for Will when they think he's dead. They only resume their quest later on, when they're gradually convinced that he's still alive.

The **midpoint** (Will's body is a fake) is simply what makes it possible for Hopper to become co-protagonist with Joyce.

Plot Point II (Brenner locates the kids) marks the beginning of logistical Act III. As is often the case, logistical Act III is made up of the last dramatic sequence(s) in dramatic Act 2, the climax and dramatic Act 3.

Dramatic Act 2 of Season 1 ends during the climax (the same in both approaches), minute 38 of Episode 8, when Joyce and Hopper rescue Will from the Upside Down. That's three-hundred-and-seventy-one minutes, so most of the season.

At the end of this dramatic action, we get an answer to the dramatic question: yes, Will is found, he's rescued and we enter **dramatic Act 3**, which shows the consequences of the action. This is only thirteen minutes long.

Of course, this long dramatic Act 2 is broken down into dramatic sequences, as we'll see shortly.

What's interesting is that while the *dramatic* approach above shows a strong connection between the inciting incident, which launches dramatic Act 2, and the climax, which marks the beginning of dramatic Act 3, there is no such connection with the *logistical* approach, which just cuts the season into more manageable logistical units.

Of course, this doesn't mean the Duffer Brothers are "wrong". As we said earlier, the methodology writers use consciously doesn't really matter as long as they do the design unconsciously, which was clearly the case here. Both conscious and unconscious approaches can work in harmony.

Looking at this, you might still be thinking that the logistical approach is more useful because it breaks the season down into more manageable blocks of two or three episodes, while the dramatic approach seems to suggest that you end up with an unwieldy dramatic Act 2 that takes up most of the season (371 minutes).

But as we know, we can use the fractal aspect of story structure in series to design episodes and break down storylines into dramatic sequences. So let's see how the Duffer Brothers have done this, consciously or not, in the first season of *Stranger Things*.

As you might remember from Storylines: Where Format Meets Structure (Chapter 1), we've defined three stages when working on storylines:

Story Design 1: Defining the Storylines
Story Design 2: Breaking the Storylines
Story Design 3: Story Weaving a One-Hour Episode

So, we're going to define the main storylines in the first season. Then, we'll see how we can break those storylines over the season, and we'll sequence one of them. Finally, we'll look at the strands map of the first episode to see how these storylines are woven together.

Defining the Storylines in *Stranger Things*

Let's go through the main storylines in *Stranger Things*.

Main Storylines in Stranger Things

A1. Will's mother, **Joyce Byers**
A2. Hawkins Chief of Police, **Jim Hopper**
A3. Will's friends: **Mike, Lucas, Dustin** (and Will himself)
A4. Will's brother, **Jonathan Byers**
B. Jane Ives, a.k.a. **Eleven (El for short)** or **The Girl**
C1. Mike's sister, **Nancy Wheeler**
C2. Nancy's boyfriend, **Steve Harrington**
D. **Dr. Martin Brenner** & the Hawkins Lab
E. **The Creature**, a.k.a. **The Demogorgon**

I've listed the first four storylines in the order in which their respective protagonists actively start to look for Will:

Joyce, Hopper, Will's friends Mike, Dustin and Lucas, and Will's brother **Jonathan**.

One or more of these four storylines (A1, A2, A3, and A4) form the **A-Story** in all episodes. Even if, for a long time, the characters work separately and not together, they are co-protagonists because they share the same goal over the season (to find Will, rescue him and bring him back alive).

Will doesn't play a big part in the development of the main dramatic action, so I've grouped him with his friends. Technically, they don't have the same goal, but he wants to stay alive and they want to rescue him, so that's close enough.

Jane Ives, also known as **Eleven** and El for short, or the girl, is the **B-Story** at season level.

Then Mike's sister, **Nancy Wheeler**, and Nancy's boyfriend, **Steve Harrington** are the **C-Story**.

Dr. Brenner and the Hawkins lab aren't technically a separate storyline because they are antagonists on the A-Story, and also obviously on El's storyline.

However, Brenner and the lab do have a couple of scenes where they act independently, so it makes sense to give them their own storyline to make it easier to visualise when they have scenes without the protagonists. They form the **D-Story** at season level.

The Creature doesn't have its own storyline either, but it's one of the antagonists on the other storylines, so I've shown it here and in the strands maps as the **E-Story** to track its limited appearances.

Breaking the Storylines in *Stranger Things*

So, now that we've identified our strands, let's take a look at each storyline in more detail and see how they are designed, so that we can break them into dramatic sequences more easily.

Identifying the Dramatic Design of Each Storyline

Knowing what the protagonist's goal is at season level and whether each storyline is plot-led, character-led or a hybrid will help you to design storylines with a strong dramatic drive and to be clear about what's at stake in each storyline. This will increase the emotional engagement of the audience.

It will also help you to break down the storylines because you'll know the main goal, which will help you to define subgoals — hence dramatic sequences — at episode level.

Joyce Byers, Will's Mother (A1)

I've placed Joyce as A1 because she's the first one to have a goal, which is to find and rescue her son.

So Joyce isn't A1 because she's more important than the other co-protagonists. She's simply the first and the main protagonist of the first episode. After that, her storyline drops down to a less important status and the boys and Eleven become the main protagonists for most of the episodes, until the final one.

Joyce's storyline is **plot-led**. We don't think that she's going in the wrong direction. We know that something bad has happened to Will, so we know that her instinct to look for her son is correct.

Information is managed in a way that allows us to be close to her emotionally. She might appear crazy to the other characters, but not to us because we know exactly what she sees and what she hears.

As a result, we never wonder whether she's paranoid or not, whether she's having visions or whether what she sees is real. There is no mystery about the reality of the danger. That's a very important part of her storyline because it makes it easy for us to identify with her emotionally, and it creates suspense.

We also know that she has a history of mental breakdowns, which makes it more difficult for her to be heard. And that brings even more conflict for her as a protagonist. Not being believed is a classic source of conflict for the protagonist in a thriller/horror.

Jim Hopper, Hawkins Chief of Police (A2)

Hopper is A2 because, prompted by Joyce, he is the second to get his goal, which is to investigate Will's disappearance and rescue him.

Hopper's storyline is **plot-led** because the main problem in his investigation (mostly Brenner and the lab) lies outside of him.

However, Hopper also needs to move on from the death of his daughter. This is a strong character-led element in his storyline, but we don't ever feel that he needs to change or that this is what's primarily at stake in his storyline, so the storyline isn't character-led.

We simply hope that he'll be able to move on — and the conflict that he experiences during the story will help him to do that.

Will's Friends: Mike, Lucas and Dustin and Will himself (A3)

The boys, prompted by Hopper, are third to get their goal, which is to rescue Will, their friend. This makes them A3.

There is nothing wrong with them doing so and the main problem is external, which makes this storyline **plot-led**.

As is often the case with co-protagonists though, they'll frequently disagree on the best way to reach their goal, which creates an interesting form of conflict within the group.

They do separate occasionally (for example when Lucas goes his own way), but they remain co-protagonists and share the same goal over the whole season.

Jonathan Byers, Will's Brother (A4)

This storyline is also primarily **plot-led**. There is nothing wrong with him trying to save his brother. It feels like he's going in the right direction.

However, there is a character-led element in this storyline, because he clearly struggles to fit in with his peers. This sub-problem is resolved eventually, through his relationship with Nancy.

Jane Ives, a.k.a Eleven (B)

Eleven wants to protect herself and others from Brenner and from the Upside Down. These are external sources of conflict, which makes this storyline **plot-led** as well.

There is also a strong character-led element because she needs to overcome her traumatic childhood and the fact that she feels responsible for what's happened, but we don't spend the whole season thinking that there is something wrong with Eleven and that she needs to change. That's because her goal is rooted at the bottom of Maslow, it's about survival and protection of others, which makes it more important than her evolution.

She's fascinating and in many ways, she's the main character in the first season. She carries most of the mystery related to the backstory and to the Upside Down, she knows more than we do, and for this reason we're not as close to her emotionally as we are to the other characters, but that's not a problem.

She's not one of the "A" storylines, because she doesn't share the goal of rescuing Will with the other protagonists. Eleven's storyline is the B-Story at season level.

Nancy Wheeler, Mike's sister (C1)

Nancy's storyline is **plot-led**. She wants to find her friend Barb, and there's nothing wrong with her trying to do so.

There is a strong character-led element though: She needs to lose some of her naivety and to realise that Steve is a jerk. This does happen as the season progresses, though Steve changes and so wins her back, which is why they are still together at the end.

Nancy and Steve's storylines form the C-Story at season level. They are apart for quite a long time, so for clarity it's best to handle them as separate storylines (C1 and C2).

Nancy and Jonathan spend a lot of time together, but they don't share the same goal (he wants to save his brother, she wants to rescue Barb). However, their goals are close enough to make them circumstantial co-protagonists.

Steve Harrington, Nancy's boyfriend (C2)

Initially, we don't see any potential for change in him, so we don't see his storyline as character-led.

He's mostly a source of conflict on Nancy and Jonathan's storylines, hence helps them to change: We want Nancy to realise that he's a jerk, and we want Jonathan to grow a backbone and stand up to him.

However, Steve surprises us and does change in the end. He apologises to both Nancy and Jonathan and finds the inner resources to join their fight against the Demogorgon. In fact, his evolution is one of the strongest in the season, and that's just the beginning.

Brenner and the lab (D)

As mentioned earlier, this isn't technically a storyline because Brenner and the lab are the main human antagonists on the A and B-Story.

However, it's definitely plot-led. Their goal is to bring Eleven back and cover up the danger they've unleashed. Brenner is an antagonist, so clearly we don't spend the whole time thinking "You really need to change and become a less horrible character".

Along with the Demogorgon, he represents the main source of danger, hence of suspense in the story. From the moment he has Benny killed in the first episode, we know that he is a very real threat, and so just seeing him after that is enough to suggest that the protagonists are in danger.

The Creature, a.k.a The Demogorgon (E)

This isn't a proper storyline either. We never see the Creature alone, it only appears as an antagonistic monster in other storylines.

The storyline is plot-led: The Creature wants to survive. To do that, it hunts and kills humans — and the occasional deer. So it's a very primal antagonist, a creature that you can't reason with, similar to the antagonists in *Alien*, *Jaws* or *The Terminator*.

Once it has killed the scientist and taken Will, we understand the danger it represents. Of course, that danger is reinforced when it takes Barb, which makes it all the more real when Nancy and the kids face the Creature later.

There is some mystery around the Demogorgon: Where does it come from? What is it? However, there's no mystery over the reality of the danger it represents, which is what generates suspense and tension every time we see it.

That's a key condition to generating suspense in a thriller or horror: you can have some mystery over the nature of the antagonist, but not over the reality of the danger it represents. A danger has to be known, whether there is dramatic irony (the audience knows about it but some of the characters don't) or not.

Breaking Down Each Storyline Into Dramatic Sequences

Now that we've defined the main storylines, let's see how we can use the fractal aspect of the dramatic 3-Act structure to divide the main dramatic action in each storyline into subgoals. This allows us to break down that long dramatic Act 2 at season level into more manageable dramatic units.

As we've seen, *Stranger Things* is plot-led because it's shaped around a main dramatic action: a group of co-protagonists trying to find Will and rescue him. Joyce is the first of the co-protagonists to be active, so her storyline shows the longest dramatic action.

It's this main dramatic action that we break down into sequences in a plot-led series, so we call this "Sequencing the Action". In a character-led series, we'd "Sequence the Evolution", and in a theme-led series, we'd "Sequence the Strands".

We don't have the space to analyse each of the storylines as we do in the companion course, but we'll set out the A1-Story, as Joyce's storyline shapes the dramatic 3-Act structure of *Stranger Things* at season level.

Dramatic 3-Act Structure in Joyce's Storyline

Here is what it looks like for the first season of *Stranger Things*, looking at Joyce's storyline:

2.5 Case Study: *Stranger Things*

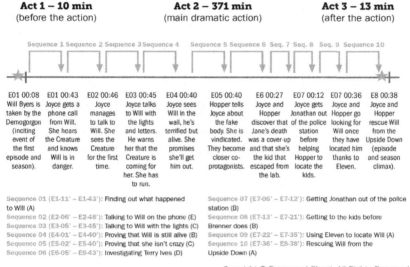

Before we see how we can break down dramatic Act 2 into sequences, let's define the dramatic 3-Act structure for Joyce's storyline.

As you can see, Season 1 lasts almost four hundred minutes in total.

Dramatic Act 1 in Joyce's storyline is only ten minutes long, which is quite standard. That's about the amount of time you have to get the main dramatic action, evolution or situation started in a first episode.

The **inciting incident** — when Will is taken by the Demogorgon — happens minute 8.

So by minute 11 (after the opening credits), we're already in **dramatic Act 2**. We know exactly what's at stake and that's one of the many strengths of the first season of *Stranger Things*: Thanks to

Joyce, the main dramatic action at season and episode level kicks in very quickly.

Dramatic Act 3 in *Stranger Things* is very short: just thirteen minutes out of almost four hundred.

So, looking at this info-graph and as mentioned in <u>Season Design</u>, you can see that we have a long dramatic Act 2 (371 minutes).

The main task for the writers is therefore going to be to break down this dramatic Act 2 into more manageable units.

Breaking Down Dramatic Act 2 in Joyce's Storyline

Because we're approaching this dramatically, instead of using logistical units (episodes, minutes or pages), we're going to use dramatic units: ten dramatic sequences for Joyce over the eight episodes of Season 1.

As mentioned in <u>Story Design 2: Breaking Each Storyline</u>, in a serial, you often have at most one dramatic sequence per storyline in each episode, because we're handling up to four or five other storylines (with their own dramatic sequences) in the same episode.

However, this isn't always the case. For Joyce, in Episode 7, there are three dramatic sequences and the beginning of a fourth one. This is why we have ten dramatic sequences over eight episodes in her storyline.

In a plot-led series, each dramatic sequence is often a way for the protagonist to reach the main goal.

So here, Joyce is trying to find Will and each sequence represents a subgoal on the way to that end goal. The climax of each sequence is going to be "yes", the protagonist has reached the subgoal (success), or "no", they haven't (failure).

Let's go through each of the ten dramatic sequences in Joyce's storyline over the whole season by defining her subgoal and its outcome in each sequence. This will help us to clarify the stakes at episode level:

Sequence 1 (A-Story in Episode 1)

Joyce is trying to find out what happened to Will.

Minute 43 in Episode 1, she gets a phone call from Will. She hears the Creature, and now she knows that Will is in danger. She doesn't know exactly where he is, but that call answers her main question in the first dramatic sequence: Her son has been taken and he is in danger.

Sequence 2 (E-Story in Episode 2)
Joyce is trying to talk to Will on the phone.

She manages to talk to him at the end of Episode 2, minute 46 (success). This climax of the sequence is also when she sees the Creature for the first time, which raises the stakes: the danger is worse than she could have imagined.

Sequence 3 (C-Story in Episode 3)
Joyce is still trying to communicate with her son.

She tries to communicate with Will, using the lights and the letters this time. She succeeds and so reaches that subgoal towards the end of Episode 3, minute 45. Will warns her that the Creature is coming for her: She has to run away.

Sequence 4 (B-Story in Episode 4)
Joyce is trying to prove that Will is alive.

This action culminates when she sees Will in the wall, terrified but alive, so she succeeds. She promises that she'll get him out.

Sequence 5 (C-Story in Episode 5)
Joyce is trying to prove that she isn't crazy.

Will is supposed to be dead and so everyone thinks that she's losing her grip on reality.

However, in the meantime, Hopper has found out about the fake body. She feels vindicated in his eyes. Now he knows that she is right about Will and that she's not deluded, so she succeeds.

They become co-protagonists from that point, so their storylines merge together. You'll see that the rest of her dramatic sequences tend to run quite close to those on Hopper's storyline.

Sequence 6 (D-Story in Episode 6)
Joyce and Hopper are trying to investigate Terry Ives. They succeed when they discover that Jane's death was a cover-up. She is the kid that escaped from the lab.

The following two sequences are those least directly connected to the main dramatic action.

Sequence 7 (B-Story in Episode 7)
Joyce is trying to get Jonathan out of the police station. She succeeds. This is a very minor sequence, just a few scenes.

Sequence 8 (B-Story in Episode 7)
Joyce, with Hopper, is trying to get to the kids before Brenner does. However, she's not closely involved. It's really Hopper who is the most active in this sequence. They succeed. Another minor

sequence for Joyce, which explains why we have more than one in this episode.

Sequence 9 (A-Story in Episode 7)

All the "A" storylines (A1, A2, A3, A4) converge during this dramatic sequence, the co-protagonists join forces and Joyce becomes part of the A-Story again. Together, they are all trying to locate Will with Eleven's help. They succeed and so they know how to get to Will.

Sequence 10 (A-Story in Episode 8)

The final sequence shows Joyce and Hopper trying to rescue Will from the Upside Down, now that they know where to look for him.

This sequence culminates towards the end of Episode 8, when Joyce and Hopper rescue Will from the Upside Down, which is the sequence climax, part of the last episode climax and also the season climax, because the main dramatic question for the whole season has been answered: Yes, the protagonists have found Will and have rescued him in time.

After this triple climax, as the main dramatic action is over, we enter dramatic Act 3 at season level.

Overall Notes

This is how the Duffer Brothers break down a very long second dramatic act — 371 minutes — into ten dramatic sequences in Joyce's storyline.

More generally, this is how we can use the fractal aspect of story structure to "Sequence the Action" (break the storylines) in a plot-led series.

Not all series — especially character-led and theme-led ones — work like that, but I chose *Stranger Things* because it uses the fractal aspect of story structure very clearly: Each storyline is broken down using dramatic sequences.

So, we've seen the ten dramatic sequences that make up Joyce's storyline. She has one dramatic sequence per episode, except in Episode 7 where she has three, the first two being minor ones.

There is a strong causality between sequences. The climax of a sequence is often the inciting incident for the next one.

Joyce is definitely part of the A-Story of the first episode. She's Will's mum and the first to actively look for him. But in the following episodes, she drops down to the E, C, B, C, or D-Story.

Stranger Things centres around its younger characters and she's no longer the main focus of the story. She returns to the front stage towards the end.

In the last episode, when Joyce rescues Will from the Upside Down, she's part of the A-Story again, because the whole season is about rescuing Will. So, the characters who are trying to rescue him lead the most important dramatic action at this point. The action around the kids trying to fight the Demogorgon and Brenner isn't less important, but is less directly connected to the overall goal of rescuing Will; it's more about Eleven saving the world, which is part of the B-Story.

So, we've identified each storyline and we've seen how we can break them down in a plot-led series, looking at Joyce's storyline in more detail, but of course that doesn't make a unified story yet.

Now we're going to see how these storylines are woven together. Let's start by looking at the strands map of the first episode:

148   2 Underlying Series Design

Strands Maps of Stranger Things: S1 E1

SCREENPLAY Unlimited — WORKSHOPS & COURSES

WRITING A SUCCESSFUL TV SERIES — How to Pitch and Develop Projects for Television and Online Streaming — With The STORY-TYPE METHOD

Strands Map of the First Season of *Stranger Things*

EPISODE 1 (48') — **Chapter One - The Vanishing of Will Byers**

Storyline / Minute in scene breakdown	OT	1	2-3	4	5	6-8	8	9-10	11-12	13	14-15	16	17-18	19-20	21-22	23	24-25	26	27-28	29	30	31-33	34-35	36	37-38	39	40	41-42	43-44	45	46	47	TOTAL (Ep. 1)
A1. Will's mother, Joyce Byers							OC		BA2				S1									S1							CS1/CH1			EC	10 min.
A2. Hawkins Chief of Police, Jim Hopper						X	OC								BA2		S1			CS1		S2		S2		S1						EC	11 min.
A3. Will's friends: Mike, Lucas, Dustin (and Will himself)						X	OC	X					BA2						BA2				S1			S1			S1		CS1	EC	18 min.
A4. Will's brother: Jonathan Byers						X	OC																						CS1/CH1			EC	5 min.
B. Jane Ives, a.k.a. Eleven (El for short) or The Girl	(X)						OC					S1		S1									S1		CS1						CH1	EC	6 min.
C1. Mike's sister, Nancy Wheeler							OC					S1																CS1				EC	7 min.
C2. Nancy's boyfriend, Steve Harrington							OC					S1																	CS1			EC	4 min.
D. Dr. Martin Brenner & the Hawkins Lab		X					OC									BA2					S1					CS1						EC	4 min.
E. The Creature, a.k.a. The Demogorgon							OC																									EC	4 min.
																																	69 min.

At Season Level:
- **X** = Inciting Incident of the strand / storyline (Season Level)
- **BA2** = Beginning of dramatic act 2 in the strand (Season Level)
- **BA3** = Beginning of dramatic act 3 in the strand / storyline (Season Level)
- **MAC** = Mid-Act Climax of the strand / storyline (at Season Level)
- **C** = Climax of the strand / storyline (at Season Level)
- **SC** = End of Season Cliffhanger

At Episode Level:
- **OT** = Opening Teaser (when present)
- **OC** = Opening Credits (marks the end of the pre-credit teaser)
- **Sn** = Dramatic Sequences
- **CSn** = Sequence Climax
- **CH** = End of Episode Cliffhanger
- **EC** = End Credits
- **FB** = Flash-Back

Main co-protagonists: Joyce, Hopper, the boys and Jonathan trying to find and rescue Will
Main (most fascinating) character and reluctant co-protagonist: Eleven, trying to protect herself and others from the Upside Down
Secondary characters and circumstancial co-protagonists: Nancy and Steve
Main antagonists: Brenner and his men, trying to bring Eleven back and to cover-up the danger they have unleashed
Monster: The Demogorgon, trying to feed itself and survive
(X) = Eleven's inciting incident isn't shown, but opening a portal to the Upside Down is the inciting event for the series

- **A-Story:** A1+A2+A3+A4 (Joyce, Hopper, Will's friends and Jonathan looking for Will)
- **B-Story:** B (Eleven trying to find food and shelter at Benny's)
- **C-Story:** C1 + C2 (Steve trying to get into Nancy's pants, and Nancy trying to resist)
- **D-Story:** D (Brenner and his men looking for Eleven at Benny's)
- **Episode Cliffhanger 1:** Joyce hears Will on the phone, so he's alive but in great danger (dramatic irony, mystery and unresolved conflict)
- **Episode Cliffhanger 2:** The boys fail to find Will in the woods, but stumble on Eleven instead (dramatic irony and unresolved conflict)

Writing a Successful TV Series

Story Weaving in *Stranger Things*

In this info-graph, you can see a summary of the series design at season level, as we've discussed in the previous sections. Now we're going to concentrate on how the different storylines are woven together in the first episode.

Identifying the Main Storylines at Episode Level

So, we've identified the main storylines at season level, but an essential part of story weaving is to **identify which storylines form the A-Story at episode level**, and which are secondary storylines. This is important because it will define your main dramatic drive for the episode, when there is one.

So for each episode, try to identify the A, B, C, D and E-Story (if present). In this first episode, they match those that we've defined at season level, but that won't be the case over the whole season.

One of the ways to identify the importance of each storyline in a produced episode is to look at the length of each storyline (here at the right of the info-graph).

Of course, if you add them all up, you end up with more than the length of the episode, because some storylines meet each other in the same scene.

If you look at the **A-Story** for the first episode, it's made of the first four storylines: **Joyce, Hopper, Will's friends and Jonathan** looking for Will. They don't start at the same time, but the protagonists of each storyline are all trying to achieve the same thing.

Joyce is on screen for about ten minutes, Hopper for eleven minutes, the boys for eighteen minutes and Jonathan has around five minutes of screen time.

The B-Story is Eleven trying to find food and shelter at Benny's. That's only six minutes.

Then you have six and four minutes respectively for **Nancy and Steve, the C-Story**.

Brenner (D-Story) only has four minutes and the **Demogorgon (E-Story)** has four minutes as well.

When it comes to writing or designing your own episodes, you'll do the same. You'll decide on your A-Story, allocate most of the time to that storyline as it will develop the main dramatic action in the episode, and then you'll split the remaining time between the other storylines, according to the space you want to give them in the episode.

In some series, for example theme-led ones such as *Big Little Lies* or *Succession*, there might not be an A-Story, you might be dealing with two or three storylines of equal importance, and a few minor ones, so you'll just adjust screen time accordingly.

Managing Focus

It's also interesting to see **when the main dramatic action in each storyline kicks in, and how we move between storylines**: Each storyline has its own design, but we move between storylines to give more pace to the story. That's part of story weaving too.

For example, we start with the incident at the lab, when the Creature escapes and kills the scientist. This is an inciting incident for Eleven because it triggers her goal to escape, survive and protect others from the Upside Down. It's also the inciting incident for the series as it triggers the main situation: The Demogorgon abducting and killing innocent victims.

And again, it's an inciting incident for Brenner, as it triggers his goal to bring Eleven back and cover up the danger they've unleashed. As is often the case in thriller or horror stories, it's the antagonist who starts the action. The protagonists react to it.

We then move the focus to Will and his friends — and are briefly introduced to Nancy — until Will is taken, which is the inciting incident for the main co-protagonists: It triggers their goal of finding Will and rescuing him.

However, even if all the co-protagonists share the same inciting event, they don't become active at the same time, so we can see that the Beginning of Act 2 (BA2) isn't the same in each storyline.

Although we're introduced to Hopper first, minute 9, it's **Joyce** who is the first active protagonist, as she starts looking for Will minute 11. This is when we enter dramatic Act 2 at season and episode level: A protagonist is actively trying to resolve the main problem caused by Will's disappearance.

Joyce manages to convince a reluctant **Hopper** to look for her son minute 18, and that's when dramatic Act 2 starts in Hopper's storyline. We understand that he's going to investigate Will's disappearance. Because of the dramatic irony (we've seen what happened to Will, so we know that Joyce is right to worry), we hope that Hopper will soon realise that Will is truly in danger.

Hopper questions **the boys** minute 24-25, which triggers their goal of finding out what's happened to their friend. That's when their dramatic Act 2 starts, which is quite late. That's not a problem though because we have active protagonists earlier in this first episode (Joyce, then Hopper).

Jonathan's dramatic Act 2 starts minute 26. He's the last one to start looking for Will.

From that point on, all the co-protagonists of the A-Story are active and we keep switching between them — as well as the B, C and D-Stories — until most of the dramatic sequences are resolved at episode level.

Checking Causality

We can also see that there is a **strong causality (cause and effect) between the storylines**: Joyce convinces Hopper to look for Will, Hopper unwittingly triggers the boys' goal by questioning them about Will, etc.

This is another part of story weaving: Designing storylines individually so that they have their own dramatic structure is great because it gives them a dramatic drive and clarifies what's at stake in each storyline, but if you stop there, the series would feel like a set of unconnected stories. You also have to create causality between the storylines, so that they form a single story.

To check for causality, try to take a storyline out of your series, season, or episode. If you can do this and if it doesn't change much, then there isn't enough causality for this storyline, so take it out or add more causality so that it becomes an integral part of the story.

The main tool used to add causality is planting and pay-off. This is discussed at length in *Screenwriting Unchained*.

Handling Dramatic Sequences

We've looked at the way Joyce's storyline is broken down into dramatic sequences at season level. Now let's look further into the dramatic sequences for each storyline in this first episode.

They unfold in parallel in the info-graph, because the storylines are woven together, yet you should be able to follow the dramatic action in each of the storylines clearly.

This is what helps the audience to remain engaged: Not only do we know what's at stake in general, we also know what's at stake at all times in each storyline. If you don't design dramatic sequences around subgoals, you often end up with "flat" or "boring" storylines, where nothing happens. Subgoals are ways for the protagonist to actively try to reach their goal.

As mentioned, **Joyce** is trying to find out from minute 11 what happened to Will (S1). This sequence climaxes minute 43-44, when she hears the Demogorgon and understands that her son has been taken. It's also the first cliffhanger (CH1).

For **Hopper**, we have two dramatic sequences. First, he starts looking for Will minute 18, prompted by Joyce, thinking nothing bad has happened (S1). But when he finds Will's bike minute 29 (CS1), he begins to investigate Will's disappearance more seriously, as Will is now a missing person (S2).

This second sequence will have its climax in Episode 2, when Hopper realises that Will's disappearance is connected with the lab, so CS2 isn't shown in this strands map for Episode 1.

Mike, Lucas and Dustin start looking for Will minute 25, prompted by Hopper. We have only one dramatic sequence (S1), which ends when they fail to find Will in Mirkwood (CS1) and bump into Eleven instead (CH2, minute 46).

Jonathan has a short dramatic sequence (S1). He's mostly tagging along in his mum's storyline, as he's looking for Will with her. His sequence starts minute 26 (BA2). The climax is minute 44 (CS1). His own storyline in this episode is just a runner (a few beats).

Nancy and Steve also have just a few scenes. Each has one sequence (S1): Steve trying to get into Nancy's pants, and Nancy trying to resist. Nancy succeeds, Steve fails minute 42 (CS1).

Brenner kicks into action minute 19, when he finds out about the disappearance of Eleven and the Demogorgon. This triggers his goal at season level, which is to get Eleven back and cover up his part in the Demogorgon's rampage. In this episode, he only has one dramatic sequence (S1), triggered minute 30 when he finds out that she's hiding at Benny's. The climax is minute 39 when he fails to capture Eleven (CS1).

Teasing with Cliffhangers

Don't forget cliffhangers, not only before leaving a storyline so that the audience wants to get back to it, but also at the end of each episode, to tease the next one. Just make sure you don't use them in a formulaic or predictable way.

This technique will differ depending on the genre, series type and story-type, but the key to a satisfying ending at episode level is to find the right balance between answering existing questions and raising new ones through managing conflict and information.

The first cliffhanger of the first episode (CH1) is when Joyce hears Will on the phone minute 43–44. Her son is alive (positive answer for Sequence 1), but he's in great danger, which is a dramatic irony (We know that Will has been taken by the Demogorgon), a mystery (Where is he? What will the Demogorgon do to him?) and an unresolved conflict (Will he survive?)

The second cliffhanger (CH2) is when the boys fail to find Will in the woods (negative answer for Sequence 1), minute 46, and they stumble on Eleven instead. This is a surprise (We weren't expecting this), it sets up a dramatic irony (We know about Eleven, the adults don't) and an unresolved conflict (What's going to happen between the boys and Eleven?)

Developing Relationships

A little aside connected to story weaving but not specific to the first episode — it's interesting to look at the way the Duffer Brothers managed to connect all the storylines to the A-Story.

In *Stranger Things*, each of the co-protagonists in the A-Story eventually pairs up with another character who doesn't necessarily share their goal, but will become an ally nevertheless.

For example, Joyce will pair up later with Hopper, once he realises that she's right. The kids will pair up with Eleven, who helps them as she tries to protect them, Will and the rest of the world from the Upside Down. And Jonathan, of course, will pair up with Nancy, whose goal is to find Barb. Together, they look for two different victims of the same monster and both will try to kill the Demogorgon towards the end.

In each of the paired storylines, at least one of the co-protagonists wants to find Will. So each pair is in some way connected to the main goal of finding Will. Even if this connection seems fairly loose for Jonathan, who seems more interested in Nancy.

This gives a strong dramatic drive to each storyline pair, because it anchors it in the A-Story overall. The audience is never lost, wondering where a storyline is going, and no storyline slows down the main story. They all move the A-Story forward.

Each of these pairs also develops a main relationship in the story: Joyce and Hopper, Mike and Eleven and Jonathan and Nancy. So we're drawn to the strong plot, but of course we're also interested in the characters' evolution. Particularly Hopper, Eleven and Nancy, whose storylines have the strongest character-led element.

The series is plot-led because the main problem is external to the protagonists, but we always care about the characters, their evolution and the evolution of their relationships.

Final Thoughts

This is how the storylines are woven together in the first episode of *Stranger Things*. It's only possible to do this effectively if the storylines have also been mapped and sequenced.

Like the Duffer Brothers, you need to have identified what your main storylines are — both at series and episode level — what's at stake in each storyline, who the protagonist is, what their subgoals in each dramatic sequence are, etc.

If you do all this, your series will have a strong dramatic drive, a fast pace, characters we can relate to, no "soft bellies" and we'll want to keep watching. We might even want to watch it over and over again.

I hope this case study starts to clarify everything in relation to series design and that it shows how the tools introduced in the first two chapters can be used in practice when designing a plot-led series.

If you'd like to look at the full case study of the first season of *Stranger Things* — which follows a wider discussion on plot-led series, and includes the scene breakdowns for all the episodes, the sequence breakdowns for all the storylines as well as the strands maps for all the episodes — or if you'd like to see how the process differs for character-led series, theme-led series and hybrids or exceptions, please see <u>Conclusion and Next Steps</u> at the end of the book.

2.6 Hands-On: What's Your Type? (Part 2)

This is the second part of the hands-on that we started in the first chapter. These three questions might take a bit more time to answer than the first two, but they should help you to further clarify the type of project you're working on, this time from a series design point of view.

What is the story-type of your first season?

Is it plot-led, character-led, theme-led, a hybrid or an exception? And, if applicable, what's the story-type of each episode? For some series, there's a clear story-type for each episode — most often that tends to be plot-led, even in character-led or theme-led series.

But sometimes you won't have a clear story-type at episode level. In that case, ask yourself what the story-type of the season or of the series is. This is one of the most useful questions to ask yourself about your project, because answering it will have many consequences from a story design point of view, as explained in How to Identify Your Story Type? at the beginning of this chapter. If you're still struggling, you might want to give our interactive story tool a try, as it's designed to help you identify your story-type. Please see If You Want to Find Out More... at the end of the book for more details.

What is the genre?

Crime, comedy, drama, thriller... Defining this will help you to design your series but also to clarify the product you're selling. When you know your product better, it becomes easier to attract the right customer.

Also, as mentioned in the section on Maslow, some genres often lead to a specific story-type.

For example, thrillers tend to be plot-led. It's extremely difficult to write a character-led thriller. You may have very strong characters or character-led elements, but from a structural point of view, thrillers tend to be plot-led because they are about survival and usually focus on a protagonist trying either not to get killed or to protect others from being killed.

A typical example of this is *The Walking Dead*. Strong characters, strong character-led elements, but the main problem is external (whether it's dead "walkers" or the succession of living antagonists). Survival and protection of family (or group) is at stake. It's a plot-led series.

Other genres, such as drama or comedy, can be plot-led, character-led or theme-led. It really depends, but it's a useful question to ask yourself because it will inform your series design at episode, season and series level.

What is the Maslow Factor (or M-Factor)?

Can you assess the various elements in your series to see if they make sense as a whole, especially when you think about the story-type, the budget, the genre and the intended audience? Does it look like they fit together, or do you have a mismatch that you need to address so that what you offer the decision-maker — and later the audience — makes sense? Thinking about the M-Factor and trying to improve it will improve your ability to sell your series, both to decision-makers and to the audience. See *Screenwriting Unchained* (including the free sampler) for a full explanation or the Story-Type Method Glossary at the end of this book for a brief definition if you're not familiar with this term.

3 Project Development

First Up

Now that we've put aside the logistical approach to story structure and have started to look into underlying series design, let's put this into practice as we explore the **pitching and development of a series**.

We won't talk that much about the development process itself as it varies significantly depending on each country, project and creative team. I'll list many references in the Recommended Reading and Watching at the end of the book that will help you explore this further.

Instead, we're going to focus primarily on the creative process leading to a successful series and we'll be getting into the nitty-gritty of designing an irresistible bible and writing a compelling pilot or first episode, using *Killing Eve* as a case study.

Let's quickly define a few key concepts, just to get the broad picture before we dig into each aspect of project development.

The creator is the writer who designs the concept, writes the bible (also called format, pitch document and a few other names) and usually writes the pilot, the first episode of the series. This can be a solo writer or a team.

Once the series is commissioned, it's usually the creator who becomes the showrunner, hires the writing team and supervises them as well as overseeing most of the creative decisions.

There is a very complex pecking order in a U.S. writing team, with associated credits. Usually, the showrunner gets a creator credit if they originated the series, a written by credit on the episode(s) they write and an executive producer credit (showrunner is not an official title).

If the creator isn't experienced enough to be the showrunner, they might stay on board and simply write some of the episodes, or they might step aside and not take a place on the writing team.

They might also be teamed-up with an experienced showrunner and share that role as co-showrunner, until they have gathered enough experience to do it on their own or realise that they can't stand the heat and decide to step out of the kitchen.

In Europe, the producer can be an informal and unofficial showrunner and take charge of most of the production side, while the creator focuses on managing the writing team and delivering episodes on time. Directors are given more power to deal with direction-related decisions, such as casting, set design, etc.

Creator, bible, you'll notice the series vocabulary has a religious undertone, perhaps because like gods, series creators create and populate a world.

The following section covers **the creation of a series bible.** This essential presentation document, selling tool or reference document can go through various incarnations and be used in different ways, depending on the development stage you're at and where the development of your project takes place. For example, it could be:

1) **A bible to pitch a series idea verbally** (usually by the writer/creator in the U.S.) **in order to get a pilot screenplay commissioned**, then a pilot produced, and then a series commissioned. In this case, the screenplay for the pilot might not be available initially. Only the arcs of the first few seasons are expected, along with a few episode loglines. A good verbal pitch for a series lasts around fifteen to twenty minutes maximum. If you don't have a strong track record, it's highly recommended to have a pilot written and ready, rather than expecting it to be commissioned, even after a successful pitch. Having a written version of the pitch to leave afterwards (see below) is also recommended.

2) **A bible to present a series in order to get the whole series commissioned** (straight-to-series). This can be done verbally or in writing, depending on the country and the circumstances. In this case, the screenplay of the first episode has often been written on spec, and the arcs for a few seasons (if a serial) might be included. The synopsis — or at the very least the logline — for all the episodes of the first season are also expected. There is no need to write the screenplay of these episodes on spec. When written, a pitch bible can be anything between ten and thirty pages, excluding the screenplay of the pilot / first episode if it's already available. The sweet spot is probably around fifteen pages. As mentioned earlier, this written

pitch bible can also be called format, book, pitch document, proposal or even TV treatment depending on the country and who you're speaking to.

3) **A bible as a written reference document that summarises all the key creative elements, once a series is commissioned and in active development or production,** so that everyone involved in the series (writers, directors, etc) can quickly catch up when they join the creative team and then be on the same page. This document usually starts with the pitching bible and then becomes a living thing, constantly updated by assistants and coordinators during production. This is what many in the industry call a "bible", while they reserve other terms for the written selling tool described previously.

As you can see, there is no industry standard, especially internationally, so when someone mentions a series "bible", a "format" or a "pitch document", make sure that you clarify what they mean, even though hopefully the context will help to avoid confusion.

Here we'll focus on the second option — a series bible as a selling tool — and on creating a written document that can be left after a verbal pitch or used to get the pilot or the whole series commissioned.

3.1 Creating an Irresistible Bible

First of all, there is no "right" way to create a series bible. If you look at the pitching bibles of produced shows, they are all different, both in content and form.

My first piece of advice is therefore to read as many of these bibles or treatments as possible (they can easily be found on the internet) and study those that are similar to your project in tone or genre, to get an idea of what other creators have done to get their series made.

Amongst many others, I recommend those of *Stranger Things*, *Fargo*, *Grey's Anatomy*, *Lost*, *New Girl* and *True Detective* as they use different approaches to convey the essence of each series.

For me, when working on a series project, the first question is: Can it run the distance? Or does this series have "legs"? I'm aware that both of these expressions are clichés, but they're clichés for a reason. It's a common problem in series — especially serials — for decision-makers to be presented with material that is not complex enough, not rich enough to justify a series.

If your series isn't limited, have you designed it so that it has the potential to succeed and continue for a long time? That's what we're going to assess together. Then, if you feel your design is lacking, we'll see how you can improve on what you have.

Overall, you want your series bible to suggest that the premise, characters and situations are so complex that a series is needed to explore them, and that they can generate dozens or even hundreds of episodes if the series is successful.

You want to convince us that we'll want to come back, week after week, episode after episode, to spend time with these characters, to explore them and the situations they encounter in their story world.

You don't want to give the impression that your series could be a long feature film (unless we're talking about a mini-series).

The main difference between a series and a feature film is that when you write a feature film, you design a story that provides definitive answers. You raise a question, you define a main problem, you explore it, and then you resolve it. A film is like an express train that takes you from A to B in the fastest and most direct way. It's exciting, but it's quick.

A series is more like a train that stops at every station. It might give you more opportunities to take a break, but it isn't artificially slowed down to make the journey longer. It's based on fast-paced storytelling that explores, in each episode, the plot-wise equivalent of a feature film in an hour or less, and does so week after week, with richer characters because you have more time to explore them.

Most importantly, a series isn't a story that brings definitive answers. It relies on a story engine that continually generates questions. Only some of these are answered as the narrative unfolds, keeping the audience hooked.

We'll see how that's done in the next section on series design, but first I'd like to go through a few elements to bear in mind when thinking about your bible and what you want to achieve.

Overarching Questions and Aims

Developing a Series
Creating an Irresistible Bible

Overarching Questions and Aims:
- Pilot commission or straight-to-series bible?
- Have you nailed your format?
- Are you thinking global from the get-go?
- Is your story engine firing on all cylinders?
- From cerebral to emotional: Where do you set the dial?
- Are you striking the right balance between mystery and suspense?
- From procedural to serial: How much mythology in your series?
- Characters in Series: How are they different?
- Are you overplanning or boxing yourself in?

Pilot Commission or Straight to Series Bible?

First, are you pitching to get the pilot commissioned or is it a "straight-to-series" bible? The document, the way you pitch the project, and the approach will all be different because the aim is not the same.

As a rule of thumb, in the U.S. you would usually go through a verbal pitch and a pilot selection process to get a series commissioned by major networks and studios. You first pitch the series to get the pilot commissioned. If the pilot is green-lit, it's used — once produced — to decide whether the first season (or the series if limited) is going to be commissioned or not.

Online streamers tend to commission "straight-to-series" and usually give more creative control to the creators, while the networks and studios involved in broadcast series are usually more hands-on during the development process of both pilot and series.

However, streamers can commission pilots too, occasionally letting their audience decide which one makes it to series, as Amazon did for *Transparent*. In 2023, after twelve years of using exclusively a straight-to-series development model, Netflix commissioned a first pilot for their single-camera comedy *Little Sky*.

European broadcasters also tend to follow a straight-to-series model but if they have doubts, they might ask the creative team to produce a low-budget or no-budget web series first instead. It might sound unfair, but it does happen. Some brave European producers even produce the pilot with their own funds, just to get the commission for the series.

Usually, that's not what happens though: You either pitch the series to get the pilot commissioned and then get the series commissioned afterwards, or you pitch the series to get a straight-to-series commission.

It's important to determine how it works in your country, for whoever you're pitching your project to, so that you're well-prepared and don't have false expectations regarding the outcome of a successful pitch.

Have You Nailed Your Format?

Next comes defining the right format, which we touched on in the hands-on at the end of Chapter 1. As we said, you want to give the story the right amount of space to breathe and come alive, not more, not less.

To achieve this, it's crucial to question the format that you've chosen for your series. You might think it's a 10 x 60 minutes, for example, but would it work better as an 8 x 45 minutes? It's much better to have a tense, efficient 8 x 45 than to have an elongated 10 x 60, unless that's the kind of feeling that you want to achieve.

So ask yourself: Have I chosen the right format for my series? If I look at the material, could each episode be shorter, or could I have fewer episodes and would that be better? Competition is fierce, so you want to give fewer opportunities for the audience to lose attention.

Look at your content and try to compress it rather than expand it, unless it needs more room to breathe in order to handle complex character arcs.

Also, how much of your current story is actually backstory and should remain backstory? Could you start the series later, without bringing in the need for a lot of exposition?

Sometimes writers don't realise that the first third or more of their story is actually backstory: Information that they needed to be able to write the story and the characters, but that the audience doesn't need to know for the most part. In such a situation, much of that information should probably remain backstory, allowing the story to start more quickly. That way, the story is shorter, it starts a lot faster and the audience is hooked earlier: It's a win-win.

So try to identify when it's best to begin your story. For example, in *Occupied*, the story starts very quickly. Many events have already taken place before the first episode: The world has experienced extreme weather events due to fossil fuel use; Norway has stopped exporting its oil and gas resources causing a crisis with Europe and Russia, etc. We are given this exposition early on, during the opening credits and the first episode, so we don't need to see the events unfold on screen. This allows the story to start the very day things get exciting, which makes the pilot / first episode more compelling.

It's always interesting to question your existing story and to ask yourself: Am I starting too late or too early? Often, it's too early. Occasionally, especially if you have a lot of essential exposition at the beginning of the story, it might be that you start too late, in which case you'll have to find a way to make the exposition palatable (often disguising it using conflict stemming from dramatic tension or humour) or start the story earlier.

Are You Thinking Global From the Get-Go?

Thanks to streaming, we can design our stories so that they reach a global audience right away. These days we don't need to design a series with the aim of reaching a sizeable audience at home first and then waiting to see if it's successful before selling it abroad or licensing the format for a remake.

From the get-go, we can design series that are intended for a global audience. This doesn't mean that they can't be rooted in a very specific place in the world, in your own country, in your own culture. Quite the contrary. But you want to design your stories and characters so that anyone, anywhere in the world can relate to them.

How do we achieve this?

First, by **using the dramatic language**, because it helps you to cross borders far more than any natural language, including the English language. Having a tight dramatic structure at series, season, storyline and episode level allows a strong emotional identification because we're able to identify with one or more protagonists.

The dramatic language is based on a universal chain of drama that every human being can relate to and identify with: Someone wants or needs something badly, and they can't get it easily. This is rooted in two universal emotions — frustration and anxiety — that we all experience.

So using the protagonist—goal—obstacle—conflict—emotion basic chain of drama at any story level (series, season, episode, storyline, sequence, scene) is one of the best ways to reach a wide audience, because anyone in the world can relate to the primal emotions it creates and relies on.

Then, **we use planting and pay-off to generate visual storytelling and enhance the emotional involvement of the audience**. We don't have the time here to cover this in detail, but the more you use planting and pay-off to generate visual storytelling (show rather than tell), the less you rely on dialogue and so the more universal the story becomes.

In the U.S., silent films helped to create a united nation populated by immigrants from all over the world, from different cultures and speaking different languages (at the expense of the native American culture, but let's not get into that here). The dialogue-free and primarily visual storytelling offered by cinema at the time was the common language that helped create the American culture.

We are in a similar situation now, especially with streaming: We can reach a global audience of people who speak different languages and come from different cultures. Visual storytelling is tremendously helpful when it comes to crossing borders.

Planting and pay-off can also be used to generate emotion, which is a universal need for the audience, hence also helps to cross borders.

Last but not least, **we use Maslow**, because the lower the main problem lies in Maslow's Hierarchy of Needs, the wider the potential audience. It doesn't mean that every story has to be about survival all the time. It just means that if your story is about something else, it helps to bring in elements that sit lower in Maslow's pyramid at storyline, episode, season and series level.

The higher the main problem sits in Maslow's pyramid, the closer it tends to cling to the original culture of the show. The lower it sits in the pyramid, the less the original culture affects whether a wider audience that doesn't share that culture and language is able to engage with the story emotionally. One of the best recent examples of this is *Squid Game*.

The culture and the language that you export to is of course relevant, as you might need subtitles or dubbing, but the story design, use of visual storytelling and the dramatic structure at episode, storyline, season and series level are far more important than anything else if you want your show to cross borders and reach a global audience.

We discuss all this at length in the first volume of the *Story-Type Method* series, <u>Screenwriting Unchained</u> and in the <u>Advanced Script Development Course</u>, and of course we've seen how Maslow applies specifically to series in <u>2.3 Use of Maslow in Series</u>.

Is Your Story Engine Firing on All Cylinders?

From story world and situation to storylines, how do you create what we're going to call the story engine of your series? How do you suggest that the story engine you've defined in your bible can generate an infinity of storylines?

Again, I'm not talking about mini-series, but otherwise can we imagine almost infinite variations of the same story?

With procedurals and sitcoms, it's fairly straightforward. You define the franchise — the common elements for all episodes, more on this later — and you pick a different case, a different plot, a different problem, a different situation in each episode. You use the same characters, in the same world, and you do this again and again until the creative team dries up or the audience gets bored (the former often leading to the latter).

Or do you have something more complex — as with serials — and does your bible define a convincing story engine? Do we get a sense of the pattern that each episode is going to follow? Of the theme that it's going to explore? Of the problems that it's trying to solve? Understanding the series type (procedural, serial etc.) and the story-type (plot-led, character-led, etc.) of your series will help you to clarify this aspect.

For example, each episode of *Money Heist* is about preparing and executing a perfect heist, and its consequences: What they have planned, what can go wrong, and how human emotions can get in the way of even the most perfect plan, thus making the story unpredictable. It's a serial and it's plot-led structurally, but ultimately it's about the characters and their relationships. The plot is different in each episode, yet every single episode follows a pattern based on the same essential elements, thanks to a well-defined story engine.

So you want to be as clear as possible about your story engine, because that's what's going to define the DNA of each episode in your series.

We'll dive into this further in the next section, where we focus on the design aspect of creating a bible.

From Cerebral to Emotional: Where Do You Set the Dial?

Next, try to figure out, in your series, where you set the dial between cerebral and emotional. One is not necessarily better than the other, but are you clear about it?

It's important to know what kind of emotional involvement you're looking to generate from the audience. You might want to create an intellectual puzzle, a cerebral piece to make the audience think, or you might want to engage the audience emotionally, make them laugh, thrill them or move them.

These two extremes are not incompatible — you can combine intellectual and emotional elements and aim for anything in between — but you need to be clear about what you're trying to achieve. Depending on your target audience and creative intentions, it's essential to ask yourself this question because it will impact on the tools you use to structure the series and design the bible.

This is almost entirely related to managing information. It means finding the right balance between mystery and suspense, questions and answers, according to genre.

For example, in a crime story, are you privileging mystery and intellectual gratification — because you're after a whodunit, a whydunit or a howdunit — or do you favour suspense or dramatic irony, which lead to the more emotional gratification that we expect from a thriller? Again, it doesn't have to be one or the other, but can you find the right balance according to genre and intended audience?

Are You Striking the Right Balance Between Mystery and Suspense?

The way you strike this balance is by making sure that you don't just raise questions, but also provide some answers. If you raise questions endlessly, the audience is going to feel more and more alienated. At some point many will tire of waiting for answers — or get confused — and give up.

So for example, if you have a mystery over your season or even the whole series and want to keep that mystery going until the end, you'll design each episode with a strong A-Story, which will define the stakes in the episode. From a structural point of view, you'll raise a dramatic question, explore it and answer it by the end of the episode. That way, even if the mystery and the main plot are still ongoing at season or series level, you're not leaving all the questions open until the end — you're providing some answers as you go along, at episode level.

If you take the second season of *The Walking Dead*, the first half of the season is about finding out what happened to Carol's daughter, Sophia, who has disappeared in the forest. Initially, it's a mystery for both the co-protagonists and the audience (closed mystery). Each episode shows the protagonists exploring various ways to try to find her. We don't get the answer to the mystery ("What happened to Sophia?") or to this main dramatic action ("Will the protagonists find her?") until the middle of the season, which makes this turning point a mid-season climax.

However, we do have other questions answered as we go through the first half of the season. Some dramatic questions, as well as surprises and dramatic ironies: We discover things that we weren't expecting in a surprising way. After that, this information is exploited as a dramatic irony: we know things that some of the characters don't. There is suspense too, as the longer it takes to find Sophia, the more danger she's exposed to and the less chances they have of finding her unhurt.

So you have a thick mystery combined with surprise, dramatic irony and suspense over the first half of the season, and a final surprise in the middle of the season.

This combination of mystery, surprise, dramatic irony and suspense is what allows the first half of Season 2 to be so strong. If you relied on mystery alone ("What happened to Sophia?") for the sake of a final surprise, it would get boring pretty quickly. Here, we still have mystery, we still have the final surprise, but we also get the thrill and excitement coming from the other tools used to manage information and conflict. I won't get into detail to avoid spoilers, but I suggest you (re)watch it. Hopefully, you'll see what I mean.

Another important element: If you have a mystery over a whole season, it can be risky not to solve it by the end of the season. For example, if you're developing a serial-procedural hybrid, with a main crime case to resolve at season level, you might want to resolve that case at the end of each season.

This doesn't mean that you can't suggest a new mystery at the end of a season, ideally using a combination of surprise and dramatic irony: giving the audience information that some of the characters don't have, in a surprising way, while still keeping some mystery. We might not know what's going to happen, but we'll be willing to wait until the next season to find out.

Playing with both **managing conflict** — to provide satisfying answers by closing a main plot at the end of each episode or season — and **managing information** — to raise new questions using a variety of tools — is what's going to help you to find that crucial balance between mystery and suspense, questions and answers, according to genre and target audience.

Examples

The first season of *Stranger Things* strikes this balance between providing answers and raising questions brilliantly. At the beginning, there is some mystery (What happened in the Lab? What is this Demogorgon monster? Who is Eleven?), but we learn a lot both through El's flashbacks and through the protagonists' investigations. There is also suspense and dramatic irony (We know what happened to Will Byers, that he's in real danger, most of the characters don't). And while the disappearance of Will Byers is solved by the end of Season 1 (*Stranger Things* was designed as a limited series initially), a couple of cliffhangers raise questions for a potential Season 2. **[Please skip the next paragraph if you haven't seen the first season and mind spoilers]**.

First, we realise that Will might not be all right after all. This is a surprise because we weren't expecting it, a dramatic irony because now we know this but other characters don't, and a mystery because we don't know exactly what's wrong with him and what will happen next. We also realise that Hopper is leaving Eggos in a cache in the woods: That's a surprise because we thought Eleven had died during her final fight with the Demogorgon. It also sets up a dramatic irony because we now know that she might be alive but other characters don't, and a mystery because we're not entirely sure that Eleven is alive, we're just hoping she might be.

This balance between providing satisfying answers and setting further questions works very well. The audience knows more than some characters do. There is still some mystery, but they don't know less than any of the protagonists — except Eleven who isn't a main protagonist to start with — so it's easy to identify with them.

Management of information is particularly important in relation to the protagonist, especially when there is mystery over important elements of the protagonist's backstory, which could prevent an emotional identification, or make it more difficult.

For example, in *Homeland*, most of the mystery on the backstory is about the shape-shifting antagonist, Nicholas Brody. This means that the mystery element in the story doesn't prevent a strong emotional identification with the protagonist, Carrie Mathison. We don't know everything about her mental health issue right away (she's bipolar), but that's exploited primarily as an internal obstacle, not a mystery.

There is little we need to know about her backstory that we don't find out early on in the story.

Both protagonist and antagonist are victims of different dramatic ironies, but we know as much as or more than the protagonist, which allows us to understand her actions, decisions, conflicts and emotions: Nothing prevents us from identifying with her emotionally. This clever design — mostly based on dramatic irony but combining suspense, surprise and mystery to find the right balance between intellectual and emotional gratification — led to eight successful seasons.

In *Sharp Objects*, although the main mystery is the whodunit (Who has committed the murders?), there is also a strong mystery over the backstory of the protagonist, Camille Preaker. While she has full knowledge of her past, we don't know enough about it to understand her actions, her decisions and her emotions. This establishes a distance between her and us, because we're unable to fully identify with her emotionally until much later in the story. We're puzzled by the case and we're interested in her intellectually, but we can't be close to her emotionally until we know enough about her past to understand her better. The acting and directing is brilliant, which led to many awards and critical acclaim, and this limited series found an audience that enjoys intellectual gratification more than emotional involvement over a single season of eight episodes. Nothing wrong with that, except that it is the right structure for a slow-burn whodunit in a limited series, not for a long-running thriller.

So be clear about what you want to achieve with your series regarding genre and target audience. Managing information is the key to finding the right balance, according to your series type and format.

From Procedural to Serial:
How Much Mythology in Your Series?

In a procedural, twenty or thirty years ago, say in a series such as the original *Magnum P.I.*, you had very little mythology (the soap element about relationships or an ongoing investigation). *The X-Files* was the exception rather than the rule. Today, in series such as *Luther* or *Grey's Anatomy*, which feature a strong procedural element, there is a tendency towards character evolution running through character-led subplots. It's entirely up to you to decide how much of that you want.

Serials, on the other hand, are all about character arcs and storylines over dozens of episodes, often weaving ten storylines or more over many seasons.

That's another essential point to think about. Is your project closer to a pure procedural? Is it closer to a pure serial? Or do you have a procedural element in your series, either at episode level — as in *Sex Education*, with the sex case of the week in each episode — or at season level — as in *Stranger Things*, with a different manifestation of the same meta-antagonist in each season?

Here again, defining the series type and clarifying its story-type will help a lot in designing a successful series.

Characters in Series: How Are They Different?

All stories are about characters. However, they don't all ask the same commitment from the audience. A feature film is a bit like having friends or family over for dinner. It's a small commitment. A series, on the other hand, is more akin to inviting them to stay in your house or going on a boat trip with them for a month. If you don't enjoy spending time with each other, it's not going to end well.

In a feature film, you might get the audience to share less than two hours with a despicable character, as in *Henry: Portrait of a Serial Killer*. A character who doesn't have any redeeming qualities, with whom we can't empathise or sympathise. It's a voyeuristic portrait, so some might find it fascinating even if there is absolutely no way to identify with the main character. Henry can't be called a protagonist, because hopefully no one is rooting for him. The only characters we can identify with are Henry's innocent victims, because they are not aware of their fate (dramatic irony) and so we lend them a lot more conflict than he ever experiences. But Henry himself is a character who at best leaves us cold and at worst disgusts us, so we're happy to leave him behind after a single serving.

In a series, we need to care about the characters. We need to relate to them so that we want to find out what's going to happen to them in each episode. So with a serial killer, you get *Dexter*, who might be a murderer but is someone the audience can identify with emotionally, because they understand his motivation and emotions.

Dexter experiences more conflict — not less — than other characters in the story and so we can relate to him over a long period of time. The writers use a classic tool to get the audience to identify with a conceptually or morally negative protagonist such as Dexter: They give him a positive motivation, lead him to experience a lot of conflict and get him to face characters that are conceptually worse than him.

Dexter's victims are murderers who haven't been adequately punished by the justice system, due to corruption or legal technicalities. This is also used in *Breaking Bad*: The drug lords and Nazi villains faced by Walter White and Jesse Pinkman over the series are far worse than them, and Walter initially became a criminal because he wanted to protect his family, a motivation that he fulfils in the end. Conceptually, Walter gets worse from a moral point of view in each season, however the antagonists get worse too. Dramatically, Walter always experiences more conflict than them, so we can still empathise with him despite his moral ambiguity.

When you have a conceptually negative protagonist and the story isn't purely character-led (so isn't primarily about their evolution or redemption), you often need villains rather than just antagonists, to establish a stark contrast with the protagonist. That's the opposite of *Henry*, where the main character *is* the villain and there is no protagonist.

Or, leaving aside serial killers and sticking with conceptually negative characters or morally dubious goals, we get *After Life* or *Money Heist*.

Even if your protagonists are conceptually negative or try to achieve something that's morally questionable, can we identify with them emotionally? If the story isn't character-led, are they facing antagonists or villains that are worse than them morally or conceptually? Do they experience more conflict than the other characters? Do we understand their actions, their emotions, their motivation, and do we want to spend time with them?

Another difference between series and feature films is that in series, you don't necessarily want to focus on the evolution of the characters, on a finite arc. What you want to focus on is the depth of the characters. And that's one of the biggest differences between feature films and TV series.

Features are about where the characters go. They start, they finish and that's it. So it's all about their evolution between the beginning of the film and the end of the film.

In series, it's a lot more about how much we can reveal about the characters as the series goes on, because you want to keep it running forever if it's successful. Again, unless it's a limited series, you don't want to suggest that we know the ending of the characters' arc by the end of the first season.

You want to imply that every time you start a new episode, or every time you start a new season, the audience will discover something new about the characters. So, can you suggest depth in the characters — revealing layers one after the other, like peeling an onion — rather than making them go through finite transformations?

It all centres on how much we can reveal about the characters as the series goes on. I'm not talking about backstory because the more backstory, the more exposition and the more you're going to struggle, because exposition is boring (especially during a pitch). I'm talking about how far can they go as characters: Where do they take us? How surprising can they be? How many different facets are there to their personality? In series, characters usually don't *change* that much, because we like them as they are. What changes is often how the audience *perceives* them.

Are You Overplanning or Boxing Yourself In?

When designing a bible, we need a good idea of the first season and a vague idea of how the following seasons might unfold if it's not a limited series or a mini-series, but there is no point in mapping them precisely because there are many things we don't know at this stage.

We don't know how long the series will last and which storylines we'll have to prune. We don't know which characters the audience will like the most or which actors will have the strongest chemistry. For example, Jesse Pinkman in *Breaking Bad* was only supposed to be in the first season, but the chemistry between Bryan Cranston and Aaron Paul was such that Vince Gilligan swiftly changed his initial plans for the character. All this and more will impact on the design of seasons to come.

The season you're writing is all you have. That's what the commissioner is interested in, and that's what you should focus on.

You want to clarify that if successful, there is plenty of potential for further seasons, but don't hold back. Don't spend too much energy designing seasons and storylines that might never be. Don't think "Wait, it's going to be so much better, so much more exciting in Season 2". TV series development doesn't work like that. Put 90% of your energy into making the best first season you can think of, and 90% of that energy into making your pilot the most exciting episode you can think of. Get your pilot commissioned, get your first season commissioned, then keep it up for as long as you can.

In a serial, clearly define which problem you're exploring in the season, and which answer you can provide by the end of the season that doesn't fully answer the larger problem, yet provides some answers and clarity. That way, we'll feel that we are in safe hands.

What you want to avoid is boxing yourself in, especially regarding the combination of series type and story-type. For example, if your series is character-led and you want more than one season, make sure that you don't fully resolve the protagonist's main internal problem by the end of the first season, as you would often do in a feature film. If you do that, you might have to change the story-type for the next season, which will alter the story-engine. This could lead to a loss of some of the original audience, without gaining a new one.

This is one of the most common issues in series projects, especially when they come from creators with feature film experience. Their first season is character-led, it fully resolves the protagonist's internal problem, and they believe that if it's successful, they'll figure out a new story with the same characters and story world. This almost never works, unless it's an anthological series or maybe a serial-procedural hybrid. For example, *The Mare of Easttown* is character-led, and that's not a problem because it's a limited series. It was a very successful show, but it's almost impossible to follow it up without breaking the story engine.

So, if your goal is a long-running series, pay attention to its story-type and series type. It's very easy to box yourself in unintentionally by choosing the wrong combination.

Sex Education and *Stranger Things* strike a perfect balance. They resolve some of the main problem at season level, but there is enough of that problem left to allow for a next season without changing the story-type, series type or story engine.

Series Design

Let's talk about series design and bible components. I've separated series design from the content of the bible because for me these are two distinct aspects of working on a bible.

The first part covers thinking about the design of your series, the story that you're telling and what you can do to make your project as strong as possible. The second part explores the best way to sell it and present it — what to put in a bible as a presentation document.

Let's start with series design:

Developing a Series
Creating an Irresistible Bible

Series Design
- Franchise and Story-Type
- Set-up and Story World
- World Building
- Genre
- Concept
- Maslow
- Theme
- Characters
- Plot

Franchise, Series Type and Story-Type

As mentioned briefly in the Film Franchise section (Chapter 1) when we discussed series types, the word "franchise" doesn't have exactly the same meaning in film and in TV, even if they cover a similar concept.

In film, a franchise often simply refers to a character — or a group of characters — that returns in different instalments (James Bond, Indiana Jones, Spider-Man, Ethan Hunt, Jason Bourne, John Wick, The Avengers). In TV, the use of the word is more precise. It refers to the series story engine: Whether it's a procedural or a serial and whatever it is that makes it possible to generate an infinity of episodes if the series is successful. It could be focused around one main protagonist (*Magnum P.I.*, *Wednesday*, *After Life*, *Fleabag*) but it could also be more complex with multiple protagonists and storylines (*Game of Thrones*, *Succession*, *Big Little Lies*, *The Walking Dead*).

Franchise and Series Type

A franchise can also define a common structure for each episode, which is often dictated by the **series type**, so let's take a look at this.

In most **procedurals and sitcoms**, there is a recurring element that starts each and every episode, often called the "springboard", because it launches the story. This is the easiest way to define a franchise.

The most well-known, common franchises are cop (solving a crime), legal (exploring a court case), medical (saving a patient), detective (investigating a case), sci-fi (supernatural situation), action/adventure (mission) and soap (relationships).

For example, the cop franchise for a cop show is quite straightforward: A murder is committed, and the protagonist solves it over the next hour. For a medical show, a patient will show up with injury/disease, and the protagonist will try to save them over the next hour. In a **soap**, each episode will explore familial or sexual relationships, affairs, betrayal, etc. In a **family show**, some drama will happen around the family relationships and will be resolved over the next hour. It's more or less the same in a **sitcom**, although it only lasts half an hour. The relationships can be family (*The Fresh Prince of Bel-Air*, *Modern Family*), friendship and dating or sexual (*Friends*, *The Big Bang Theory*), workplace (*The Office*) and so on.

Historically, procedurals were fairly straightforward. Audiences expected such franchises to deliver predictable episodes where a problem was introduced, explored and resolved within one hour. At first, a few procedurals evolved to add a "soap" franchise element, for example in *ER* or *Hill Street Blues*. Over the last twenty or thirty years, this has become the norm and now most series tend to include a "soap" element (a relationships franchise).

Things get more complicated with **serials**, especially when the series is theme-led overall, such as *Game of Thrones*, *Succession* or *Occupied*.

Today, not all series have a franchise with a clear "springboard" — a recurring element that starts every episode and gives each episode a similar structure — but all successful ones still have a specific DNA that applies to most episodes. Some even combine different franchises.

Franchise and Story-Type

So now that we've looked at the way the series type (procedural, serial, sitcom etc) impacts on the franchise, let's see how the **story-type** of contemporary series often defines a significant part of the franchise, and which other elements of your series design can help to clearly establish its DNA.

As we said, some of the **main franchises are plot-led**: cop, legal, medical, detective franchises are all about resolving a case of the week (someone dies, a patient gets ill, a new client walks in, etc.). Their main problem tends to lie at the bottom of Maslow's Hierarchy of Needs (survival, protection).

This is also the case for action/adventure/thrillers, such as *24* or *Prison Break*. These often use a unifying goal to shape one or more seasons.

The difficulty for newcomers lies in defining a series goal that can remain active over many episodes but doesn't lead to an inflated budget due to constantly changing locations: It's harder to get *The Fugitive* or *24* financed than a series based on a single location. However, you can be clever about this. For example, *Money Heist* (one of the most watched non-English language series on Netflix) looks on the surface like a show with high production value, but in reality it's fairly contained, with a single main location — the mint in which the heist takes place — and a few studio interiors — the police HQ and the main protagonist's HQ.

Some franchises are about power, for example in *The West Wing*, *The Sopranos*, *Succession* or *Game of Thrones*, where various groups, clans, families — or members of the same family — fight for power. **These tend to be theme-led** and can explore any level in Maslow's pyramid.

The soap franchise tends to be character-led, at least at storyline level. It's all about relationships — family, friendship, sexual intimacy, love/belonging. These explore primarily the middle of Maslow's pyramid.

However, **the sitcom franchise is usually plot-led.** It also explores the middle of Maslow's pyramid, but each episode is closed-ended and there is nothing clearly at stake at season or series level as episodes can be watched intermittently or out of order.

Other franchises can be based on genre (for example, hunting a different monster in each episode as in *Buffy*).

Some combine different franchises, often a pure procedural element with a soap element, so that you have procedural cases in the A-Story but serial relationships in the B and C stories, or vice-versa.

While it's often less obvious than for procedurals, sitcoms or soaps, you can still have a franchise element in **serials**. For example, there is a medical franchise element in *Sex Education*: The teaser in each episode introduces the main sex therapy case that's going to be solved over that specific episode. It's not necessarily the A-Story, but that's part of the series DNA.

Often the music and the opening credits — slowly evolving as the story world changes through each season — contribute to defining the franchise (*Game of Thrones*, *The Walking Dead*). You watch the opening of an episode and you're immersed in the story world right away.

Overall, a strong franchise will help you convey the idea that your story couldn't be a feature film or a mini-series. You want your franchise to suggest that you won't be telling just one story but a multitude, both simultaneously (storylines) and chronologically (episodes and seasons), yet will create a coherent piece.

Set-Up and Story World

The next element of story design that is worth thinking about is what we're going to call the set-up, which also introduces the story world — we'll focus more specifically on that element in the next section.

Very simply, the set-up defines **the time** — when the story happens — **the place** — where it takes place — **what's at stake** — usually a main dramatic action or evolution — and **the world** the characters inhabit: Is it reality? Fantasy? A combination of both?

In a series, you have about ten minutes in the first episode to sell the next fifty. That's when you introduce the story world and get the story started. It's crucial to get this right, because it's one of the main elements of story design. We'll discuss this further when we talk about writing a compelling pilot, but I recommend you watch the first episodes of successful series to check what a good set-up looks like: *The Walking Dead, The Night Agent, Sex Education, Stranger Things, Breaking Bad, Occupied, The Queen's Gambit, Lost* are all great examples.

In many ways, the first episode sets up the series, but you really can't afford to have a set-up that takes the whole of the first episode. The worst way to start a series is to have a first episode that feels like a long first dramatic act: a slow introduction to the story world and the characters, before we finally understand what's at stake and who wants or needs what and why. You really need to get one main action, evolution or situation started early in the first episode.

Especially with the hundreds of other series you're competing with, if you don't hook the audience within five to ten minutes, your series will be dead in the water.

Sometimes you might need more than ten to fifteen minutes to introduce the story world and your characters. In that case, consider using something like a teaser flashback: Starting with a snippet from later in the story — when things are really interesting and exciting — and then going back to the beginning to introduce your story world. That's what *Breaking Bad, Occupied, The Walking Dead* or *The Queen's Gambit* do. It allows you to "earn" a longer set-up: You hook the audience from the start, which means you can then afford to take a bit more time to introduce your characters and story world.

Alternatively, you can make sure that you get the story started before the end of a longer-than-usual set-up.

For example, the set-up of *Stranger Things* is eight minutes long, which would be almost too long, especially as it includes a fairly uneventful scene introducing the boys playing Dungeons & Dragons. To make up for this, 1) the writers set up a strong dramatic irony *before* that scene, during a short teaser — there is a monster on the run! — so that they can generate tension during a scene that might otherwise feel a bit dull and 2) they design a strong dramatic sequence that shapes the second half of this slightly long set-up (Will trying to escape from the Demogorgon before it takes him). In other words, the storytelling — using the three dimensions of screenwriting, including managing information — has started *before* the end of the set-up, right from the teaser: We don't have to wait for the main dramatic action (here finding and rescuing Will) to start to be thrilled, intrigued and entertained.

It's getting harder and harder to hook people and to keep them watching. So it's one thing you try to achieve right away. You get the main dramatic action, evolution or situation started as soon as possible or, if you need more time, you use a teaser flashback or an ironic/dramatic sequence in the first dramatic act to hook the audience as quickly as you can.

World Building

The next element is world building, which is often an essential part of series design. We could easily spend a whole chapter on this if it was our main topic.

There are different ways to approach this.

Sometimes, when a story is based in a real world setting or on a true story, it's more about defining that setting — time and place — and researching the facts. Take a fantastic series such as *Chernobyl*: You start with Chernobyl, 1986, research the events meticulously, find an original take on it, and you have built your world from the facts upwards (I wish it was as easy as I make it sound, obviously it's not, *Chernobyl* is artfully crafted).

In other series, creators have to build a world from scratch, with a complex mythology, and most importantly, its own set of rules. It could be a dystopian or apocalyptic future, as in *The Handmaid's Tale* or *The Last of Us*, or it could combine genres in a unique mix, such as sci-fi and western in *Westworld*.

Either way (real or invented world), building an original, compelling world represents a lot of work. This is often one of the unique selling points of the series, so creators invest a significant amount of time in developing it.

Sometimes, creators will adapt an existing story world, such as the Addams Family franchise in *Wednesday*. More often, they create rich, complex environments to transport the viewers to new worlds and to keep them immersed in the stories that they're watching. And in a way you get hooked, you get addicted to the story world, just like you get addicted to the characters.

Take a supernatural period piece, a horror/thriller, such as *Stranger Things*. Defining the story world doesn't stop at defining the place — Hawkins, Indiana — and the time — 1984 for the first season. The Duffer Brothers also create a fictional universe with a complex mythology and make it feel real. The key to achieving this —

building an invented world that feels real — is to focus on small details, to add authenticity to the storytelling.

You need to define rules and stick to them, especially if your world is invented — based around fantasy or the supernatural. And you need to think about the details of that world, about that era, and how they tie in together so that we'll feel like it's coherent and credible. Visual effects can help to bring an invented world to life, but the details in the costumes and the production design are also going to make a difference.

Of course, your project doesn't have to be a high budget period piece with special effects to benefit from this aspect of design. For example, a series like *Sex Education* creates a slightly off world that makes a British school look almost like an American campus. It's supposed to take place today. It has modern gadgets, mobile phones and so on, but it also has a unique and kind of universal "retro" feel.

It's a more subtle kind of world building than say *Stranger Things*, *Westworld* or *The Handmaid's Tale* and it's more about production design than writing, but it definitely helped the series to cross borders and reach a wider audience abroad, especially in the U.S.

Again, we could spend a lot more time discussing world building, but it's a key part of series design, so give it the attention it deserves and make sure you define a compelling story world. Just as we'll go back to a show if we fall in love with the characters, we'll also go back to a show if it takes us to a world that we want to return to.

Genre

Historically, the five main genres for procedurals were cop shows, legal shows, medical shows, private investigators and family shows. Of course, other genres were developed, such as western, sci-fi, fantasy, monster, superhero, vampire, etc.

At least in the U.S., most "genre shows" have a supernatural element. Cop shows or western shows aren't seen as genre shows, even if they belong to a specific genre, like thriller or comedy.

Today, while pure genre series are still made, the definition isn't as strong and new genres come and go. Nordic Noir (*The Bridge*, *The Killing*), western sci-fi (*Westworld*), etc.

If your series fits a genre or combines two or more genres (hybrids), it doesn't hurt to mention it, but if it doesn't that's not a problem. Drama is not really a genre, but a lot of people love it, so that's okay too.

What you want to avoid is selling your project with the promise of a genre that you don't deliver in the material. Yes, you'll likely generate interest more easily if you brand your project a thriller, a comedy or a horror, but you'll probably disappoint the reader or the audience if you don't deliver on that promise. Announcing a genre raises interest (at least from the market and a crossover or mainstream audience), but also expectations. As with advertising, no genre is better than false genre.

The most important thing is to be clear about the format and the nature of the recurring element in the franchise (when present). The genre is the cherry on the cake that will help your readers or pitchees to get a grasp on your project more quickly and marketing departments to sell it more easily, but you can leave it out if the cake doesn't need it.

Concept

A concept is an idea for a show that's developed so that its potential for a series becomes obvious, and it's possible to identify from this concept what makes it unique and different from previous shows in the same genre.

It's not easy to come up with a strong concept. A high concept is a story that can be pitched in one minute and not only sold to those who are going to commission your series, but once it's bought and produced, can be sold easily to the audience too.

That's why decision-makers love high-concept projects: It makes their job much easier.

It also makes the job of creators easier, as a high-concept not only helps them to sell their project, it also helps them to have a clear understanding of its dramatic backbone and to define its franchise more easily, so they are less likely to get lost or break something unwittingly during the development process.

Many successful series aren't high-concept, which isn't necessarily a problem. It's just more difficult to encapsulate the essence of the series in an elevator pitch or a short logline.

So anything that clarifies your concept and makes your project high-concept can be a tremendous help in getting it made, as long as it doesn't destroy its very nature of course.

High-concept series often use managing information — especially dramatic irony — in one way or another. I explore this further at the beginning of the book, in The Three Dimensions of Screenwriting.

Maslow

As we saw earlier in 2.3 Use of Maslow in Series, Maslow can be a great help when designing a series, so it doesn't hurt to mention it again here.

Once you've defined the main problem in the story, can you position it on Maslow's Hierarchy of Needs? It should give you an idea of the size of your potential audience. You can then check if the story-type, budget and genre fit together.

If the main problem sits at the top of Maslow's pyramid — which suggests a limited audience — yet your project needs a high budget, look at other elements in your story, look at the problems in each storyline and try to ensure that these sit lower in the pyramid.

For example, if there aren't likely to be many people that will care about the main problem — because it's thematic or spiritual, for example — but if each storyline explores problems that are located lower in Maslow's pyramid, then you'll be introducing ways for a wider audience to relate to and engage with your story.

Theme

Do you know what the series is about? You're not necessarily aware of that early in the development process, sometimes it will only appear to you after a couple of drafts, but once you've identified your theme, can you make sure that it's encapsulated in every situation, scene, episode, storyline and season?

Sometimes, when you're struggling, it's because you're focusing on the plot or the characters, but your story isn't about anything at its heart. And few people want to spend hours of their lives watching a story that's got nothing to say.

Also, will the story resonate with a contemporary audience? Ideally with any future audience as well, so that we can keep selling and replaying it, but at the very least with an audience today.

It doesn't have to be about current events, but does your series explore a theme that is relevant to a large audience? Even if it's set in the past or takes place in the future, whether it's a sci-fi or a sitcom, what does it tell us indirectly about the world, society, people, relationships, today?

Thinking about the theme is going to help you to reach your audience. The plot and the characters have to be exciting, but check that the theme explores elements that are relevant to a modern audience, not only for your local audience but also abroad.

Character Design

As we said earlier, if we don't care about the characters, the series is dead. We don't have to like them or approve of their actions (sympathy), but we have to relate to them, to understand them, to care about them, to identify with them (empathy).

From a design point of view, we tend to identify with the character or characters who experience the most conflict in a story. This conflict can be generated using the classic protagonist—goal—obstacle chain of drama, or using managing information, especially dramatic irony (information that the audience has, but not some of the characters).

If you use dramatic irony, for example, you can generate conflict even if the characters don't experience any, which means that you can achieve a more subtle kind of conflict than characters fighting, arguing or yelling at each other.

Also, remember that conflict leads to change. We tend to resist change, so what forces us to change, what leads us to change is the conflict that we experience. Especially if you have a story with strong character-led elements, you want to make sure that the conflict the characters experience is connected to their evolution, in other words that their evolution springs from the conflict that they experience in the story.

This evolution (also called a character arc) can be a *change* or a *growth*: The protagonist of a series or a storyline may need to *change* because they're going in the wrong direction, or they might just need to *grow* because they're going in the right direction, but need to become stronger in order to reach their goal. Or they will grow, they will evolve as a result of having tried to achieve this.

Finally, one of the most important characters is your antagonist, especially if the series is plot-led. You won't necessarily have an antagonist but when you do, make sure that they are strong and memorable. They might even be charismatic. Think of an antagonist such as Negan Smith, who significantly raises the stakes and renews our interest from Season 6 in *The Walking Dead*. Or Gustavo "Gus" Fring, who does the same from Season 2 of *Breaking Bad*. A great antagonist can make a series, just like a weak one can break it.

Of course, most of your characters need to have a drive, a goal, a motivation. They also need to have defining characteristics, such as a dominant trait that really defines them, and secondary traits that make them different from all the characters who have that same dominant trait.

For example, if your character's dominant trait is jealousy, great, but we have 10,000 jealous characters in the repertoire. So, what makes your jealous character different from Othello, Salieri in *Amadeus* or Amy in *Little Women*, who are all very different jealous characters themselves?

Another important part of character design in relation to the protagonist that is worth repeating: we don't have to identify with them conceptually. We don't have to like them or approve of them. We just need to be able to understand them, their conflict and their motivation so we can empathise with them, see some truth in them. We can be fascinated by them, root for them, feel for them even if what they try to achieve is morally reprehensible, as long as they experience more conflict than the other characters in the story.

This is where Maslow really helps, because whatever their goal, making sure that their motivation is rooted towards the base of the pyramid can help the audience to identify with a character that they might otherwise not necessarily feel close to.

If you think about it, that was a huge part of the success of shows such as *Breaking Bad* or *Squid Game*. This is why historical genres, such as cop shows, medical shows, legal and private investigator shows did so well: they are rooted in a lower layer of Maslow. And if you have that, if you have a motivation that everyone can understand, you can make your character much more complex or ambiguous.

On the other hand, if you don't have that, if you have a protagonist who isn't nice and has a motivation that no one cares about — especially if they experience less conflict than other characters in your story — then you're most likely in trouble.

Plot

This comes last because in some ways plot is the least important. Plot isn't structure, it's only part of structure. Of course, we need a strong plot and a good story engine is a plot-generating machine, but it will only be efficient if we care about the characters.

Sometimes, a writer will spend a lot of time designing a sophisticated plot, and yet the story will feel empty because there is no theme, the characters are too shallow, or we don't understand their motivation. Sadly, all that work on the plot is lost simply because it's not enough on its own to interest us, move us or entertain us.

We're rarely primarily interested in the plot. The plot is often what's going to make us willing to keep watching, but in the end, it's always about the characters.

When you work on the plot, one of the most important things to have in mind is causality: cause and effect. Is there enough causality in the story? Do events happen because of what's happened before, in the same storyline or in some of the other storylines in your series? And do events have an impact on what happens later in the story?

When you have causality in a story, you give the audience the feeling that watching matters: They can't miss an episode or even a few minutes because if they do, they won't understand what's going to happen later.

Strong causality in the story means that the audience will want to watch each and every episode. Even in a procedural where you don't have to watch all episodes and can watch them in any order, causality within the episode is really important, because that's what's going to make us feel like we'll be lost if we miss a few minutes.

Another element to check in relation to plot: If we have different storylines, are they connected to each other, either thematically or dramatically?

Everything that happens should be both surprising and unavoidable. This can only happen if the plot springs from the characters, from their motivation, from their decisions and their emotions. Obstacles, conflict, twists and reversals are always welcome in a story, but they have to feel organic to the story.

And this is how and why plot is so strongly related to characters. If you just have plot (things happen) and if it doesn't spring from the characters (X happens because character Y does Z), it will feel very artificial. The opposite isn't true: Characters rarely spring from the plot — even though their actions and reactions often do.

This is important at episode level, at season level and at series level, especially with serials.

Causality is strongly connected to planting and pay-off, which we study at length in *Screenwriting Unchained* (book or online course).

Bible Components

Whether verbal or written, a bible can be useful as a selling tool to get the pilot and the series commissioned, but also as a reference tool for all those involved in the project, especially once the show goes from pilot to series and a writing team is assembled. As we said, we're not going to discuss that kind of bible here. We're focusing instead on the selling/pitching bible.

Although there is no industry standard, and their contents can vary from country to country, contemporary bibles or pitch documents will include many similar elements.

I'm going to focus on elements that you can find both in the U.S. and the European market. They should be relevant for most countries, although they might not be found in the same order or given the same importance.

The following components can be part of a fifteen-to-twenty-five-minute verbal pitch to a potential buyer or as a written "bible" document or pitch deck containing the key design of a series.

Developing a Series
Creating an Irresistible Bible

Bible Components
- Series title
- Series logline
- Series overview (or one-sheet)
- Character breakdowns and story world
- Pilot story
- Arc of the first season (and possibly more)
- Arc of the series
- Tone, genre and style
- Episode loglines or synopses
- Package / Pitch Deck

Series Title

Along with the writer's name, the title is the only mandatory element of a pitching bible, so make sure they are both on your title page. You could also add a quote or a table of contents, but these are entirely optional.

Your title is crucial because it's your first hook. When you're looking at a series that you might want to watch, the first thing that you see on the Netflix or Amazon wall — or in any TV guide — is a picture and the title. Because it's your first hook, you want the title to encapsulate the tone and the essence of your series, of its concept, while ideally suggesting if not the main conflict, at least some kind of conflict.

Think of your title as an up-to-three-word pitch to start selling your series to your target audience. When you see it in the middle of the series wall or TV Guide, what does the combination of picture and title achieve? Is it enough to make someone curious enough to pick that series before even reading the logline? It's as simple as that.

Let's look at a few titles from recent successful series: *Sex Education*, *Breaking Bad*, *Occupied*, *Killing Eve*, *Stranger Things*, *Fleabag*, *Squid Game*. They are great titles, very short, true to the show, yet they make us want to find out more because they suggest mystery or conflict.

Another approach, which is a bit more risky because it supposes that the audience knows a little about the series, is to craft an ironic title that creates a contrast between the content and the title.

It could play on a double meaning. For example, *Happy Valley* doesn't suggest conflict, but it's an ironic title that refers to the amount of drugs trafficked in the story world.

Transparent works in a similar way. It doesn't suggest much conflict, but it plays on a double meaning: "Transparent" means something you can easily see through, but it also refers to life as a trans parent, which is the subject of the series, based on the creator's personal story.

One last example: *Life in Pieces* refers both to the fact that the characters' lives are in pieces — which suggests conflict — and the fact that each episode of the series shows four separate pieces of their lives, which is actually one of its unique selling points.

So think like a salesperson: Take time to design this first hook that you can use to sell your project and make someone want to read the logline, which is your next selling element.

Series Logline

Moving up from three words, we now have up to three lines to get the audience to want to give your series a try. And again, the "audience" can be the decision-maker you would like to send your project to so that they read the bible or so that you get a chance to pitch it to them, or it could be the actual audience sitting in front of the series wall, at home, deciding what they're going to watch next.

If you're lucky and are dealing with a plot-led series or a character-led series, your logline should give a sense of who wants or needs what and why, and what stands in their way, as well as what's at stake if they fail. Often you can't do that because your story is theme-led or multi-stranded and you have more than one protagonist, or because the show is more complex.

Either way, a good logline is an essential selling tool that will help you to draw people in at any stage.

Series Overview (or One-Sheet)

This is a brief summary of the show and what you intend it to deliver. Like the rest of the bible, it should be written in your own voice, and you want to adapt the style and tone to the project, so that it reflects the genre for example.

It shouldn't be an overview of the pilot. It should be an introduction to the series world and the backbone of the story. Is it a quest? Is it a transformative arc? Does it explore a problem in society? Remember, you're not trying to summarise the plot in your overview.

A good overview could include an idea of the format — so the broad genre, comedy or drama followed by the number and the length of the episodes — as well as the series type, if you know it: Is your project a procedural, a serial, a serial-procedural hybrid, an anthology, a mini-series, a sitcom?

It can also include an opening statement, for example to establish the creator's personal connection to the material, or what inspired them to write it.

When you do that, it also subtly reinforces the creator as being the most qualified person to develop the project. This can be a discrete way to tie yourself to the show so that no-one says, "Oh, great idea, but let's get it developed by someone else". Not that this happens often, but a personal connection just makes it more obvious that you're the right person to develop this show.

This personal statement could have its own section if you need to expand on it a bit.

In your overview, you also want to convey the following elements from the design: the time, the place, the genre — if there is one — the tone, the theme — what the series is about — the context and the characters. Mention all the main characters, make sure they're cast-able, but keep this description brief, because you're going to have a separate section on characters. You could also, if necessary, have a separate section on tone, genre and style.

That's about it. I don't recommend specifying the story-type or anything too technical from a structural point of view because if the reader doesn't share the same theoretical references or disagrees with your assessment, it could sidetrack the discussion into a fruitless dead-end. When bibles venture into this territory — *Stranger Things*, *Fargo* — they keep it simple and accessible.

Character Breakdowns

This section often comes after the overview. As we said earlier in Characters in Series: How Are They Different?, series are all about characters, so it's an essential section in your bible, much more so than the plot. We come for the plot, but we stay for the characters.

You can take up to one page for the three to five main characters in your series and less space for others. I would try not to overload the pitchee or the reader. Simply show that you have a good grasp of your characters, that you know who they are and what their function in the story is. In other words, convey their essence. Your goal is to make us feel that each character is unique, yet relatable.

You don't need pages to describe each character if you define them clearly. If you know what they want or need, their motivation, where they come from, what their main character traits are, you can describe their essence in just a few paragraphs, starting with their name and approximate age. We've discussed this and a few other elements in Character Design.

When you present your characters in the bible — especially your protagonists — try to think about how you're going to get the reader to engage with them. Charismatic actors can do wonders with troubled protagonists, but unfortunately you don't have that on the page.

Overall, using all the above, you want to convey the feeling that the design of these characters is such that we won't tire of seeing them week after week, even if they never change. Focus on clarity, complexity and originality.

Story World

Although you could include elements related to the story world in the previous section — for example, settings connected to each character or group of characters — sometimes it can be a good idea to dedicate a specific section to the story world, especially if it's particularly complex, original or sophisticated.

When present, this section could be as simple as a series of descriptions of the main locations, for example in a sitcom. You could also elaborate on worlds, rules or even aspects of production design or costumes to give a sense of the geography, the scale or the unique look of the show.

Don't get bogged down in detail though, the idea is to help the reader to visualise your story world and convey its originality, not to lose them in irrelevant nuances. You're brushing the big picture, not briefing the art department.

Pilot Story

This is where you summarise your pilot, your first episode.

Usually, it's a synopsis of three to five pages that tells the whole story of the pilot (not just the beginning). It can be a little shorter or longer, but when present that's roughly the length expected in a bible. As always, check if the expectation in your own country is different, and follow the format your local decision-makers expect.

You'll find more tips about writing a synopsis in the "6.1 Selling Documents" section of *Screenwriting Unchained*.

Arc of the First Season (and Possibly More)

Next, we'll expect to see an arc (summary) of the first season and possibly a sketch of the seasons to come if it's a serial.

Unless we're dealing with the adaptation of a well-known existing work, where the audience is familiar with the original material and expects to find key story elements in the series, there isn't much point in going beyond Season 2 in detail. This is because everyone knows that things are likely to change not only after the first season but even during its production. Anything can happen, and experienced showrunners often try to develop episodes by blocks of five or six, so that they can adjust to unexpected changes as a production unfolds.

Casting in particular can have a big impact on the direction of a second season. You pick actors that you think are right for the series, but you don't know how the audience is going to react to them and whether they will like one character more than another.

This can impact even a first season. We've already mentioned the example of Jesse in *Breaking Bad*, who was supposed to die after a few episodes. Being flexible is a key quality of a showrunner. You have to adapt to what the set, the cast chemistry or the audience is telling you.

You're less likely to make such big changes during production for streaming or when each season is commissioned and written in advance. But the fans' reaction to social media, which characters, which storylines they enjoy the most, can still influence story design for the next season.

For example, the Twitter hashtag #JusticeforBarb and associated campaign influenced the plot of Season 2 of *Stranger Things*, after Barbara's death early in Season 1.

This being said, all you have is the current season. It makes sense to have some knowledge of what's going to happen in your storylines and where you'll land in future seasons, but none of that will matter much if the series is not renewed. This is why many showrunners throw everything they have in the current season, with the confidence that they'll sort out the next season when the show is renewed.

For some shows, you need to map ahead and for some others (especially procedurals and mini-series series), it really doesn't matter that much. So, try to make a call regarding your series and decide whether you need more than the arc of the first season in your bible, and how much detail to provide.

Regardless of how many season arcs you put in your bible, each season should end on a hook, unless it's a procedural, a sitcom, a limited series, a mini-series anthology or similar. Usually, this hook will be a cliffhanger of some sort. So try to include one in each arc to raise the curiosity of the reader regarding what might come next.

Arc of the Series

If the series is a procedural or a sitcom, there is less of a need to give it an arc in the bible. First, because characters don't really change between seasons, second because we want to believe that the show can keep running for many years.

With serials, although the story will most likely undergo change, providing a series arc might suggest that you know where you're going and that you have a handle on the material. However, no one expects it to be written in stone. Showing rigidity regarding what might happen in Season 5 when you've not even got the first season commissioned is more likely to trigger alarm bells. Pick your battles, and in this case their timing.

You want to convey the idea that there is life in the show after the first season. So instead of a series arc, you could also write about themes you'd like to explore or the characters and stories you intend to develop in future seasons.

Tone, Genre and Style

Although this can be addressed in the overview, a separate section on tone, genre and style is sometimes included if necessary.

For example, if it's a straight sitcom, you don't need to spend much time on tone or genre, but if you're developing *The Office* or *Fleabag*, you might want to clarify the specific tone: talking to the film crew, mockumentary-style, or how breaking the fourth wall and talking to the camera generates comedy and drama, etc.

This will help decision-makers to read the episode loglines or synopses (and the pilot, if available) with the right frame of mind.

When you describe these story elements, make sure they are congruent with the style of the bible. If you're pitching a comedy, make it funny and use the same tone as the material. If you're selling a thriller or a horror, ensure that the pitch contains suspenseful or horrifying moments.

If you haven't done so in the overview, it might also be a good idea to mention here the primary target audience for the show, the most common ones in the U.S. being kids 6-11, teens 12-17, adults 18-34, 18-49, 25-54 or 55+ and whether it's primarily boys/girls or men/women.

You could also expand on theme, structure, mythology, format or anything else if you feel that it wasn't addressed properly in the overview and think it deserves more space here or even in a separate section, but really you want to keep it short and sweet. Try not to break the flow: Sell the sizzle, not the sausage.

Episode Loglines or Synopses

For serials, we usually have eight to fifteen episode loglines. For a mini-series or limited series, it can be as few as two, though in that case we'll most likely have more detailed synopses.

Some serials will include the loglines for all the episodes of the first season in the bible. You don't have to do that, but it might be a good idea, especially if you don't have many of them and if you know what's going to happen.

In more developed bibles, you can also find a short synopsis for all the episodes in the first season. In that case, each episode will be summarised in about one page. You can see an example of this approach in the bible for *Grey's Anatomy*.

Some sitcoms or procedurals will include a logline or synopsis for just a few episodes, to give an idea of how the franchise works — what the recurring element of the series is.

If the story world and the characters are rich enough, if the franchise and springboard are clearly defined, we should be able to imagine an infinity of episodes without needing to see lots of detailed loglines. Having to write dozens of loglines or synopses might not be a good sign...

Package

The package includes everything at pitching stage that's not about the story itself: producer, creator, showrunner, writers, actors, budget, visual elements, moodboards, etc.

It's best not to mention specific actors for a part unless 1) You're sure you can get them and 2) You know that they would be seen as an asset for this particular show by the specific company, broadcaster or network you're going to pitch the project to.

Of course, mentioning well-known actors as casting examples to give a better idea of the characters is fine.

If there is a strong visual aspect to your project, don't hesitate to show it and include some examples in moodboards, storyboards etc. This can help generate interest and visualise the world of your series. You might even want to go a step further and present your bible as a pitch deck instead.

Pitch Deck

A pitch deck is not a separate component. It's simply a more visual version of the bible, including the same sections but with less text and more pictures, often organised in slides in a smaller or larger format than usual, or using a landscape rather than portrait orientation. Anything that will give the document a distinctive look that conveys the essence of the project.

The visual elements in the bible of *Stranger Things* were very strong, so the Duffer Brothers decided to create a pitch deck using the same font as a Stephen King novel from the same period, etc... These visual clues really helped to convey the mood and the style of the series, playing on its retro factor. They also included a moodboard and mentioned earlier films and shows that inspired them.

The video distributors went a step further in the same direction and used fake VHS tape cases for the Blu-rays of the series. Everyone made the most of the distinctive visual style of *Stranger Things*, both to get it commissioned and then to sell it to the audience.

Using a pitch deck is a no-brainer when the project has a strong visual element, whether it's because it's an adaptation of a graphic novel, because of stunning locations or because it's visually distinctive in any other way.

A good story should stand by itself, but visual aids can enhance even the strongest bible — as long as they look good and match the style of the project. So consider a pitch deck if your series has a distinctive look or tone that is best conveyed visually. It can be a fantastic selling tool.

3.2 Writing a Compelling Pilot / First Episode

Let's get into how to write a compelling **pilot / first episode**, which is a key part of your series project. It's unlikely your show will be commissioned if you don't have a great pilot demonstrating not only how the creator writes, but also how they have set up the series and the franchise. This is especially true if they don't have a strong track record.

In other words, the quality of the pilot will often determine whether the series lives or dies, so we're going to spend quite a bit of time on this topic. Here are the main points we're going to discuss:

Developing a Series
Writing a Compelling Pilot

Writing a Compelling Pilot
- Goals for the pilot
- Premise or midstream pilot?
- The premise
- Opening image
- Teaser or 3-minute hook?
- 10-minute hook
- Complications
- End-of-episode hook
- Final check: Does the pilot introduce and service the franchise?

First, we'll talk about your goals for the pilot: What is this crucial document supposed to achieve?

Then, we'll make the distinction between the two main types: Are we dealing with a premise or a midstream pilot?

We'll also look at the main components of a compelling pilot: its opening image as well as various hooks and complications.

We'll then illustrate all this with a short case study of *Killing Eve* before going through a final project work exercise: 3.4 Hands-On: Pilot Checklist.

Goals for the Pilot

A pilot has two main aims.

First, it's to set the right creative start for the series, get the series commissioned and then produced. Then, once produced, it's to hook the audience into the series.

Let's drill into this in more detail:

Developing a Series
Writing a Compelling Pilot

The goals for the pilot are to:
1. Get the series commissioned
2. Hook the audience from the beginning
3. Keep the audience interested as we introduce the story world and characters
4. Make sure that by the end of the pilot we care both about the characters and the story
5. Define the stakes
6. Show that drama is a struggle, not a statement
7. Set the right balance between hope and fear
8. Provide a satisfying ending
9. Establish a theme relevant to the audience
10. Demonstrate the series franchise

So, what are the main goals you want to achieve in a pilot?

1) Get the series commissioned. Sometimes, the pitch bible will lead to the series being commissioned (this is what we call a "straight-to-series" commission). Sometimes, only a pilot will be commissioned (if it's not been written on spec already) and produced, and then a decision will be made to greenlight the rest of the series or to stop there.

This decision can be made by studio/network executives, and occasionally by the audience.

2) Hook the audience from the beginning so that they want to know what's going to happen next, first in the pilot itself, then in the rest of the series. This is essential. The pilot is not just about making the audience want to watch the rest of the series. You have to hook them right away so that they watch the first episode until the end, *then* want to watch the rest of the series.

3) Keep the audience interested (both at an intellectual and an emotional level) as you set up the story world, introduce the characters, establish the genre and define the main storylines, so they aren't tempted to switch to a different show.

4) Make sure that by the end of the pilot, we care about both the characters and the story. The pilot has to make us fall in love with strong, original, unique characters: Protagonists, antagonists, returning characters… If we don't want to know what's going to happen to the characters, the series is dead. Again, this doesn't mean we have to like them. Just that we understand them and can relate to their conflict, especially for the protagonists. Usually, this means that we understand who wants or needs what and why, and what stands in the way in each storyline. Even if the pilot introduces a long-term goal, can the protagonist of each storyline be active short-term? This is why the fractal aspect of story structure is such a key aspect of series design, as we've seen in the case study of *Stranger Things*.

5) Define the stakes: What happens if the protagonist fails to reach the goal or to change? Do we care? This is where Maslow can really help. What's at stake in each of the storylines? How many people can relate to these stakes? It's not enough to know what your protagonist wants or needs. You also have to convey, in the pilot, what happens if they fail to change (if the series is character-led) or if they fail to reach their goal (if it's plot-led). And you want to do this at series, season and episode level, as well as in each storyline.

6) Illustrate that drama is a struggle, not a statement. Does the pilot introduce a formidable antagonistic force, whether it's an **external antagonist** in a plot-led story, the **protagonist themselves** in a character-led story, or **society** in a theme-led story? If we agree that a good story is a problem-solving process, do we understand the main problem explored in the series, and are we interested in it? If the main problem is not clear, does your series work as an exception or a hybrid, and if so, how?

7) Strike the right balance between hope and fear. Do we *fear* that the protagonist might fail because the sources of conflict are strong enough, but also *hope* that they stand a chance of succeeding? We can relate to characters who experience conflict, that's in fact the main way to generate identification, but most of us won't relate to passive victims, because it's alienating. So, can the protagonist take action (consciously or not) to resolve the internal or external problem introduced in the pilot? Also, make sure that the strength of the obstacles — or the strength of the antagonist if there is one — matches or exceeds the strength of the protagonist.

8) Deliver a satisfying ending that provides an answer to the main dramatic question of the pilot, without answering every question so that we still want to find out what's going to happen next if we're talking about a serial or a limited series. This is classically achieved with a cliffhanger (an unresolved conflict) and is often tightly linked to management of information. Does the ending, for example, conclude a dramatic action while setting up a mystery or a dramatic irony that raises interesting questions about the rest of the story? Or, does it resolve a mystery or a dramatic irony that sets up new subgoals? Is the ending both surprising and organic to what happened before (does the story suggest causality)? Very often, if a pilot feels flat, predictable or linear, it's due to weak management of information.

9) Define what the story is about (theme), making sure it's relevant to a contemporary audience. Especially if your series is set in the past or in the future, or in a weird, original or different world. Is it relevant to most people, not only those in your own country sharing your language and your culture, but to almost anyone, anywhere? That's the audience that you can reach with modern series, especially with streaming: As we said earlier, stay local but think global.

10) Demonstrate the series franchise. This is especially important for procedurals, where you really want to show that you've nailed your franchise and have clarified the DNA of each episode. The pilot should reflect that. Even serials or hybrids should give a sense of their story engines, of their DNA. So, does the pilot already give a taste of how each future episode will explore the series concept and deliver the promise of the premise? If it's a heist story (*Money Heist*), has the heist started? If it's about occupation (*Occupied*), has the foreign invasion taken place? If it's about two women playing a deadly game of cat and mouse (*Killing Eve*), have they met and has the game begun? And so on: The main elements that are going to be characteristic of every single episode in your series should be in place.

If a pilot achieves all this, it's far more likely to be put into production and for the series to get commissioned. There is no guarantee, of course, but you will stack the odds in your favour, because it will give a sense that you're in control of your material and know how to involve the audience in the storytelling. Many pilots fail to hit at least one of these goals.

Premise or Midstream Pilot?

There are two main types of pilots:

A **premise pilot** shows the beginning of the story, before the main action starts or the main concept is introduced. That's how *Stranger Things*, *Sex Education* or *Breaking Bad* begin. The main story in a premise pilot hasn't really started yet. So we see the normal world of the protagonist(s) before the story starts proper, even if the episode itself starts with a teaser flashback, as in *Breaking Bad*.

A **midstream or 3rd episode pilot** shows the story already under way, without showing its starting point. That's how *The Office* begins, both in the original UK series and the U.S. remake. Same for *Fleabag*.

If the first episode sets up the story world before the series defining or recurring element is introduced, make sure you don't wait until the end of the episode to introduce the inciting incident of the series or its main dramatic action or evolution.

If you need more than ten minutes to set up your story, use a teaser flashback or any other device to hook the audience within the first ten minutes, ideally less than that. You can't afford to have a pilot that's just a long first dramatic act.

Breaking Bad and *The Queen's Gambit* illustrate this approach. They use a teaser flashback to give a more gripping opening to their premise pilots, then take their time to set up the story world.

The Walking Dead is a successful hybrid, so let's see how it works. **[Please watch the first episode before reading the end of this section to avoid spoilers if you mind them.]** It combines a teaser and a semi-cold start in a premise pilot that feels like a midstream pilot.

The episode starts with a short teaser that sets up the tone and genre (post-apocalyptic zombie horror drama). Then it takes about ten minutes to reveal Rick Grimes' backstory through a series of flashbacks to "the world before". This is a great way to make sure the audience is hooked early on yet catches up quickly with the relevant part of the main protagonist's backstory: He's a cop; he has a rocky relationship with his wife, Lori; he has a son, Carl and a best friend, Shane (also a cop). This short exposition sequence ends with Rick being shot on the job, minute twelve. Fifteen minutes in, he wakes up in his hospital room and we have a semi-cold start. The protagonist knows as much as we do (i.e. nothing) about what's happened while he's been in a coma: the zombie apocalypse. In fact, we know a bit more than him for a while, thanks to the teaser, which increases the suspense and tension.

This is a masterful way to manage information, because it makes sure that the audience catches up alongside the protagonist, yet the main action (survival and finding his wife and son) kicks in very quickly. As a result, we don't have too much exposition regarding the zombie events at the beginning of the series; it's handled gradually through action, dialogue and short flashbacks as the story unfolds. Also, we never feel that the protagonist knows more than we do over a long period of time, which would prevent a strong emotional identification.

The Premise

A premise is a set of conflicts, complex enough to be explored over the course of a hundred episodes if we're talking about a procedural, a serial, a sitcom and so on.

This can be achieved by a straightforward franchise that defines a "case of the week", or a sitcom that sets up the recurring characters, situations and tone.

Or it can be achieved with a more general question (a mystery, a character study, a quest) that will be ongoing over many episodes.

What you want the pilot or first episode to achieve is to define and service a franchise based on the premise.

Sex Education is an interesting example because it's a serial with a strong procedural element. The premise is simple enough: Otis, the teenage son of a sex therapist, finds that he also has a knack for the subject and secretly begins to charge his peers for advice.

Because this is a covert operation, there is a strong dramatic irony that creates conflict (we know what Otis is doing but his mother and the college headmaster don't).

By the end of the pilot, we know that the story is about Otis and his inability to have sexual intimacy, even with himself, which makes the fact that he becomes a sex therapist highly ironic too. The sex clinic has been set up, and it's clear it will allow Otis to spend time with Maeve, the girl he's falling for, who is out of his league.

We have both a long-term quest linked to the romantic element (Will Otis overcome his issue? Will he and Maeve end up together?) and a procedural element (a sex case for each episode). The pilot itself illustrates the first sex case solved by Otis and Maeve, introduced by the teaser as in every episode, so the pilot services the franchise based on the premise before it's even defined.

Overall, a good premise raises the right questions, questions that the audience demands to see answered in the rest of the series. Unlike a feature film, a pilot should define processes, not offer immediate solutions. Nail the premise and half the work is done.

Pilot Components

Let's take some time now to look at the way pilots are designed.

First, put logistical acts aside — at least for a while. By all means, use them later on if you're familiar with them, and follow whichever format the broadcaster or the showrunner asks you to use.

But from a design point of view, from a structural point of view, from a dramatic point of view, put logistical acts aside during the design.

Instead, focus on defining, breaking and weaving the storylines, as well as on designing a dramatic 3-Act structure for the episode around the A-Story — the main dramatic action for the episode — as explained in Storylines: Where Format Meets Structure (Section 1.3 in Chapter 1) and illustrated in the case study of *Stranger Things*, at the end of Chapter 2.

That chapter — along with the Series Design part of the 3.1 Creating an Irresistible Bible section — explores all the dramatic tools you can use in series design, including your pilot.

Once you've done that, make sure you nail the most important moments and the main hooks in your first episode and your chances of having designed a compelling pilot will have gone through the roof!

Let's see how this works.

Developing a Series
Writing a Compelling Pilot

Pilot Structure:
Put aside Logistical Acts, Sequence the Storylines and Nail the Hooks

1. Opening Image
2. Teaser or 3-minute hook?
3. 10-minute hook by the end of the set-up
4. Complications and resolutions
5. End-of-episode hook

Opening Image

What do you open your pilot with? It often helps if you can come up with an opening image that's striking, original, puzzling. Something visual that conveys more than what's on the surface, so not just a stunning landscape. Your mission is to hook the audience from the first moment, visually. You don't need a strong opening image for every episode, or in every series, but it can really help to find a striking one for the pilot that sets the theme, the genre, the tone.

Whether it's puzzling, intriguing, shocking or fascinating, it should be something that makes us want to stay and give the story one to three minutes. I know it's harsh to hear for writers, but that's what you'll get at best when your pilot starts: one to three minutes of attention from the audience.

So think of something visual that conveys more than what's on the surface:

In *Occupied*: a man walking in a Nordic landscape, disoriented, with traces of blood in the snow. Who is this man? What did he do, or what happened to him?

In *Breaking Bad*: a pair of khaki trousers floating gracefully through the air and landing in the desert dirt, right before an RV runs them over. Whose trousers are they? What happened to the person wearing them?

In *Sex Education*: two teenagers having sex; the ceiling light, rocking in the room below. No stunning landscape here, but it's enough to catch our attention.

All these examples are visually striking, but they also suggest conflict, raise questions, set the tone and the theme, etc.

Teaser or 3-Minute Hook

Once you've hooked the audience from the opening image, the next step is to have a teaser or a three-minute hook, so that by the time you've reached the three-minute point, the audience won't be tempted to try a different series. They have no choice but to keep watching yours. They're hooked.

This three-minute limit means that if your story needs longer to get exciting, it might benefit from a teaser flashback, as in *Breaking Bad*, *The Queen's Gambit* or *Occupied*. Or it could be a simple teaser, as in *Stranger Things* or *Sex Education*. Anything that allows you to buy more time from the audience before a longer than usual set-up.

However, you don't need a teaser to meet this three-minute deadline if you start a main dramatic action or evolution quickly. For example, in *The Night Agent*, the protagonist is introduced and a main dramatic action starts within the first three minutes (there is a bomb on the train). Past that point, it's hard to stop watching if you're part of the intended audience, simply because you want to know what will happen to the characters that have just been introduced. The suspense (immediate danger) has hooked us. This shows how quickly a good 3-minute hook can kick in.

Whether you use a teaser or not as a hook, just make sure that the first two to three minutes of your pilot are so compelling that there's no way we're going to stop watching after minute three if we should be part of your target audience.

10-Minute Hook

The next stage is what I call the 10-minute hook, which is the end of the set-up. For me a good set-up is five to ten minutes. That's how much time you have before you get the A-Story, the main dramatic story in the pilot started. The first ten minutes sell the next fifty.

By this point, you want to have started the main conflict in the episode — if not of the season or of the series — so that the audience knows what's at stake, why they should keep watching.

If we understand "Who *needs* or *wants* what and why?" by minute ten, if we're aware of the main dramatic action or evolution in the episode, through managing conflict, then we'll know why we should keep watching.

Otherwise, you could consider setting up a mystery or a strong dramatic irony. Something that hooks us for the rest of the episode through the "Who *knows* what and when?" part of the story, through managing information. Instead of wondering whether the protagonist will get what they want or what they need, we might wonder how and when the victim of a strong dramatic irony will find out what we know and they don't.

From a story structure point of view, we're usually in dramatic Act 2 by minute ten. Again, unless you use a teaser flashback or a dramatic sequence in Act 1 to give a shape to that longer first dramatic act.

If you don't achieve this by minute fifteen, preferably minute ten, or find a way around that by managing information, your chances of the pilot being pushed back to the bottom of the pile or being tossed in the bin go up exponentially.

In *The Walking Dead*, the 10-minute hook is when Rick Grimes, the protagonist, gets shot around minute 12. This turning point is strong enough for us to want to find out what's going to happen to him. It comes a bit later than minute ten, but the teaser flash-back has bought enough time for us to get to know Rick so that we can root for him as he tries to find his wife and son — his first goal in the series.

In *Stranger Things*, as we've seen, the 10-minute hook takes place minute 7, when Will Byers is taken by the Demogorgon, just before the opening credits. It's the inciting incident that triggers the co-protagonists' goal to find and rescue Will over the first season.

In *Occupied*, the 10-minute hook is minute 13, when Prime Minister Berg is abducted. A bit later than the 10-minute landmark, but as in *The Walking Dead* or *Breaking Bad*, a teaser flashback buys the writers some time at the beginning of the episode.

So the 10-minute part of this hook shouldn't be taken literally. It's just a way to make sure that by minute ten — or minute fifteen if you've found a way to buy a bit more time — the audience feels that the story has started and can commit to watching the rest of the pilot and, hopefully, season.

Complications

Once we've got the audience on board past minute ten, they'll start to care about the characters, especially if you get the protagonist(s) to experience a lot of conflict.

Over the rest of the pilot, we'll explore a fascinating story world, meet new characters and we're going to come up against various obstacles, complications, twists, cliffhangers etc. both in the main plot (A-Story) and in the subplots (B-Story and so on).

These turning points don't have to happen at a specific page number or at a specific minute, especially when you're dealing with streaming or premium channels. On the contrary. The more you follow set milestones, the more it's going to make your story feel predictable and formulaic.

Still, when you have a clear main plot, for example in a procedural, writers will usually break the A-Story first and then fit the other storylines around that, as explained in <u>Storylines: Where Format Meets Structure</u> (Section 1.3 in Chapter 1) and illustrated in the case study of <u>*Stranger Things*</u>, at the end of Chapter 2.

Often these turning points will match the end of logistical acts (so around minute 15, 30, 40, 50 in a classic logistical 5-Act structure) to make it so that the audience will want to come back to the show after the commercial breaks. But these aren't really about structure, they are about format, as explained in Chapter 1.

Today, most writers and showrunners developing series for streamers have given up on the logistical 5-Act structure. They have reverted to a logistical 3-Act or 4-Act structure, focusing on character development and they simply breakdown the main storylines (say A, B, C) around their respective goals / what's at stake in each strand, before weaving them together in the most effective way.

If your showrunner, broadcaster or commissioner insists on following any logistical format, that's absolutely fine. That's the way they consciously approach series design, and if that works for them, great. Remember, it's only the size of the sausages.

Just make sure that the actual structure underneath is sound: Who wants or needs what and why, who knows what when, whether a main problem is defined in the A-Story, whether secondary problems are defined in the B and C stories. We've discussed this in Storylines: Where Format Meets Structure (Section 1.3 in Chapter 1) and we've seen how it works in the case study of *Stranger Things* at the end of Chapter 2.

End-of-Episode Hook

Unless we're talking about a procedural or a sitcom, you want to have an end-of-episode hook by the end of the pilot, because this episode will be the first of many more to come: It has to sell the rest of the series.

So by the end of the pilot you might have answered the main dramatic question at episode level (A-Story for the episode), but you shouldn't have answered every question (for example, ongoing mystery, dramatic irony or main dramatic action at season or series level), again unless it's a procedural (closed-ended episode) or a sitcom. Even then, you probably have a few ongoing character relationship subplots going on if it's a modern series including a "soap" element.

In a limited series or a serial, the main dramatic question is obviously still open, which is one of the many possible hooks, at least until the *finale*.

We saw a powerful end-of-episode hook in *Transparent* when we discussed cliffhangers in Chapter 1, and another one in the case study of *Stranger Things* at the end of Chapter 2. We'll see one more example in the case study of *Killing Eve* that concludes this chapter.

3.3 Case Study: *Killing Eve*

Let's take a look at the pilot of *Killing Eve* to see how all these elements are implemented, starting with the series **title**, along with the **poster** and the **logline**. You might want to (re)watch the first episode before reading the rest of the section to make the most of it and avoid spoilers.

If I look at the title and the poster, personally, I'm intrigued. I'll give a few minutes of my time, at least to read the logline:

"*Killing Eve* topples the typical spy action thriller as two fiercely intelligent women, equally obsessed with each other, go head-to-head in an epic game of cat and mouse".

It sounds original, interesting enough. I've seen spy action thrillers with an epic game of cat and mouse before, but not based around two fiercely intelligent women equally obsessed with each other.

This logline is cleverly designed because it mentions the **genre**, which provides an immediate connection between the storytellers and the audience. It helps potential viewers to gauge whether it might be for them or not. I'm always ready for a good spy action thriller, so count me in.

The logline also contains the **premise** and the **franchise** of the series: "Two fiercely intelligent women, equally obsessed with each other, go head-to-head in an epic game of cat and mouse". Every single episode in the series will be about that.

It suggests original, intriguing characters and a lot of conflict. So I'm sold and I have a pretty good idea of what the series is about. For me, the DNA of the series lies in these few lines. That's what you want to achieve in a logline.

Let's spend a bit more time on the franchise: A game of cat and mouse, attraction/repulsion between a detective and an assassin. The pilot introduces and services this franchise: All the elements are there by the end of the episode, including Eve and Villanelle meeting for the first time. This premise, this franchise has already started to be exploited in the pilot.

Next, the **opening image**. It's not striking in any way, but when you start a spy thriller, opening in Vienna is an efficient way to convey the genre. It might be cliché, but it works.

Now let's look at the **set-up**.

Killing Eve is an example of a premise pilot: It introduces the premise. The story has not started yet when this first episode begins. We are introduced to Villanelle through her interaction with a child in a café. We're not supposed to like Villanelle or to identify with her, but we're supposed to find her interesting. Her behaviour is odd and intriguing, so we want to know more. That's the **3-minute hook**.

Interestingly, we meet Villanelle first, though she's the antagonist, not the protagonist of the series. Eve is the protagonist because she experiences more conflict than Villanelle. Villanelle is possibly the main character, because she's fascinating, but she's not the character who experiences the most conflict. Even when she commits crimes, it doesn't particularly affect her because she's so good at her job. Villanelle is the character who causes most of the conflict for Eve, hence the antagonist. It's a protagonist/antagonist situation.

For most, *Killing Eve* is a plot-led series with the evolution of their relationship as a character-led subplot. The main problem at series level, introduced in this first episode, is: How is Eve going to find a way to stop Villanelle before she kills more people, risking her life and the lives of her teammates at the same time?

The **10-minute hook** takes place around minute 11, when Villanelle's handler sends her to tie up loose ends in London — kill the witness that Eve has been asked to protect. That's when we understand that the story has started, that Eve and Villanelle are bound to face each other, and we want to see what's going to happen when they do.

The **set-up** defines a clear main plot, a strong A-Story for the pilot. It achieves this within a very short amount of time: It introduces the characters, gives Eve her main goal at episode level — which is to protect her witness — and this all happens within the first ten minutes of the episode. It's an effective set-up.

After many **twists and complications**, Villanelle kills the witness and three other people, which is the climax of the A-Story for the pilot. Eve has failed to reach her goal in this first episode and she gets fired as a result, which is a huge conflict for her. It also feels like an undeserved punishment, which reinforces our identification with her. This climax is not conflictual for Villanelle at all — which isn't a problem as she is the antagonist — but it brings a lot of conflict for Eve because she feels responsible for the death of four people. So conflict is managed efficiently in order to help the audience know who they should be identifying with emotionally.

Now let's look at the **end-of-episode hook**: the main cliffhangers of the pilot that complete the franchise set-up.

Because of Eve's action during the episode — raising the right questions, being inquisitive, having the correct intuition about Villanelle — she is offered a new job. That's the first cliffhanger at the end of the pilot: We know that she'll be challenged further. We also know that Villanelle will be involved, because the second cliffhanger is Villanelle being assigned a new mission in Italy.

While we understand that Villanelle is a skilled assassin, we've not seen her at work yet — we've only seen the bloody aftermath. One of the reasons why this second cliffhanger works is because it makes us curious to see Villanelle in action, knowing that because she's good at her job, this will cause conflict for Eve.

So we don't know exactly what Eve's job is going to be other than that it's going to be connected to stopping Villanelle. Neither do we know what Villanelle's mission is, except that it's in Tuscany. We are left wanting to find out more. These two main cliffhangers make up the end-of-episode hook in the pilot.

By the end, the pilot has reached most of the goals that we defined. One of the most important ones being striking the right **balance between hope and fear**. This is achieved perfectly in *Killing Eve* because Eve is completely out of her depth: She's not a field agent, she's being asked to do something that she's not trained to do. She's not a super-cop or a superhero. She's a protagonist who isn't well-equipped for the job that she's going to have to do, which we understand is to stop Villanelle, a skilled assassin. So we *fear* for Eve.

At the same time, we have *hope* because she's clever, resourceful and she has good instincts. We get a sense that yes, it's going to be difficult for Eve to reach her goal, but at the same time she has qualities that make us believe that she could succeed, which gives us hope.

This is the balance that you want to strike by the end of a pilot. We understand what's at stake. We get what the character is going to try to achieve. We know what they are facing — here a formidable antagonist, but it could be mostly themselves in a character-led series — and we're aware that although they are very likely to fail, they might just about stand a chance of reaching their goal.

Of course, *Killing Eve* is not for everyone, but if you're part of its potential audience, this first episode does a great job at keeping you watching until the end. Once you have, you'll most likely want to watch the rest of the season. That's what a compelling, well-designed pilot achieves for the audience, and it can do the same for decision-makers, before it's even produced.

3.4 Hands-On: Pilot Checklist

Here is a checklist that summarises all the elements we've discussed to help you through your pilot or first episode. As you're familiar with it now, we'll use *Killing Eve* to illustrate how it's done.

Writing a Series: Writing a Compelling Pilot

Checklist: By the end of the first episode / pilot of your series,
1. Do we care about the characters and the story?
2. Do we understand who wants or needs what and why?
3. Do we understand the stakes?
4. Does the pilot introduce a formidable antagonist?
5. Does the pilot achieve the right balance between hope and fear?
6. Does the pilot provide a satisfying ending?
7. Do we know what the story is about (theme) and is it relevant to a contemporary audience?
8. Does the pilot demonstrate the series franchise?
9. Most importantly, are we hooked? Do we want to know what's going to happen next?

1. Do we care about the characters in the story? By the end of the pilot, we do care about Eve because of all the conflict she's experienced. She's failed at her mission and is responsible for the death of four people. She's also lost her job, which feels like an undeserved punishment because we know she did everything she could to avoid this outcome. Yes, she's failed, but we don't feel she's entirely responsible. We don't identify with Villanelle, which of course doesn't matter because she's the antagonist, but we find her intriguing if not fascinating, so she doesn't leave us cold.

2. Do we understand who wants or who needs what and why by the end of the pilot? In *Killing Eve*, we know that Eve wants to stop Villanelle. We also understand that, at a personal level, she needs change in her life, and that being challenged by Villanelle might bring her that. We also get that this might be the same for Villanelle.

3. Do we understand the stakes? What happens if the protagonist fails to reach the goal? It's clear that if Eve doesn't stop Villanelle, more people will die. That's what's primarily at stake. On a more personal level, Eve will be unhappy if her life doesn't become more exciting.

4. Does the pilot introduce a formidable antagonist? Definitely. Villanelle is an original, fascinating antagonist and main character who has already caused a great deal of conflict for Eve.

5. Does the pilot achieve the right balance between hope and fear? As we've just seen, this is one thing that the *Killing Eve* pilot does brilliantly: Eve is out of her depth and Villanelle is a mighty antagonist, but Eve is also clever and resourceful, so we fear that she might fail, but we hope she'll succeed.

6. Does the pilot provide a satisfying ending? Although Eve fails (which is a negative conclusion to the A-Story of the pilot), it's still a satisfying ending because the two cliffhangers launch the franchise: the cat and mouse game between two fiercely intelligent women. Some questions are answered at episode level (Eve fails to protect her witness) but new questions are raised at season level: Will Eve stop Villanelle? How is their relationship going to evolve? Will they simply fight each other, or will they complete each other?

7. Do we know what the story is about, the theme, and is it relevant to a contemporary audience? The main thematic problem actually sits quite high on Maslow's pyramid because it's about self-actualisation. Both of these modern, independent women are frustrated. They are very different, but they also have something in common: There is something missing in their lives. Could it be each other? This is what the story is really about. What happens when we're attracted to someone who's dangerous, who could destroy us? What happens when we're afraid of something that might be exactly what we need? Many of us can identify with and relate to this, which makes the story more relevant. Of course, the thriller element lies much lower on Maslow's pyramid, which widens the potential audience.

8. Does the pilot demonstrate the franchise? By the end of the first episode of *Killing Eve*, the two women have already started their game of cat and mouse, and Eve has lost the first round. Her new "team" hasn't been assembled yet, but the two cliffhangers clearly suggest what's to come, so yes, the pilot demonstrates the franchise.

9. Do you believe that the audience is hooked by the end of that episode? Do we want to know what's going to happen next? Of course, this is subjective, some people might be bored by the end of the pilot. This doesn't matter. You're not trying to please everyone; you just want to hook *your* audience. Personally, I'm hooked and I want to watch the rest of the series. Hopefully, anyone else in the target audience will feel the same.

If your pilot passes this checklist, there's a good chance that your project will stand out in any decision-maker's reading pile and reach the top one percent. It won't guarantee a commission, of course, but assuming everything else is up to scratch, it will definitely give you an edge.

The vast majority of pilots fail at least one of these checks, yet each of these elements is essential to establish the potential of your series and write a compelling pilot / first episode.

After this last hands-on, it's now time to wrap this up…

Conclusion and Next Steps

I hope you enjoyed reading this book, that you found it informative and, in some ways, entertaining; that you feel better equipped to design, write, pitch and assess series and that this new understanding of how series are designed will be a defining step towards your own success.

If you'd like to take this journey into series design to the next stage, especially regarding project work, I invite you to look at the following online courses (www.screenplayunlimited.com/online-courses/):

The **Advanced Script Development Course** covers the same ground as the first volume in this series, *Screenwriting Unchained*, adding dozens of clips, training videos, quizzes and gamification for a total of fifteen hours of interactive content. If you haven't read *Screenwriting Unchained*, it's the best way to make the most of any volume in the *Story-Type Method* series, including this one.

The **TV Series Add-On Course** builds on the main course and is designed as a companion course for this third volume in the series, particularly if you're developing serials or limited series.

The first three training modules (**Foundations**, about four hours of content) follow the content of this book fairly closely. However, the next five modules (**Advanced Development**, about six hours of content) dive much deeper into series design through additional topics and detailed case studies of successful series, which unfortunately could not be included in this book as following them on paper would have been tedious and unpractical.

We study in-depth one series per story-type (*Stranger Things*, *Sex Education* and *Big Little Lies*) as well as a few hybrids and exceptions: *Fleabag*, *Mr. Robot* and *Happy Valley*. There is also a bonus case study of *Occupied* that looks at a successful non-English language series.

These advanced case studies provide a structural analysis at episode, season and even series level, in a way that's simply never been done before.

They include detailed scene breakdowns for all the episodes in a season; strand maps showing visually how the storylines are defined, broken and woven together; and info-graphs revealing the dramatic structure of each storyline at season level. These documents are available to download from within the course, along with additional resources.

In the course, you go through the content at your own pace with training videos, video clips, interactive quizzes and even a Writers' Room game to keep you motivated and entertained, while applying first-class tools and techniques to your project through hands-on videos, each one focusing on a particular aspect of series development. There is even an interactive assistant tailored to each of our courses, available 24/7 to answer any questions you might have about the content, while you explore or revisit it. This makes the experience truly interactive.

The course ends with a final hands-on that sets you on the path to your series rewrite:

You'll find a discount code for both online courses in the "*If You Want to Find Out More*" section at the end of this book. This is in addition to any existing discount.

Just before that, you'll find a list of *recommended reading and watching*. I've selected a few titles that give the points of view of talented and experienced showrunners, producers and writers on the series development process.

Remember, all the elements we've discussed should help you to prevent or get out of difficult situations and hopefully get your series made, but they are only tools, techniques and principles. They don't replace talent or inspiration. I just hope they'll help you figure out the approach that works best for you, your team and your projects.

Ultimately what's going to get your project made is your passion for it and whether you'll find a unique way to communicate it to others.

Passion is a fire that sometimes needs to be revived or protected, but it's also a beacon that you can always trust and follow. When in doubt, follow your passion. Trust your instinct, be inspired, be original, be daring, be challenging and never, ever try to please everyone.

I wish you the best of luck with your projects and I hope you'll let me know when your next creation hits the small or big screen, possibly in some ways thanks to this little book.

Here is to your successful series!

Story-Type Method Glossary

Note: When a definition references another **term** from this glossary, it will appear in *italics* the first time it's mentioned in the definition. When a definition references chapters from this book (or other volumes in the series), these links are underlined. Most of the terms and concepts related to the *Story-Type Method* are defined and introduced along with the method itself in the first volume in the series, <u>Screenwriting Unchained</u> as well as in the <u>Advanced Script Development</u> online course (<u>www.screenplayunlimited.com/online-courses/</u>). Please see <u>Conclusion and Next Steps</u> for more details.

0-9

3-Act Structure: See *Three-Act Structure (Dramatic)* and *Three-Act Structure (Logistical)*.

3rd Episode Pilot: See *Pilot / First Episode*.

A

Act: Main division in a screenplay. This division can be logistical, which means based on an arbitrary number of pages or minutes (30-60-30 Three-Act paradigm or its 25-25-25-25 Four-Act variant with a *midpoint* in a feature screenplay) or the number of commercial breaks in a TV episode / TV movie (leading to two, four, five or seven acts). These *logistical acts* only apply to the whole screenplay. They are about format rather than structure. See *Three-Act Structure (logistical)*. Act divisions can also follow a more flexible dramatic structure, for example before, during and after a main *dramatic action* or *evolution*. These *dramatic acts* have no predetermined length and apply not only to the whole story, but also to its parts: *dramatic scenes and sequences, subplots, strands, storylines, episodes and seasons*, thanks to the *fractal aspect of story structure*. See *Three-Act Structure (dramatic)*, <u>The Dramatic 3-Act Structure</u> in <u>A Quick Overview...</u> (How to Make

The Most of This Book), Underlying Series Design (Chapter 2) and also the following problems in *The Screenwriter's Troubleshooter*: 03 The Story Takes Too Long to Start, 19 The Script Feels Formulaic and 35 The Script Is Unnecessarily Complex.

Action: See *Dramatic Action*.

Antagonist: *Character* (or group of characters sharing the same *goal*) whose objective is in direct opposition to the protagonist's goal, hence constitutes the main source of conflict for the *protagonist*. Not all stories need an antagonist. In *character-led* stories, where the main problem lies within the protagonist, the protagonist *is* the antagonist, and we have instead a *catalyst character*. An antagonist isn't the same as a *villain*. See Character Design in Series Design (Chapter 3) and the following problems in *The Screenwriter's Troubleshooter*: 18 There Is No Clear Protagonist, 24 There Is No Clear Antagonist and 26 The Villains or Antagonists Are Weak or Unconvincing.

Anthology Series: An Anthology series brings a new world and set of characters in each episode. In the past, series such as *Twilight Zone* or *Alfred Hitchcock Presents* were anthologies. *Black Mirror* is a more recent example. Episodes tend to be one hour, but they can be half an hour too, in any genre. See Anthology Series in 1.2 Series Types.

Anthological Limited Series: See *Mini-Series Series*.

Anti-Climax: Disappointing, underwhelming or predictable *ending* — usually of a story, but it could be of a *dramatic sequence, storyline, episode or season* — often due to a lack of *conflict* or because of a *deus ex machina*. See the following problems in *The Screenwriter's Troubleshooter*: 22 The Ending Is an Anti-Climax, 23 The Ending Is a Deus Ex Machina and 10 The Ending Doesn't Work.

Arc: In series, an arc is a continuous *storyline* that spans across multiple episodes or seasons. It usually involves the development and transformation of a *main character* or a group of characters, as well as the progression and resolution of a major conflict or problem. An arc can also be used to describe the overall structure and direction of a series, from the *inciting incident* to the *climax* and the *ending*. A character arc describes the transformation of a character over a story (season, series, feature film). There is a misguided rule that all characters need to have an arc, or that the *protagonist* is the character who changes the most. This can be the case, but it's not always true.

For example, in sitcoms, you might have a relationship arc (say Rachel and Ross in *Friends* or Jim and Pam in *The Office*), but the characters don't change significantly. See Characters in Series: How Are They Different? in Overarching Questions and Aims, Character Design in Series Design, Arc of the First Season (and Possibly More) and Arc of the Series in Bible Components (all in Chapter 3), as well as Sitcom in 1.2 Series Types.

B

Backstory: See *Character Backstory*.

Beginning: According to the logistical *Three-Act Structure* paradigm, the first twenty-five to thirty minutes of a two-hour screenplay. In the *Story-Type Method*, it's the first ten to fifteen minutes of the film or TV series *first episode / pilot*, also called the *set-up*. One of the most important parts of a story, along with the *ending*. It usually introduces the *characters* and the *story world*, and sets up a main *dramatic action* (*plot-led story*), *evolution* (*character-led story*) or *theme* (*theme-led story*). Ideally, it gives an indication of *what's at stake* in the story. See Setup / Story World in Series Design (Chapter 3) and the following problems in *The Screenwriter's Troubleshooter*: 03 The Story Takes Too Long to Start, 02 We Don't Care About the Story and 19 The Script Feels Formulaic.

Bible: In series writing, a bible is a document that contains information on the *characters*, settings, themes, tone, style, *structure*, and *storylines* of a show. It is used to pitch a series idea to producers, networks, or studios, as well as to guide the writers and *showrunners* during the production process. A bible usually includes a logline, an introduction, a summary of each episode, a breakdown of the main characters, a description of the story world, and a vision for future seasons. A pitching bible can also be called format, book, TV treatment, pitch document or proposal. Finally, it can be a reference document used to keep track of key information about the show during its production so that everyone in the creative team can get up to speed and stay on the same page. See Overarching Questions & Aims, Series Design and Bible Components in 3.1 Creating an Irresistible Bible.

Breaking the Fourth Wall: Writing technique that involves a *character* or an actor acknowledging the presence of the audience or the camera, which results in breaking the illusion of the fictional world. It's usually done by looking directly at the camera or the audience, or by addressing them directly. Breaking the fourth wall can have various effects, such as creating humour, intimacy, metafiction, or shock. It can also be used to comment on the story, the characters, or the medium itself. Some examples of breaking the fourth wall can be found in *Fleabag*, *House of Cards*, *Deadpool* and *Ferris Bueller's Day Off*. See <u>Story-Type</u> in <u>2.3 Use of Maslow in Series</u> and <u>Tone, Genre and Style</u> in <u>Bible Components</u> (Chapter 3).

C

Catalyst Character: *Character* who pushes, forces or helps the *protagonist* to change in a *character-led* story (or in the *character-led subplot* of a *plot-led story*). They often look like an antagonistic character because they tend to oppose the protagonist's *conscious goal*. In fact, catalyst characters are *co-protagonists* on the protagonist's *unconscious need* to change. Examples: Maeve in *Sex Education*, Tiffany in *Silver Linings Playbook*, Driss in *The Intouchables*, Jonathan "The Duke" Mardukas in *Midnight Run*. See the following problems in *The Screenwriter's Troubleshooter*: <u>01 We Don't Care About the Protagonist</u>, <u>05 The Characters Are Flat, Two-Dimensional</u>, <u>16 The Scenes Are Aimless, There Is No Dramatic Conflict</u>, <u>19 The Script Feels Formulaic</u> and <u>24 There Is No Clear Antagonist</u>.

Causality: Cause and effect. When events happen in a story as a result of what has happened before, and when they also cause further events in a story, there is causality. When events happen due to chance, luck or coincidence, and when they have few consequences later, there isn't enough causality. To check for causality in a story, write a step outline (the whole story over a few pages with one paragraph per step) and see if you can take out or swap some of these steps without disrupting the whole story. If this is possible, get rid of these steps or find a way to connect them with what has happened previously and what happens next. Pay extra attention to *subplots*, *strands* or *storylines* and verify that they are sufficiently connected to the *main plot*. See <u>Plot</u> in <u>Series Design</u> (Chapter 3) and the following problems in *The Screenwriter's Troubleshooter*: 25 The Narrative Is Episodic or Repetitive and 38 The Plot Is Contrived.

Character: The central element of story, along with *plot* (what happens in the story) and *theme* (what the story is about). Story *is* character. If we don't care about the characters, we won't care about the story. See Characters in Series: How Are They Different? in Overarching Questions and Aims, Character Design in Series Design, Character Breakdowns in Bible Components (all in Chapter 3) and the following problems in *The Screenwriter's Troubleshooter*: 01 We Don't Care About the Protagonist, 02 We Don't Care About the Story, 05 The Characters Are Flat, Two-Dimensional, 06 The Character Logic Is Fuzzy, 12 The Characters Are Too Similar, 13 The Characters Are Stereotypes or Clichés.

Character Backstory: What happened to the *character* before the story started. Writers need to work on the characters' backstories to be able to write about them, but the audience doesn't need to be given all this information. This is why it's called backstory. Most of it should remain in the background and there's no need to bring it to the front, except the part that, if unknown, could prevent an emotional identification. See Surprise, Mystery, Dramatic Irony and Suspense in Managing Information in Series (Chapter 2) as well as the following problem in *The Screenwriter's Troubleshooter*: 14 The Characters' Backstories Are Irrelevant / Pointless.

Character Change: When a *character* doesn't follow the right path, they need to change. This often means that they have to move on from a traumatic event in their past that is holding them up, or to become aware of an internal flaw and correct it. The audience will only want a character to change if they believe that there is hope they might do so, and if the character isn't happy (consciously or not) with the way they are. Usually, a character change is associated with the protagonist's *evolution* in a *character-led story*. See Character Growth, Steadfast Character, 2.1 Underlying Story Structure and Story-Type in Use of Maslow in Series (Chapter 2), Characters in Series: How Are They Different? in Overarching Questions and Aims, Character Design in Series Design (both in Chapter 3) as well as the following problem in *The Screenwriter's Troubleshooter*: 05 The Characters Are Flat, Two-Dimensional.

Character Growth: When a character follows the right path, they don't need to change because there is nothing wrong with them or with what they're trying to achieve. However, they might need to grow (get stronger, resolve a minor internal issue, face an internal fear) in order to stand a chance of reaching their *goal*. Alternatively, they might grow as a consequence of the conflict they have experienced while trying to reach their goal. A character growth is often associated with the protagonist's *evolution* in a *plot-led story*. See *Character Change, Steadfast Character*, 2.1 Underlying Story Structure and Story-Type in Use of Maslow in Series (Chapter 2), Characters in Series: How Are They Different? in Overarching Questions and Aims, Character Design in Series Design (both in Chapter 3) as well as the following problem in *The Screenwriter's Troubleshooter*: 05 The Characters Are Flat, Two-Dimensional.

Character Evolution (or **Character Arc**): When a character is different at the end of the story, they have evolved. This evolution can be a change or a growth (see above). Usually, the *protagonist* of a *character-led story* changes (or fails to change if it's a tragic ending) while the protagonist of a *plot-led story* grows (or remains steadfast). Not all characters need to evolve. A character who doesn't evolve is called a *steadfast character*. See *Character Change, Character Growth*, 2.1 Underlying Story Structure and Story-Type in 2.3 Use of Maslow in Series, Characters in Series: How Are They Different? in Overarching Questions and Aims, Character Design in Series Design (both in Chapter 3) as well as the following problem in *The Screenwriter's Troubleshooter*: 05 The Characters Are Flat, Two-Dimensional.

Character Inciting Event: Event that triggers the unconscious need to change in a character. See *Inciting Event (or Inciting Incident)* and also the following problem in *The Screenwriter's Troubleshooter*: 03 The Story Takes Too Long to Start.

Character-Led Story: A story where the main problem lies within the *protagonist*. In such a story, the protagonist *is* the *antagonist*. Most of the *conflict* comes from within the protagonist. What's primarily at stake is whether the protagonist will change or not, whether they'll find a way of overcoming their inner flaw. The backbone of the story is the *main dramatic evolution* of the protagonist. Because we resist change, we need conflict to force the character to evolve. Usually, this conflict comes from a *catalyst*, a character who pushes, forces or helps the protagonist to change. In a character-led story, the protagonist might be the character who changes the most, but that's not necessarily true for other story-types. See A Quick Overview... (How to Make The Most of This Book), 2.2 How to Identify Your Story-Type? as well as the following problem in *The Screenwriter's Troubleshooter*: 18 There Is No Clear Protagonist.

Character-led subplot: See *Subplot*.

Cliffhanger: An unresolved *conflict* at the end of a *scene* or a *sequence* in a script, a storyline, an episode or a season in a series or before we leave a *strand* in a *multi-stranded narrative*. This is usually achieved by leaving the protagonist in a difficult situation, or by dropping an information-bomb (*surprise*, set-up or resolution of a *dramatic irony*, resolution of a *mystery*) that leaves the audience wanting to know what's going to happen next. See Cliffhangers in 1.3 Conventional Series Design and Pilot Components in 3.2 Writing a Compelling Pilot / First Episode, as well as the following problems in *The Screenwriter's Troubleshooter*: 04 The Story Is Linear, Feels Predictable and 34 Too Many Questions Are Left Unanswered.

Climax: The moment, scene or sequence towards the end of a story during which you provide an answer to the *dramatic question* that shaped it. As soon as we understand who wants or needs what and why in a story, we enter *dramatic Act 2* and start wondering "Will the protagonist reach their *goal*?" This is the dramatic question. The climax, usually the most conflictual moment in the story, brings an answer to this question and marks the end of the main *dramatic action* or *evolution* that shaped the story if it was *plot-led* or *character-led*. We enter *dramatic Act 3* in a story after the climax. Thanks to the *fractal aspect of story structure*, we can also find a climax at the end of a *dramatic scene, sequence, subplot, strand, storyline, episode or season* if they are designed using a *dramatic Three-Act Structure*. See A Quick Overview... (How to Make The Most of This Book), 2.1 Underlying Story Structure and the following problems in *The Screenwriter's Troubleshooter*: 10 The Ending Doesn't Work, 22 The Ending Is an Anti-Climax and 23 The Ending Is a *Deus Ex Machina*.

Closed-Ended Series: See *Procedural*.

Closed Mystery: A TV industry term used to describe a story based on a main mystery: We don't know what happened, and we are trying to figure it out with the protagonist (who, hopefully, doesn't know more than we do about what happened). A classic example is a *whodunit*, or murder mystery, such as *Broadchurch*, *Sherlock* or *Mare of Easttown*. See *Whodunit*, *Mystery* and *Open Mystery*, as well as 2.4 Managing Information in Series.

Character Arc: See *Arc*.

Co-protagonists: When two or more *characters* share the same *conscious goal* or *unconscious need*, they are co-protagonists if this group of characters experience the most conflict in the story. For example, in *Saving Private Ryan*, all the soldiers led by Captain Miller have the same *goal*, stated in the title. In *Little Miss Sunshine*, all the family members have both the same conscious goal (to get Olive to the pageant in time) and the same unconscious need (to become less dysfunctional). In *Stranger Things*, Will's mother, brother and friends — joined by Hopper — have the same goal, which is to find Will and rescue him. In *The Walking Dead*, Rick Grimes is the first and main protagonist, but all the survivors that are part of his constantly evolving group are co-protagonists as they share the same goal: staying alive while protecting each other. See *protagonist*, Storylines: Where Format Meets Structure (Section 1.3 in Chapter 1) and the following problem in *The Screenwriter's Troubleshooter*: 18 There Is No Clear Protagonist.

Coming Next: Brief summary at the end of an episode showing what's coming in the next one. Feels more and more unnecessary and outdated, especially with streaming where the whole show is available and can be binge-watched right away. See Teaser, Recap and Coming Next in 1.3 Conventional Series Design.

Conflict: One of the main elements of drama, mostly used to generate realism, interest, *identification*, *emotion* and cause an *evolution*. A conflict can be serious or humorous (most gags are conflicts). Conflict can be used to disguise *foreshadowing* or to make *exposition* more palatable. It usually comes from the opposition between a *goal* and *obstacles*, whether they are external or internal. Conflict can also be generated through *managing information*, for example using *dramatic irony*. See A Quick Overview: The Three Dimensions of Screenwriting (How to Make the Most of This

Book), the following problems in *The Screenwriter's Troubleshooter*: <u>20 The Conflict Is Artificial or Inconsequential</u>, <u>04 The Story Is Linear, Feels Predictable</u> and <u>16 The Scenes Are Aimless, There Is No Dramatic Conflict</u>.

Cold Start: When a story starts with a *protagonist* who doesn't know where they are or how they ended up there and doesn't remember their past due to some condition — usually amnesia but it can also be a coma or a repressed memory — we have a cold start. This sets up a *mystery* about the protagonist's past, but because we know as much as the protagonist, it doesn't prevent emotional *identification*. On the contrary, we team up with the protagonist to resolve this mystery. A cold start often leads to flashbacks gradually revealing the missing information about the protagonist's past, as they start to remember their past or put the pieces together. Examples: *The Walking Dead*, *The Bourne Identity*, *Predators*, *Before I Go to Sleep*, *The Maze Runner*, *Cowboys & Aliens*. See <u>Premise or Midstream Pilot?</u> in <u>3.2 Writing a Compelling Pilot</u> and the following problems in *The Screenwriter's Troubleshooter*: <u>03 The Story Takes Too Long to Start</u> and <u>01 We Don't Care About the Protagonist</u>.

Conceptual Identification: See *Identification*.

Conscious Goal: What a character consciously wants, what they are trying to achieve actively. This isn't necessarily the same as their *unconscious need*. The protagonist's conscious goal defines the *main dramatic action* in a *plot-led story*. See <u>A Quick Overview...</u> (How to Make The Most of This Book) and the following problem in *The Screenwriter's Troubleshooter*: <u>05 The Characters Are Flat, Two-Dimensional</u>.

Contrived: When events happen in a story to serve the plot or the theme, rather than stemming from the characters and what has happened to them previously, we say that the plot is contrived. See the following problem in *The Screenwriter's Troubleshooter*: <u>38 The Plot Is Contrived</u>.

Creator: The writer (or writing team) who designs a series concept and puts the series *bible* together. They also usually write the screenplay of the *pilot* or first episode, and often become *showrunner* of the series and oversee its development. See <u>First-Up</u> in <u>Project Development</u> (Chapter 3).

D

Deus Ex Machina: An unplanted element that helps the *protagonist* to get out of trouble at the end of a story, an episode, a storyline, a *dramatic sequence*, or a *dramatic scene*. Initially, the expression comes from ancient plays, where the plot was resolved by gods being lowered onto stage on a mechanical platform: "Deus ex machina"—a god from a machine. See the following problem in *The Screenwriter's Troubleshooter*: 23 The Ending Is a *Deus Ex Machina*.

Dialogue: What the characters say. Good dialogue is an important asset in any screenplay; poor dialogue can easily put the reader off. However, from a story design point of view, it's the least important part. Bad dialogue is often caused by too much *exposition*, not enough *visual storytelling* and "on the nose" dialogue, what a character says to explain something to the audience in an obvious way, when no human being would. See the following problems in *The Screenwriter's Troubleshooter*: 15 The Dialogue Is Cheesy, Full of Action Movie Clichés and 21 The Dialogue Is Stilted and Unnecessarily Verbose.

Dogmatic: See *Formula, Formulaic*.

Dramatic Act: See *Three-Act Structure (dramatic)*.

Dramatic Action: Action defined by what the *protagonist* consciously wants. In a *plot-led story*, the protagonist's *goal* usually remains the same over the entirety of *dramatic Act 2*, so we have a main dramatic action that shapes the whole story. This main dramatic action is often cut down into more manageable units called *dramatic sequences*, which are a succession of scenes connected to the same *subgoal* (way to reach the goal). See A Quick Overview... (How to Make The Most of This Book), Storylines: Where Format Meets Structure in 1.3 Conventional Series Design and the following problems in *The Screenwriter's Troubleshooter*: 02 We Don't Care About the Story, 07. The Story Sags in the Middle.

Dramatic Evolution: An evolution defined by the *protagonist's* unconscious need to change or grow. In a *character-led story*, the protagonist's need to change usually remains the same over the entirety of *dramatic act 2*, so we have a main dramatic evolution that shapes the whole story. This main dramatic evolution is often cut down into more manageable units called *dramatic sequences*, which are a succession of scenes connected to the same *subgoal* (what the protagonist consciously wants in the sequence). These are ways for the protagonist to experience the *conflict* that is going to force them to change, one step at a time. The sequences can all be connected to the same *dramatic action* if the protagonist has the same conscious goal over the whole story. A dramatic evolution, usually connected to the protagonist's need to grow, can also shape a character-led *subplot* in a *plot-led story*. See *character change*, A Quick Overview... (How to Make The Most of This Book) and the following problem in *The Screenwriter's Troubleshooter*: 05 The Characters Are Flat, Two-Dimensional.

Dramatic Irony: When the audience knows something that at least one character on screen is unaware of. This can be used to generate *suspense* in a thriller (Hitchcock's "bomb under the table"), humour in a comedy (most of the characters in *Tootsie* are unaware that Dorothy Michaels isn't a woman), and tension in drama (the characters at the beginning of *Stranger Things* don't know that there is a Demogorgon on the run and that it has taken Will Byers). A character kept in the dark is the victim of a dramatic irony. It works in three steps: 1) Set-up, when you give the audience the information, 2) Exploitation, when you make the most of the conflict (humour, drama) generated by the dramatic irony and 3) Resolution, when the victim finds out. Dramatic irony is one of the most powerful tools in the writer's toolbox and is linked to managing information, along with *mystery*, *surprise* and *suspense*. See A Quick Overview... (How to Make The Most of This Book), Surprise, Mystery, Dramatic Irony and Suspense in 2.4 Managing Information in Series and the following problems in *The Screenwriter's Troubleshooter*: 04 The Story Is Linear, Feels Predictable and 19 The Script Feels Formulaic.

Dramatic Question: The main hook that keeps the audience interested during *dramatic Act 2*. In a *plot-led story*, it's "Will the protagonist get what they want?" In a *character-led story*, it's "Will the protagonist get what they need?" This applies to the whole story but also to its parts when there is something clearly at stake in each dramatic unit (season, episode, act, strand, storyline, dramatic sequence or scene). See A Quick Overview... (How to Make The Most of This Book) and the following problems in *The Screenwriter's*

Troubleshooter: 02 We Don't Care About the Story, 04 The Story Is Linear, Feels Predictable and 16 The Scenes Are Aimless, There Is No Dramatic Conflict.

Dramatic Scene: A scene where something is clearly at stake, i.e. we understand who wants what and why in the scene and what stands in the way. A new dramatic scene starts when the *protagonist* or the *goal* changes. A new logistical scene starts when the location or the time changes. As a result, a dramatic scene can be made up of many logistical scenes. For example, a single dramatic scene can start in the kitchen, continue in the bathroom and end in the bedroom. This would be three different logistical scenes, but a single dramatic scene if the protagonist and the goal remain the same over the three logistical scenes. See A Quick Overview... (How to Make The Most of This Book), Storylines: Where Format Meets Structure in 1.3 Conventional Series Design and the following problem in *The Screenwriter's Troubleshooter*: 16 The Scenes Are Aimless, There Is No Dramatic Conflict.

Dramatic Sequence: A succession of *dramatic scenes* where the *protagonist's goal* in each scene is connected to the same *subgoal*, either as a way of reaching it, or as a way of dealing with the consequences of having reached it (or having failed to reach it). A dramatic sequence can also be designed around a *dramatic irony*, in which case an *ironic question* (How and when will the victim find out, and how will they react?) replaces or supplements the *dramatic question* (Will the protagonist of the sequence reach the subgoal?). The protagonist of a dramatic sequence is usually the story protagonist, but occasionally it can be a different character, especially in a *multi-stranded narrative* or TV series. There is no set number of dramatic sequences in each *act*, and there is no set duration for each dramatic sequence. A dramatic sequence can be as short as a few minutes, and as long as sixty minutes or more. See A Quick Overview... (How to Make The Most of This Book), Storylines: Where Format Meets Structure in 1.3 Conventional Series Design and the following problem in *The Screenwriter's Troubleshooter*: 07 The Story Sags in the Middle.

Dramatic Structure, Dramatic 3-Act Structure: See *Three-Act Structure (dramatic)*.

E

Emotion: What we want to deliver to the audience through storytelling, along with entertainment and meaning. Emotion is usually generated using *conflict*, through the basic chain of drama: Protagonist—Goal—Obstacles—Conflict—Emotion, as explained in *Screenwriting Unchained*. The most moving moments in a story (for example the ending) tend to *pay off* what has happened before in the story and are often delivered using *visual storytelling*. See <u>Storylines: Where Format Meets Structure</u> (Section 1.3), <u>2.4 Managing Information in Series</u>, <u>Are You Striking the Right Balance Between Mystery and Suspense?</u> (Section 3.1) and the following problems in *The Screenwriter's Troubleshooter*: <u>27 The Script Is Cold, Unemotional</u>, <u>35 The Script Is Unnecessarily Complex</u> and <u>10 The Ending Doesn't Work</u>.

Emotional Identification: See *Identification*.

Encore Twist: A surprise at the beginning of *dramatic Act 3* that relaunches the same *dramatic action* for the protagonist, when we thought the action was over because it looked like the protagonist had succeeded, or had failed and given up. See the following problems in *The Screenwriter's Troubleshooter*: <u>10 The Ending Doesn't Work</u>, <u>17 The Script Loses the Plot in the Third Act</u>.

Ending: What you leave the audience with, so one of the most important parts of a story, along with the *beginning* (also called the *set-up*). We can enjoy both happy and unhappy endings. What's key is whether the ending is satisfying or not, as most of the meaning of the story is conveyed through its ending. A satisfying ending is key to getting positive word-of-mouth. An unsatisfying ending can ruin an otherwise good story. See <u>End-of-Episode Hook</u> in <u>Pilot Components</u> (Chapter 3) and the following problems in *The Screenwriter's Troubleshooter*: <u>10 The Ending Doesn't Work</u>, <u>17 The Script Loses the Plot in the Third Act</u>, and <u>34 Too Many Questions Are Left Unanswered</u>.

Episodic: A story is episodic when it feels like a succession of disconnected episodes that could be easily removed or swapped without changing much in the story or its meaning. Poorly designed biopics often suffer from this when they try to tell the whole life of the main character instead of focusing on a main event or finding a different protagonist. Repetition in a story isn't necessarily an issue, it can even be rewarding. For example, in *Russian Doll*, *Groundhog Day*, *Edge of Tomorrow* or *Source Code*, the story repeats itself but this is part of a *high-concept* idea based on *dramatic irony* and *foreshadowing*. Each repetition adds something to the narrative, hence the story isn't seen as episodic. See <u>Plot</u> in <u>Series Design</u> (Chapter 3) as well as the following problem in *The Screenwriter's Troubleshooter*: <u>25 The Narrative Is Episodic or Repetitive</u>.

Evolution: See *Dramatic Evolution*.

Exception or Hybrid: When a story isn't *plot-led* (the main problem lies outside of the *protagonist*), *character-led* (the main problem lies within the protagonist) or *theme-led* (the main problem lies in society), it might be an exception or a hybrid. Exceptions often have no main problem, or have more than one. They can also be designed using *dramatic irony* (*Fleabag*, *The Departed*, *The Court Jester*, *Happy Valley*, *The Hand That Rocks the Cradle*), or with a non-linear or multi-stranded aspect (*The Secret in Their Eyes*, *This is Us*, *Citizen Kane*, *Mr. Robot*, *L.A. Confidential*, the first season of *True Detective*). A hybrid uses more than one story-type over the story. For example, *Edge of Tomorrow* starts as character-led (a coward needs to grow a backbone), then becomes a plot-led story (a former coward tries to save the world). *Breaking Bad* starts as plot-led (a dying man trying to protect his family), then gradually becomes character-led (a criminal with an ego problem needs to realise he's destroying the very thing he set out to protect: his family). See <u>A Quick Overview...</u> (How to Make The Most of This Book), <u>2.2 How to Identify Your Story-Type</u> and the following problems in *The Screenwriter's Troubleshooter*: <u>18 There Is No Clear Protagonist</u> and <u>19 The Script Feels Formulaic</u>.

Exploitation: See *Dramatic Irony*.

Exposition: Telling the audience what happened before the story started, or what has happened between scenes. It can be useful and even necessary, but it's the literary part of drama and when there is too much of it or when it's not handled properly, the audience gets bored. See <u>Set-Up / Story-World</u> in <u>Series Design</u> (Chapter 3) and the following problem in *The Screenwriter's Troubleshooter*: 30 The Script Contains Too Much Exposition.

F

Free Ad-Supported Streaming Television (FAST): Fairly recent and growing media content distribution model where users get free access to linear television channels via the internet and the revenue is generated by targeting advertisements to users as part of the viewing experience. Examples: Pluto TV (Paramount), Peacock (NCBU), Tubi (Fox), The Roku Channel (RokuTM).

Filler Episode: An episode of a series that does not advance the plot, develop the main characters, or derive from the original source material. It is often unrelated or tangential to the main story arc. It may be used to take up space or lengthen a story. Filler episodes are more common in anime fandoms, where filler more precisely refers to anything that isn't in the original source material. Filler episodes are usually considered to be of lower quality or interest than plot-related episodes. There are quite a few filler episodes towards the end of Season 10 of *The Walking Dead*, for example Episode 21, "Diverged".

First Act: See *Three-Act Structure (dramatic)*, *Three-Act Structure (logistical)*, A Quick Overview... (How to Make The Most of This Book) and the following problem in *The Screenwriter's Troubleshooter*: 03 The Story Takes Too Long to Start.

First Episode: See *Pilot / First Episode*.

Foreshadowing: see *Planting*.

Format: In TV series lingo, the format simply defines the length and broad genre of the episodes in a series. The two most common formats are the one-hour drama and the half-hour comedy. Format can also have a second meaning, which is the underlying concept or the underlying rights for the adaptation of a foreign series or IP. For example, in order to adapt *The Office* or *The Bridge* in the U.S., studios bought the format from the UK or Danish rights holders. Finally, some call a pitching bible a "format", keeping the term "bible" for the reference document compiled and updated during the production of a show. See *Bible*, Format in 1.2 Series Types as well as First Up and Have You Nailed Your Format? in 3 Project Development.

Formula, Formulaic: Any attempt at convincing creators that all stories should follow the same structure or paradigm in a prescriptive, dogmatic way. Usually based on a mandatory number of *logistical acts* or *sequences* of fixed duration, along with steps or plot points supposed to happen in every story at a specific page number: three-act, four-act, five-act, seven-act, eight sequences, fifteen beats, twenty-two steps, etc. The primary consequence of any formula or paradigm is that it reduces the writer's creative freedom and makes the story predictable—hence boring—for the audience. It's fine to use any paradigm that helps with the writing from a productivity point of view, but formulas are about story *format*: they should not be mistaken for *story structure*. See A Quick Overview... (How to Make The Most of This Book), 1.3 Conventional Series Design as well as the following problems in *The Screenwriter's Troubleshooter*: 19 The Script Feels Formulaic, 03 The Story Takes Too Long to Start, 17 The Script Loses the Plot in the Third Act, 38 The Plot Is Contrived and 10 The Ending Doesn't Work.

Fractal Aspect of Story Structure: A property of dramatic structure that means we can design both the whole story and its parts in the same way: If we use the *dramatic structure* to design the whole story around a main *dramatic action* or *evolution*, we define three *dramatic acts* (before, during and after a main dramatic action or evolution). We can use this same tool to design *dramatic acts, sequences, scenes, subplots, strands, storylines, episodes and seasons*. This is a key aspect of the *Story-Type Method* developed in *Screenwriting Unchained*. See A Quick Overview... (How to Make The Most of This Book), Storylines: Where Format Meets Structure (Section 1.3 in Chapter 1), 2.1 Underlying Story Structure and the following problems in *The Screenwriter's Troubleshooter*: 07 The Story Sags in the Middle as well as 19 The Script Feels Formulaic.

Franchise: In film, a franchise is often simply a character — or a group of characters — that returns in different instalments (James Bond, Indiana Jones, Mission Impossible, Bourne, John Wick, The Avengers). In TV, the franchise refers specifically to the series story engine: Whether it's a *procedural* or a *serial*, what makes it possible to generate an infinite number of episodes if the series is successful? A franchise often defines a common structure or template for each episode, which can be helped with the use of a *springboard*. See Franchise, Series Type and Story-Type in Series Design (Chapter 3).

G

Goal: What a *character* wants (*conscious goal*) in a story. Same as Objective. What the protagonist wants over the whole story is the main goal. See *Unconscious Need, Subgoal* and the following problem in *The Screenwriter's Troubleshooter*: 01 We Don't Care About the Protagonist.

H

Hero: A conceptually positive *character* who fights — and is often ready to sacrifice themselves — for the greater good. A hero isn't the same as a *protagonist*, as the latter doesn't need to be conceptually positive, they only need to experience more conflict than the other characters in the story. See A Quick Overview… (How to Make the Most of This Book) and the following problems in *The Screenwriter's Troubleshooter*: 37 The Protagonist Is a Conventional Hero and 26 The Villains or Antagonists Are Weak or Unconvincing.

Hierarchy of Needs: See *Maslow's Hierarchy of Needs*.

High-Concept: When a story features a striking and easily communicable plot or situation, it's high-concept. Executives and producers love high-concept projects because they are easy to pitch, both to potential partners and to the audience. A high-concept story summarised in a few lines can make someone want to read the script or watch the film/series. High-concept stories are often designed around *dramatic irony* (the audience knows something that at least one character isn't aware of). For example, an out-of-work actor pretends to be an actress in order to get a part and discovers what being a woman really means (*Tootsie*). An emotionally wounded woman shares her most intimate self-loathing thoughts with the audience, except the reason why she's broken, and the result is both moving and funny (first season of *Fleabag*). See Concept in Series Design (Chapter 3) and the following problem in *The Screenwriter's Troubleshooter*: 35 The Script Is Unnecessarily Complex.

Howdunit: When there is a *mystery* around how a crime was committed in a story. See *Whodunit, whydunit and whobeendun* as well as 2.4 Managing Information in Series.

Hybrid: See *Exception*.

I

Inciting Action: Sometimes in a story, we don't have an *inciting event* (see below) but an inciting action: a succession of events in the first *dramatic act* that trigger the *goal* of the *protagonist*. For example, in *Misery*, the car accident isn't an inciting event in itself because it only triggers the main situation: Writer Paul Sheldon being looked after by Nurse Annie. Paul also needs to realise that Annie is a nutter before his goal to escape and survive is triggered. We understand this before him, and this *dramatic irony* (we know that Annie is a nutter, he doesn't) shapes some of what would otherwise be a long first *dramatic act*, as we give him the unconscious goal of realising that he's in more trouble than he thinks. In *Occupied*, the whole of the first episode is an inciting action for the rest of the series. See the following problem in *The Screenwriter's Troubleshooter*: 03 The Story Takes Too Long to Start.

Inciting Event (or Inciting Incident): The event in a story that triggers the *protagonist*'s *goal*. There is not always an inciting event in a story. Sometimes, the protagonist is already trying to reach their goal when the story starts. In *character-led* stories (where the main problem lies within the protagonist), you can look for two inciting events: the *plot* inciting event, that triggers the *conscious goal* of the protagonist, and the *character* inciting event, that triggers their *unconscious need* to change. You can have either, both or none in such stories, but it's interesting to know what to look for. See A Quick Overview... (How to Make The Most of This Book) and the following problem in *The Screenwriter's Troubleshooter*: 03 The Story Takes Too Long to Start.

Identification: In a story, we're after emotional identification — the ability for the audience to feel empathy, to root for one or more *protagonists*. This is not the same as conceptual identification, feeling sympathy, which means that we like the characters or approve of what they are doing. See A Quick Overview... (How to Make The

Most of This Book), Storylines: Where Format Meets Structure (Section 1.3), 2.4 Managing Information in Series, Are You Striking the Right Balance Between Mystery and Suspense? (Section 3.1) and the following problems in *The Screenwriter's Troubleshooter*: 01 We Don't Care About the Protagonist, 02 We Don't Care About the Story and 18 There Is No Clear Protagonist.

Ironic Question: When a *dramatic irony* is set up in the story (the audience knows something that at least one character, the *victim*, isn't aware of), the audience wonders: How and when will the victim find out, and how will they react? This defines an ironic question, which is answered when the dramatic irony is resolved. It's important to be aware of such a question when a strong dramatic irony is exploited over most of the story, because it can be more important than the *dramatic question* (Who wants or needs what and why?). For example, in *Tootsie*, the ironic question is part of the climax of the film, as we want to know how the victims will react when they find out that Dorothy Michaels is a man, not a woman. In *Breaking Bad*, we want to know how Walter's wife, son and brother or sister-in-law will react when they find out that he's the criminal mastermind hunted by the DEA. See *Dramatic Irony*, A Quick Overview... (How to Make the Most of This Book) and the following problems in *The Screenwriter's Troubleshooter*: 10 The Ending Doesn't Work.

L

Limited Series: See *Mini-Series*.

Logistical Acts: See *Three-Act Structure (logistical)*.

Logistical Scene: See *Dramatic Scene*.

Logistical Three-Act Structure: See *Three-Act Structure (logistical)*.

M

Main Character: The most important *character*, the character whose life story we're telling, the most fascinating character in a story. Not necessarily the same as *protagonist*. We tell the story of a main character, and we identify emotionally with a protagonist. The protagonist is often the main character as well, but not always. For example, in the first season of *Stranger Things*, the protagonist is the group of characters looking for Will Byers, while the main character (and occasional co-protagonist) is Eleven. In many thriller, horror or monster movies/series, we identify with the protagonist, but the antagonist is the main character, the most fascinating character in the story: Nurse Annie in *Misery*, Villanelle in *Killing Eve*, the alien in *Alien*, the shark in *Jaws*... This is why the antagonist is often — but not always — referenced in the title of such films or series. See 3.3 Case Study: Killing Eve and the following problems in *The Screenwriter's Troubleshooter*: 28 The Protagonist Is Not Strong Enough, 01 We Don't Care About the Protagonist and 18 There Is No Clear Protagonist.

Main Dramatic Action: See *Dramatic Action*.

Main Dramatic Evolution: See *Dramatic Evolution*.

Managing Conflict: An essential part of *story structure* related to defining *who wants or needs what and why* in a story. The main tool used for managing conflict is what we call the basic chain of drama (protagonist—goal—obstacles—conflict—emotion): a *character* trying to reach a *conscious goal* or an *unconscious need*, meeting *obstacles*, which generates *conflict* and *emotion*. See A Quick Overview... (How to Make The Most of This Book) and the following problem in *The Screenwriter's Troubleshooter*: 20 The Conflict Is Artificial or Inconsequential.

Managing Information: An essential part of story structure related to defining *who knows what when* in a story. The main tools used for managing information are *mystery, surprise, dramatic irony* and *suspense*. See A Quick Overview... (How to Make The Most of This Book), 2.4 Managing Information in Series and the following problem in *The Screenwriter's Troubleshooter*: 04 The Story Is Linear, Feels Predictable.

Maslow's Hierarchy of Needs: A theory of human psychology defined by Abraham Maslow in 1943. It establishes five levels of human needs, from the most basic (physiology), shared by all human beings, to the most sophisticated (self-actualisation). In between, we find safety, love/belonging and esteem. Maslow proposes that lower levels need to be fulfilled before higher levels can be reached. This has many direct applications to screenwriting regarding audience, genre, story-type, identification and getting the project made. This is detailed in "Is Maslow Running the Show?" in the first chapter/module of *Screenwriting Unchained* (the book or the online course). See also *Maslow Factor (or M-Factor)*, 2.3 Use of Maslow in Series, 2.5 Hands-On: What's Your Type? (Part 2) and Maslow in Series Design (Chapter 3).

Maslow Factor (or M-Factor): An indicator used in the *Story-Type Method* to estimate the market appeal and potential audience of a feature film or TV series project / produced work. It's obtained by looking at the target audience, genre and story-type in relation to *Maslow's Hierarchy of Needs*, as well as the budget. The more those elements fit together, the higher the M-Factor. The more there is an inconsistency, the lower. The scale goes from one to five and it's always a subjective approximation, not an exact value. Still, a low M-Factor can help to identify issues that need to be addressed in order to increase the market appeal of a project and the chances of seeing it commissioned and produced. This is detailed in "Is Maslow Running the Show?" in the first chapter/module of *Screenwriting Unchained* (the book or the online course). See also *Maslow's Hierarchy of Needs*, 2.3 Use of Maslow in Series, 2.5 Hands-On: What's Your Type? (Part 2) and Maslow in Series Design (Chapter 3).

Mid-Act Climax: In some stories, it's not possible to have the same *goal* for the *protagonist* over the entirety of *dramatic Act 2*. In that case, we can shape the first half of dramatic Act 2 over a first goal, give an answer to the first *dramatic question* during a mid-act climax, then have the protagonist pursue another goal—logically connected to the first—during the second half of the story. This second *dramatic action* will be resolved towards the end of dramatic Act 2, in the *climax* of the story. For example, heist movies are often designed with a mid-act climax. The first half of the story is shaped around the preparation of the heist; the heist itself is a mid-act climax (success or failure of the operation); then a second half of the story deals with the logical consequences of the first half: escaping from the police, fighting over the loot, etc. There is a mid-act climax in *Life is Beautiful* and the pilot of *Occupied*. There is a mid-season climax in the second season of *The Walking Dead*. A mid-act climax isn't the same as a *midpoint*. See A Quick Overview… (How to Make The Most of This Book), Storylines: Where Format Meets Structure (1.3

in Chapter 1), 2.1 Underlying Story Structure and the following problem in *The Screenwriter's Troubleshooter*: 07 The Story Sags in the Middle.

Midpoint: Some say that every story should have a midpoint in the middle of a script, so around minute sixty in a two-hour film or minute thirty in a one-hour episode. This mandatory plot point is used in the *logistical Three-Act Structure*, but this is about story format, not story structure. In a good screenplay, something important happens every few minutes, so if you look for a midpoint, you'll find one, but it's unlikely to be significant from a structural point of view. The midpoint can be safely ignored if you find it confusing. Instead, consider using an optional *mid-act climax*, which is a more useful tool. See A Quick Overview... (How to Make The Most of This Book), 2.1 Underlying Story Structure and the following problem in *The Screenwriter's Troubleshooter*: 07 The Story Sags in the Middle.

Midstream or 3rd Episode Pilot: See *Pilot / First Episode*.

Mini-Series (or Limited Series): A mini-series or a limited series has a fixed number of episodes (more than one and less than thirteen, usually four to eight) and tells one story with a beginning, middle and end in a single season. The distinction between mini-series and limited series is blurred as often the terms are inter-changeable and many people use one or the other indifferently and mean the same thing. When a distinction is made, it's usually that a mini-series is closer to a few episodes of feature-length (two or three episodes of ninety minutes to three hours each), while a limited series is usually six to eight episodes of one hour. Examples: *Bodyguard, The Night Manager, Chernobyl, The Queen's Gambit, Mare of Easttown, Unbelievable*. See Mini-Series (or Limited Series) in 1.2 Series Types.

Mini-Series Series (or Anthological Limited Series): To create a mini-series series or anthological limited series, you take *limited series* (closed-ended stories at season level), and you make series of them. This is a fairly recent evolution, each mini-series bringing different characters and story world in each season, but each mini-series being linked thematically or by genre to the others. Examples: *True Detective, Fargo, American Horror Stories*. See Mini-Series Series (or Anthological Limited Series) in 1.2 Series Types.

Multi-Stranded Narrative: A story that doesn't have a main *plot* because it has no main *dramatic action* or *dramatic evolution*, but only *subplots* called *strands* connected to the same *theme*, which often leads to *theme-led* stories. However, many TV series have a strong multi-stranded element, yet are *plot-led* because all the *storylines* show *co-protagonists* facing the same external problem and trying to reach the same *goal*, as in *Stranger Things*, *The Walking Dead* or *Chernobyl*. See *Theme-Led Story*, A Quick Overview... (How to Make The Most of This Book), 2.1 Underlying Story Structure as well as the following problems in *The Screenwriter's Troubleshooter*: 19 The Script Feels Formulaic, 18 There Is No Clear Protagonist and 39 The Theme Overshadows the Story.

Mystery: A mystery is set up when the audience is given enough information to understand that there is something they don't know, but not enough to know what it is. It can provide a good hook to start a story, as the audience will want to find the answer, out of intellectual curiosity. It can even be used over a whole TV series, for example when a slow-burn mystery is resolved over a season. However, it can be off-putting if it lasts too long and can even work against the emotional involvement of the audience, unless other tools linked to *managing information* (*who knows what when* in the story) are used as well: *surprise, dramatic irony* and *suspense*. The worst kind of mystery is when the *protagonist* knows more than the audience over a long period of time about information that is needed in order to understand their actions, decisions or emotions, for example some elements of their *backstory*. This makes an emotional *identification* with such a protagonist difficult if not impossible. See *Open Mystery, Closed Mystery*, Surprise, Mystery, Dramatic Irony and Suspense in 2.4 Managing Information in Series, From Cerebral to Emotional: Where Do You Set the Dial? and Are You Striking the Right Balance
Between Mystery and Suspense? (both in Section 3.1).

Mythology: The part of a procedural series about an ongoing investigation or story development that carries over multiple episodes, occasionally leading to a serial-procedural hybrid. For example, *The X-Files* alternates procedural episodes and mythology episodes about the Syndicate, whose goal is to create a human-alien hybrid and hide the truth about extraterrestrials. See Serial-Procedural Hybrid in 1.2 Series Types.

N

Narrative: The form chosen to convey the *plot* in a story. See Plot in Series Design (Chapter 3) and the following problem in *The Screenwriter's Troubleshooter*: 25 The Narrative Is Episodic or Repetitive.

O

Objective: See *Goal*.

Obstacle: Something that stands in the way of a protagonist's *goal* in order to generate conflict. Obstacles can be internal (coming from the *protagonist*), external (coming from other characters or nature) or external with an internal origin (from other characters but triggered by the protagonist's actions, decisions or evolution). See A Quick Overview... (How to Make The Most of This Book) as well as the following problems in *The Screenwriter's Troubleshooter*: 01 We Don't Care About the Protagonist, 20 The Conflict Is Artificial or Inconsequential, 24 There Is No Clear Antagonist and 31 The Drama / Conflict Is Told But Not Shown.

On Spec: Writing a screenplay "on spec" means writing a script on your own time, without being hired or commissioned by a producer or a studio. It's a way for writers to showcase their talent and creativity, hoping to sell their script or get representation. Writing on spec can also help writers practice their craft and find their voice. Some examples of successful spec scripts include *Buffy the Vampire Slayer*, *The Hangover*, and *Juno*. While there was a huge market for spec scrips in the 90s, today a good spec script is more likely to get a writer some work than to get that spec project made. See First-Up in Project Development (Chapter 3).

Open-Ended Series: See *Serial*.

Open Mystery: A TV Industry specific term to define a series based on a main dramatic irony rather than a *whodunit*: We know who has done it, but the characters (including the protagonist) don't know. So there is no mystery for the audience, at least regarding the main dramatic action. The mystery is for the protagonist and how they will resolve the case. Classic examples are *Happy Valley* and *Columbo*. Many series are neither closed nor open and combine dramatic irony and mystery, for example, *Stranger Things* and *Homeland*. See *Mystery* and *Closed Mystery*, as well as 2.4 Managing Information in Series.

P

Paradigm: See *Formula, Formulaic*.

Pay-Off: See *Planting* below.

Pilot / First Episode: Technically, the difference between a pilot and a first episode screenplay is that you only have a pilot if the first episode is written before the others, and if once produced it leads to the series being commissioned. If your project is commissioned "*straight-to-series*", it means that the first episode is not produced as part of the decision-making process, hence you don't have a pilot, just a first episode. This distinction only matters before the series is produced. Once it's produced, there are only first episodes. In this book, as often in the real world, we use pilot and first episode indifferently, though we might favour pilot simply because it's shorter. A pilot can be a **premise pilot** if it establishes the story before the main problem, situation or concept is introduced. For example, the first episodes of *Sex Education*, *Stranger Things*, *Killing Eve*, *Occupied* or *Breaking Bad* are premise pilots (even if the latter starts with a teaser flashback). The first episodes of *The Office* or *Fleabag* are **midstream pilots** (or 3rd episode pilots), because the story has already started when we meet the characters for the first time. *The Walking Dead* illustrates a successful hybrid between these two approaches. See 3.2 Writing a Compelling Pilot / First Episode for more details and examples in 2.5 Case Study: *Stranger Things* and 3.3 Case Study: *Killing Eve*.

Pitch Deck: A pitch deck is a document that is used to sell a TV show idea to potential buyers, such as networks or studios. It usually includes a synopsis of the show and the story, information about the characters, some plot scenes, the target audience, production details, and the creative team behind the project. A pitch deck can also be accompanied by a pilot episode or a treatment (a document outlining the proposed show's storylines and characters). It's a more visual version of a bible. For example, the Duffer Bothers created a pitch deck for their project *Montauk* — which would become *Stranger Things* — that included a moodboard and references to other films and shows that inspired it. See Pitch Deck in Bible Components (Chapter 3).

Planting (or **foreshadowing**): Introducing an element in a story (object, *character*, *dialogue*, song) so that the audience either accepts it or understands its meaning later in the story, when that element pays off. Useful in order to add *causality* to the story, facilitate *visual storytelling* or avoid a *deus ex machina*. Planting can also be used to generate emotion. See Planting and Play-Off in the first chapter/module of *Screenwriting Unchained* (the book or the online course) as well as the following problems in *The Screenwriter's Troubleshooter*: 25 The Narrative Is Episodic or Repetitive, 31 The Drama / Conflict Is Told But Not Shown, 23 The Ending Is a Deus Ex Machina.

Plot: The sequence of connected events (not necessarily in chronological order) that happen in a story. One of the main components of story structure, along with *character* and *theme*. Not exactly the same as *Narrative*. See Plot in Series Design (Chapter 3) and the following problems in *The Screenwriter's Troubleshooter*: 17 The Script Loses the Plot in the Third Act, 25 The Narrative Is Episodic or Repetitive, 29 The Plot Is Slowed Down By Unconnected Storylines, 38 The Plot Is Contrived.

Plot Inciting Event: See *Inciting Event (or Inciting Incident)*.

Plot-Led Story: A story where the main problem lies outside the protagonist—in other characters or nature. See *Story-Type Method*, A Quick Overview... (How to Make The Most of This Book), 2.2 How to Identify Your Story-Type? as well as the following problem in *The Screenwriter's Troubleshooter*: 18 There Is No Clear Protagonist.

Premise: Idea or argument on which the story is based. See The Premise and Premise or Midstream Pilot? in 3.2 Writing a Compelling Pilot and the following problem in *The Screenwriter's Troubleshooter*: 40 The Premise Is an Artificial Excuse For Action.

Premise Pilot: see *Pilot / First Episode*.

Procedural (or Closed-Ended Series): A problem is introduced, investigated and solved within one closed-ended, self-contained episode. A complex case can run over a few episodes, but that's the exception, not the rule. They stem from four of the most common genres in TV series history: cop shows, medical shows, legal shows and private investigator shows. Examples: *CSI, Law and Order, House M.D., Magnum P.I., ER, Luther*. See Procedural (or Closed-Ended Series) in 1.2 Series Types.

Protagonist: The *character* who experiences the most *conflict* in the story, hence the character with whom we identify the most at an emotional level. The word comes from the Greek *protagonistes*, which means "the one who fights in the first row". A helpful image. It can be a group of characters — called *co-protagonists* — if they share the same goal (*conscious want* or *unconscious need*), as in *Stranger Things, The Walking Dead, Saving Private Ryan* or *Little Miss Sunshine*. If we can't identify with one or more protagonists, we're usually in trouble. See A Quick Overview... (How to Make The Most of This Book), Characters in Series Design (Chapter 3) as well as the following problems in *The Screenwriter's Troubleshooter*: 01 We Don't Care About the Protagonist, 18 There Is No Clear Protagonist, 28 The Protagonist Is Not Strong Enough and 37 The Protagonist Is a Conventional Hero.

R

Raising the Stakes: See *What's at Stake?*

Recap: A brief summary at the beginning of an episode or a season that recaps what happened in the previous one. More useful for seasons than episodes today. See Teaser, Recap and Coming Next in 1.3 Conventional Series Design.

Repetitive: See *Episodic*.

Resolution: See *Dramatic Irony*.

Runner: Minor *storyline* made of just a few beats (three to five in an episode). Such storylines are usually not designed using a *dramatic 3-Act structure*, as they are too short. See Storylines: Where Format Meets Structure in 1.3 Conventional Series Design and Jonathan's storyline in Story Weaving in *Stranger Things* at the end of 2.5 Case Study: *Stranger Things* for an example.

S

Scene: See *Dramatic Scene*.

Season Arc: See *Arc*.

Second Act: See *Three-Act Structure (dramatic)*, *Three-Act Structure (logistical)*, A Quick Overview… (How to Make The Most of This Book) and the following problem in *The Screenwriter's Troubleshooter*: 07 The Story Sags in the Middle.

Sequence: See *Dramatic Sequence*.

Serial (or Open-Ended Series): In serials, *storylines* are serialised over many open-ended episodes and seasons, until a finale. They tend to include a "soap" element, i.e. serialised storylines about relationships (family, friendship and/or sexual). The number of episodes is in theory infinite. Serials are currently the predominant form of modern TV series, and one that requires a different structural design compared to feature films, simply because of the number of storylines and the fact that they span over many episodes. While a procedural episode is built almost like a mini-plot-led movie, serials have a more complex design. See Serial (or Open-Ended Series) in 1.2 Series Types and the following problem in *The Screenwriter's Troubleshooter*: 29 The Plot Is Slowed Down By Unconnected Storylines.

Serial-Procedural Hybrid: A *procedural* that alternates "case of the week" episodes and "mythology" episodes (character relationships, thematic arc, ongoing investigation, etc.), such as *Dexter* or *The X Files*. Alternatively, it could be a *serial* that has a procedural element at season level, such as *Broadchurch*, *Stranger Things*, *24* or *The Wire*. It could also be a serial that has a procedural element in each episode, such as the sex case in *Sex Education*, or a procedural with strong serial elements, such as *Grey's Anatomy*. See Serial-Procedural Hybrid in 1.2 Series Types and the following problem in *The Screenwriter's Troubleshooter*: 29 The Plot Is Slowed Down By Unconnected Storylines.

Series Arc: See *Arc*.

Series Type: The overall form of a series, based on its structure at episode, season and series level: *procedural, serial, serial-procedural hybrid, limited series, sitcom, anthology,* etc… See 1.2 Series Types.

Set-Up: A set-up is the first step in *foreshadowing*, when we plant an element before it pays off later (see *Planting*), and in *dramatic irony*, when we give the audience information that at least one character (the victim) isn't aware of. In comedy, when we set up a gag, we misdirect the audience. Then with a *surprise* we turn the situation around (*pay-off* or punchline). The set-up can also be the *beginning* of the story (first ten to fifteen minutes in a feature film or first episode / pilot in a series), when we introduce the *characters*, the *story world* and *what's at stake.* See Beginning, 2.4 Managing Information in Series, Setup / Story World in Series Design (Chapter 3) and the following problems in *The Screenwriter's Troubleshooter*: 04 The Story Is Linear, Feels Predictable, 25 The Narrative Is Episodic or Repetitive and 03 The Story Takes Too Long to Start.

Showrunner: The writer (with an executive producer credit as showrunner isn't an official title) in charge of overseeing the development and production of a TV series. Often the creator of a series, if they are experienced enough. The showrunner can be a solo writer or a writing team. See First-Up in Project Development (Chapter 3).

Sitcom: a series that is a situation comedy, where the humour comes from situations and characterisation. See Sitcom in 1.2 Series Types.

Springboard: In TV, the springboard is the recurring element often present in procedurals and sitcoms that starts each and every episode. It's called "springboard" because it launches the story. This is one of the easiest ways to define a *franchise*. For example, the cop franchise for a cop show is very simple: a crime is committed, and the protagonist solves it over the next hour. See Franchise, Series Type and Story-Type in Series Design (Chapter 3).

Stakes: See *"What's at Stake?"*

Steadfast Character: A character who doesn't change or grow, who remains essentially the same from the beginning until the end of the story, which isn't necessarily a problem, for example in *sitcoms.* See *Character Evolution*, Sitcom in 1.2 Series Types and the following problem in *The Screenwriter's Troubleshooter*: 05 The Characters Are Flat, Two-Dimensional.

Story Format: See *Formula, Formulaic*.

Story Structure: A combination of *plot*, *character* and *theme*, as well as *managing conflict* (Who wants or needs what and why?) and *managing information* (Who knows what when?). Not to be confused with story format. See If You Want to Find Out More... to download a free sampler (first seventy pages) of *Screenwriting Unchained*, as this is developed in the *Introduction* and the first chapter: *The Story-Type Method, a New Framework for Developing Screenplays*. Alternatively, see A Quick Overview... (How to Make The Most of This Book), 2.1 Underlying Series Design and the following problems in *The Screenwriter's Troubleshooter*: 19 The Script Feels Formulaic and 35 The Script Is Unnecessarily Complex.

Story-Type, Story-Type Method: According to the *Story-Type Method*, there are three main story-types: *plot-led*, where the main problem lies outside the protagonist (in antagonistic characters or nature); *character-led*, where the main problem lies within the protagonist; *theme-led*, where the main problem lies in society and is usually not solvable, which leads to a *multi-stranded narrative*, a collection of storylines exploring the same *theme*. Not all stories have to fit one of the main story-types, which are mostly templates to stimulate creativity. Many stories are *hybrids* or *exceptions*. See If You Want to Find Out More... to download a free sampler (first seventy pages) of *Screenwriting Unchained*, as this is developed in the *Introduction* and the first chapter: *The Story-Type Method, a New Framework for Developing Screenplays*. Alternatively, see A Quick Overview... (How to Make The Most of This Book), 2.2 How to Identify Your Story-Type in Series and the following problems in *The Screenwriter's Troubleshooter*: 02 We Don't Care About the Story, 19 The Script Feels Formulaic and 35 The Script Is Unnecessarily Complex.

Story World: The story world defines the setting, the environment in which the story takes place. It can be anything from an everyday environment in a contemporary drama, to an entirely invented world in a fantasy or science-fiction story. Whether the story takes place in the real world or in an invented world, in the past or in the future, the rules of the story world should be consistent and make sense. See

Setup / Story World and World Building in Series Design (Chapter 3) as well as the following problem in *The Screenwriter's Troubleshooter*: 36 The Supernatural Element Is Too Vague.

Storyline: Part of a series that follows a *character* or group of characters sharing the same *goal, subgoal* or need. It's not a *subplot*, because there is not necessarily a main *plot*, and it's not a *strand* either, because some or all of the storylines could be part of the same main plot, as in *Stranger Things* or *The Walking Dead*. We call them strands in a multi-stranded narrative where there is no main plot, hence no subplots. In practice, the terms strands, subplots and storylines are often used indifferently and mean the same thing: a sub-story within the story. Thanks to the fractal aspect of story structure, storylines can be designed in the same way as scenes, episodes, seasons or feature films, using the d*ramatic three-act structure*. See *Strands*, A Quick Overview... (How to Make The Most of This Book), Storylines: Where Format Meets Structure (1.3 in Chapter 1), 2.1 Underlying Story Structure and the following problem in *The Screenwriter's Troubleshooter*: 29 The Plot Is Slowed Down By Unconnected Storylines.

Straight-to-Series: When a series (all the episodes in a season) is commissioned upfront, without testing through a pilot first. See *Pilot / First Episode*, First Up in 3 Project Development and 3.2 Writing a Compelling Pilot / First Episode.

Strand: Each individual *storyline* in a *multi-stranded narrative* is a strand. It's similar to a *subplot* in a conventional *narrative*, but as there is no main plot (no main *dramatic action* or *evolution*), there can't be subplots, so they are called strands and are usually connected to the same theme. In TV series, strands are called *storylines*, but it doesn't mean there is no main plot. See *Storyline*, Storylines: Where Format Meets Structure (1.3 in Chapter 1), A Quick Overview... (How to Make The Most of This Book), 2.1 Underlying Story Structure and the following problem in *The Screenwriter's Troubleshooter*: 29 The Plot Is Slowed Down By Unconnected Storylines.

Structure: see *Story Structure*.

Subgoal: A way for the *protagonist* to reach the *goal*. It often defines a *dramatic sequence*, which is a succession of scenes connected to the same *dramatic action*. See Storylines: Where Format Meets Structure in 1.3 Conventional Series Design, A Quick Overview... (How to Make The Most of This Book) and the following problems in *The Screenwriter's Troubleshooter*: 25 The Narrative Is Episodic or Repetitive and 07 The Story Sags in the Middle.

Sub-Subgoal: A way for the *protagonist* to reach the *subgoal*. It often defines a *dramatic scene*, which is a succession of beats connected to the same *dramatic action*. See *Subgoal*, Storylines: Where Format Meets Structure (3.1 in Chapter 1), A Quick Overview... (How to Make The Most of This Book) and the following problem in *The Screenwriter's Troubleshooter*: 16 The Scenes Are Aimless, There Is No Dramatic Conflict.

Subplot: A *storyline* exploring a problem less important than the problem explored in the main plot (*main dramatic action* or *evolution*) but connected to it. Usually, we don't have more than two or three subplots in a story, unless we're dealing with a multi-stranded narrative or a TV series. Subplots are often used to explore a *theme* (what the story is about). In a *plot-led story*, there is often a *character-led* subplot, a smaller internal problem that the protagonist needs to resolve. This subplot usually defines a need for the protagonist to grow. When there is no main plot, for example in a *multi-stranded narrative*, subplots are called *strands*. In TV Series, they are called *storylines*. See Storylines: Where Format Meets Structure in 1.3 Conventional Series Design, 2.1 Underlying Story Structure and the following problem in *The Screenwriter's Troubleshooter*: 29 The Plot Is Slowed Down By Unconnected Storylines.

Surprise (or **Twist**): A piece of information that the audience doesn't expect. Surprise is one of the tools linked to *managing information* (Who knows what when?) in a story, along with *mystery*, *dramatic irony* and *suspense*. See A Quick Overview... (How to Make The Most of This Book), Surprise, Mystery, Dramatic Irony and Suspense in 2.4 Managing Information in Series and the following problem in *The Screenwriter's Troubleshooter*: 04 The Story Is Linear, Feels Predictable.

Suspense: To generate suspense, the audience needs to know where danger — physical, emotional or psychological — is coming from. Hitchcock, the "Master of Suspense", uses the following situation to explain it: If two characters are talking about the weather, there is no suspense, but if you then show the audience that there is a bomb under the table, suddenly, we want to yell at the characters "Get out!". In this example, Hitchcock uses *dramatic irony* (telling the audience something, in this case about a danger, that at least one character is unaware of) to generate suspense. However, we can have suspense without dramatic irony. As long as the audience knows where the threat comes from, there is suspense, even if all the characters are aware of the danger. Suspense is one of the tools linked to *managing information*, along with *mystery, surprise* and *dramatic irony*. See A Quick Overview... (How to Make The Most of This Book), Surprise, Mystery, Dramatic Irony and Suspense in 2.4 Managing Information in Series and the following problems in *The Screenwriter's Troubleshooter*: 04 The Story Is Linear, Feels Predictable and 10 The Ending Doesn't Work.

T

Teaser: A short scene or sequence (usually no longer than three to five minutes) that teases the audience at the beginning of a series episode, usually ending with a cliffhanger or a surprise, before the opening credits. It can also be a flash-back or a flash-forward that adds context or sets up a mystery or a dramatic irony. For example, many episodes of *The Crown* start with a flash-back or flash-forward teaser that adds historical context. Each episode of *The Walking Dead* starts with a teaser. Each episode of *Sex Education* starts with a teaser that introduces the sex case of the episode (the procedural aspect of the series). See *Teaser Flashback*, Teaser, Recap and Coming Next in 1.3 Conventional Series Design and Teaser or 3-minute Hook in Pilot Components (Chapter 3).

Teaser Flashback: When we need to take some time to introduce our characters or the story world, it might be helpful to start the narrative (film, episode) in the middle or even towards the end of the dramatic action, before going back to the beginning. This teaser could show an exciting event, a conflictual or desperate situation or reveal a puzzling piece of information that will not only grab the attention of the audience but also set up interesting questions, often using *mystery* or *dramatic irony*. That way, when we go back to the beginning of the story, not only is the audience hooked, but they can watch the unfolding events with the additional knowledge, curiosity or anticipation of conflict to come brought by the teaser. Frequently used in TV series, for example in *The Walking Dead*, *Breaking Bad*, *The Queen's Gambit* or *Occupied*. Just be careful not to provide an answer to the *dramatic question* in the teaser, as this could undermine the emotional involvement of the audience during the rest of the story. For this reason, if the teaser comes from the end of the story, it's usually a good idea to choose a moment before or during the *climax* (*Run All Night*) rather than after it (*John Wick*). See Teaser and Teaser, Recap and Coming Next in 1.3 Conventional Series Design as well as the following problems in *The Screenwriter's Troubleshooter*: 01 We Don't Care About the Protagonist, 03 The Story Takes Too Long to Start and 30 The Script Contains Too Much Exposition.

Time-Lock: We have a time-lock when there is a limited amount of time for the *protagonist* to reach a *goal*. This increases the tension and raises the stakes. A classic time-lock is a bomb about to blow-up in an action movie, but you can use more subtle time-locks, for example if you give your protagonist only *Two Days, One Night* to get her job back, or 24 hours to stop a terrorist plot — each episode showing one hour in real time — in the TV series *24*. See the following problems in *The Screenwriter's Troubleshooter*: 07 The Story Sags in the Middle and 10 The Ending Doesn't Work.

Thematic Acts: See *Theme-Led Story*.

Theme: What the story is about. One of the essential elements of story structure, along with *character* and *plot*. See *Theme-Led Story* below, A Quick Overview... (How to Make The Most of This Book), Theme in Series Design (Chapter 3) and the following problem in *The Screenwriter's Troubleshooter*: 39 The Theme Overshadows the Story.

Theme-Led Story: A *multi-stranded narrative* where the main problem usually lies in society. This problem could be spiritual or philosophical. Often, it can't be resolved. In a theme-led story, there isn't one *protagonist* over the whole story, as there isn't one *character*—or group of characters—experiencing more conflict than the others. There is no main *plot* as there is no main *dramatic action* or *evolution*. There can't be *subplots* when there is no main plot, so we call each storyline a *strand*. In a theme-led story, we don't have three *dramatic acts* as there is no main dramatic action or evolution, but we have three thematic acts: Act 1, before the audience understands what the theme is; Act 2, while the theme is explored; Act 3, the consequences of this exploration. Examples: *Game of Thrones, Deadwood, Occupied, Big Little Lies, Succession, Crash, Magnolia, Dunkirk, Parenthood.* Some theme-led stories, such as *Cloud Atlas*, are also non-linear. See *Story-Type Method,* A Quick Overview... (How to Make The Most of This Book), 2.2 How to Identify Your Story-Type and the following problems in *The Screenwriter's Troubleshooter*: 19 The Script Feels Formulaic, 18 There Is No Clear Protagonist and 39 The Theme Overshadows the Story.

Third Act: See *Three-Act Structure (dramatic), Three-Act Structure (logistical)* and the following problem in *The Screenwriter's Troubleshooter*: 17 The Script Loses the Plot in the Third Act.

Three-Act Structure (dramatic): A story is structured in three *dramatic acts* when it's designed around a main *dramatic action* or a main *dramatic evolution.* In this case, we have three dramatic acts because we have what happens before the audience understands what the *protagonist* wants or needs (dramatic Act 1); then we have a dramatic Act 2 that shows what happens while the protagonist tries to reach their *goal (conscious want* or *unconscious need).* This triggers the *dramatic question*: Will the protagonist reach their goal? Towards the end of this dramatic Act 2, during the *climax,* we provide an answer to this dramatic question: Yes, the protagonist reaches the goal or No, the protagonist fails. After the climax, once the protagonist has succeeded or failed and given up, we enter dramatic Act 3, which shows the consequences of the dramatic action or evolution in the story world. Before, during and after a main dramatic action or evolution: This is what defines a dramatic 3-Act structure. These dramatic acts have no fixed length, though Act 1 tends to be fairly short (usually around five to fifteen minutes) and Act 3 very short, as once the main action or evolution is over our attention drops. Act 2 usually covers most of the story and is divided into *dramatic sequences,* often designed around *subgoals,* which are ways for the protagonist to reach the goal. Not all stories are designed this way, for example *theme-led stories, hybrids* or *exceptions* don't use the 3-Act structure at story level, but all stories can use the dramatic 3-Act structure to design their parts: dramatic *scenes,* sequences, acts, *subplots, strands, storylines,* episodes and seasons, thanks to the *fractal aspect of story structure.* This is detailed in

Screenwriting Unchained, using many info-graphs and examples. Alternatively, see A Quick Overview... (How to Make The Most of This Book), 2.2 How to Identify Your Story-Type? as well as 2.1 Underlying Story Structure and the following problems in *The Screenwriter's Troubleshooter*: 01 We Don't Care About the Protagonist, 19 The Script Feels Formulaic, 02 We Don't Care About the Story and 16 The Scenes Are Aimless, There Is No Dramatic Conflict.

Three-Act Structure (logistical): A story formatted following a logistical 3-Act structure is divided into three acts according to an arbitrary number of pages or minutes. Act I (beginning) covers twenty-five percent of the story, Act II (middle) fifty percent, Act III (end) twenty-five percent. The second act is divided in two equal parts by a *midpoint* in the middle of the story. So, in a two-hour feature film, according to the logistical 3-Act paradigm, Act I is thirty minutes long, Act II sixty minutes long (two halves of thirty minutes each), and Act III is thirty minutes long. This division in three logistical acts has no real justification and is about format, not structure. Usually, a dramatic structure can be found underneath if the story is well-designed. For example, a Shakespeare play is divided into five logistical acts, but is designed in three dramatic acts. A one-hour procedural episode in a TV series is formatted in five acts because of four commercial breaks, but is designed in three dramatic acts. A 90-minute TV movie is formatted in seven logistical acts because of six commercial breaks, but is designed in three dramatic acts. Understanding this difference between logistical and dramatic acts is crucial. Talented writers might be using logistical acts consciously, but they will be using dramatic acts unconsciously, not only to design the whole story, but also its parts. This is detailed in *Screenwriting Unchained — the book or the online course* — using many info-graphs and examples. Alternatively, see *Three-Act Structure (dramatic)*, A Quick Overview... (How to Make The Most of This Book), 2.2 How to Identify Your Story-Type as well as the following problems in *The Screenwriter's Troubleshooter*: 19 The Script Feels Formulaic, 02 We Don't Care About the Story, 03 The Story Takes Too Long to Start, 07 The Story Sags in the Middle and 17 The Script Loses the Plot in the Third Act.

Twist: See *Surprise* and *Encore Twist*.

U

Unconscious Need: When the character needs to change, to move on, we call this their unconscious need. The *conscious want* of a protagonist (goal) defines the *dramatic action*, while the unconscious need defines the *dramatic evolution*. In *character-led stories, what's at stake* is the unconscious need of the protagonist. In *plot-led stories*, it's the conscious want, although there is often an unconscious need as well that defines a *character-led subplot*. See A Quick Overview... (How to Make The Most of This Book), 2.2 How to Identify Your Story-Type as well as the following problems in *The Screenwriter's Troubleshooter*: 05 The Characters Are Flat, Two-Dimensional.

V

Victim: See *Dramatic Irony*.

Villain: Conceptually negative *character* who opposes a conceptually positive *protagonist (hero)*. A Villain isn't the same as an *Antagonist*, and not all stories need a villain. In fact, most modern ones don't. See Characters in Series: How Are They Different? in Overarching Questions & Aims (Section 3.1 in Chapter 3) and the following problems in *The Screenwriter's Troubleshooter*: 26 The Villains or Antagonists Are Weak or Unconvincing and 37 The Protagonist Is a Conventional Hero.

Visual Storytelling: Essential tool used to convey the story visually as opposed to using dialogue (show rather than tell). This can usually be achieved using *foreshadowing*. Visual storytelling can help your story to cross borders and can contribute to generating emotion. This is explored in Visual Storytelling / Planting and Pay-off in the second chapter of *Screenwriting Unchained*. See Are You Thinking Global From the Get Go? in 3.1 Creating an Irresistible Bible as well as the following problems in *The Screenwriter's Troubleshooter*: 11 The Screenplay Is Written Like a Novel, 31 The Drama / Conflict Is Told But Not Shown and 09 The Screenplay Is Too Dry or Not Visual Enough.

W

Web Series: A low budget or no-budget series of short episodes released on the web, usually on a YouTube channel. They are often used as a calling card to get a higher-budget, more complex version commissioned and produced by a network or a streamer. See <u>Web Series</u> in <u>1.2 Series Types</u>.

What's at Stake? The question most often asked by development execs or producers when they don't care about a story. It means "Why should we want to know what's going to happen next?" If this isn't clear, the story starts with a significant handicap. To identify what's at stake in a story, answer the following question: What will happen if the *protagonist* fails to solve the main problem in the story? Or, more generally, what happens if the main problem in the story isn't solved. Make sure this defines something that makes us feel sad, anxious or terrified, or any negative feeling you can come up with. It should be something that we don't want to see happen to the *characters*. For example, in *Silver Linings Playbook*, if Pat doesn't change, he goes back to jail or to hospital and he doesn't get to spend the rest of his life with Tiffany. In *The Walking Dead*, *Squid Game*, *Gravity* or *Misery*, the protagonist's life is at stake. In the first season of *Stranger Things*, it's Will Byers' life as well as the Hawkins community as a whole that's at stake. In order to increase or renew the interest of the audience in the story, it can be useful to keep raising the stakes: make it so that the consequences of the protagonist failing get even worse as the story progresses. You can raise the stakes over the whole story, but also over a storyline, dramatic sequence or scene, depending on what the *subgoal* or *sub-subgoal* is. See <u>Storylines: Where Format Meets Structure</u> (1.3 in Chapter 1), <u>Goals for the Pilot</u> in <u>3.2 Writing a Compelling Pilot</u> and the following problem in *The Screenwriter's Troubleshooter*: <u>02 We Don't Care About the Story</u>.

Whobeendun: Term made up in this book that stands for "Who [has] been done?". Derived from w*hodunit*, it's used when there is a mystery around who the victim of a crime is. For example, in the first season of *Big Little Lies*, we have both a whodunit (we don't know who has committed the murder) and a whobeendun (we don't know the victim's identity either). See *Whodunit, howdunit and whydunit* as well as 2.4 Managing Information in Series.

Whodunit (or closed mystery): Stands for "Who [has] done it?" and is used to describe a story in which there is a *mystery* around the murderer's identity, usually only revealed at the end in a final *surprise*. The mystery is closed because the audience doesn't know who the murderer is (in opposition to an *open mystery*, where the audience knows thanks to the use of *dramatic irony*). Classic murder mysteries such as Agatha Christie's novels are whodunits. So are most Sherlock Holmes novels (and episodes of the *Sherlock* TV series). Recent whodunits, such as *Knives Out*, have successfully renewed the genre, using a wider diversity of tools to manage information, including dramatic irony. See *closed mystery, whydunit, howdunit,* and *whobeendun* as well as 2.4 Managing Information in Series for more examples.

Whydunit: Term that stands for "Why [have they] done it?". Derived from *Whodunit*, it describes a story featuring a *mystery* around the reason why a crime was committed, the motivation of the murderer. For example, the sci-fi thriller *Minority Report* is a whydunit where the protagonist is accused of being about to commit a crime — in a future where murders can be predicted — yet has no idea of what his motivation could be as he doesn't even know the victim, so he spends the whole film investigating this in order to avoid a life sentence. See *Whodunit, howdunit and whobeendun* as well as 2.4 Managing Information in Series.

World Building: The action of building a fictional world for a series through research if the story takes place in the real world or through invention if the story takes place in a fantasy or sci-fi world. It's a key part of series design. See Set-Up / Story World and World Building in Series Design (Chapter 3).

Worst Point: A plot point in conventional series design, especially procedurals, where the protagonist reaches an apparent dead-end. It's the equivalent to the "All is lost" prescriptive beat in the *Save the Cat* approach to feature film writing. Not at all necessary in modern series writing, even if it usually makes sense to subject the protagonist to an increasing amount of conflict as the episode or film progresses. See Worst Point in Conventional Series Design (Chapter 1).

Writers' Room: Space where writers of a TV series gather to pitch, brainstorm, and workshop episode ideas together. It is a collaborative model for writing shows that is common in the U.S. TV industry and is gathering momentum in Europe and elsewhere. The writers' room is usually led by the *showrunner* or the executive producer of the series, a senior writer — often the *creator* of the series — who has the final say on creative decisions. The writers' room can also include co-executive producers, supervising producers, producers, co-producers, and staff writers, who have different levels of experience and responsibility, following a strict and well-established hierarchy. Some examples of TV shows that used the writer's room model include *The X-Files*, *The Daily Show*, *Breaking Bad*, and *Game of Thrones*. See First-Up in Project Development (Chapter 3).

Recommended Reading and Watching

Television Development by Bob Levy, Focal Press

Excellent overview of the U.S. TV development process, from a producer's point of view. Very clear and detailed explanation of the industry, the processes and the culture.

TV Writing On Demand by Neil Landau, Focal Press

Useful tips on the craft, lots of interviews, thoroughly documented, especially relevant for streaming.

Writing the TV Series Drama by Pamela Douglas, Michael Wiese Productions (San Francisco)

Great overview of the TV development process from a writer's point of view. Primarily from a U.S. perspective, although one chapter gives a view on fifteen other countries.

The TV Showrunner's Roadmap by Neil Landau, Focal Press

Insightful interviews with some of the most talented and successful showrunners.

Writing the Pilot – Creating the Series by William Rabkin, Moon & Sun & Whiskey Inc.

Excellent volume dedicated to the writing of a TV series, along with a brief history of U.S. Television.

Screenwriting Unchained by Emmanuel Oberg, Screenplay Unlimited Publishing (London), 2016

Introduction to the Story-Type Method, #1 bestseller in TV Screenwriting on Amazon U.S. and in many other countries. Recommended to learn more about the tools and principles that apply to any kind of screenwriting, including TV series. Every book in the Story-Type Method collection builds on the advanced techniques detailed in this first volume.

The Screenwriter's Troubleshooter by Emmanuel Oberg, Screenplay Unlimited Publishing (London), 2019

Tactical handbook for anyone involved in the script development process for Film, TV and streaming. #1 bestseller in TV Screenwriting on Amazon U.S. and in many other countries.

Showrunners: The Art of Running a TV Show by Des Doyle, available on DVD as well as on Amazon Prime Video and Apple TV+.

First ever feature-length documentary to explore the world of U.S. television showrunners and the creative forces they employ. Very entertaining and insightful overview of the TV creative process, featuring interviews with some of the best showrunners in the business.

The Children of Tendu by Jose and Javi, available on iTunes / Apple Podcasts

Lively podcast where Javier Grillo-Marxuach (Emmy Award-winning writer/producer on *Lost* and creator of *The Middleman*) and Jose Molina (writer/producer on *Sleepy Hollow*, *Firefly*, *Castle* and *Law & Order: SVU*) share their hard-earned experiences, giving practical, straight-shooting advice on breaking into television and staying there! Episode 4 — The Writers' Room: How do I Work This? is particularly insightful.

If You Want to Find Out More...

If you enjoyed
WRITING A SUCCESSFUL TV SERIES

You'll LOVE its companion course that includes detailed case studies of hit shows such as *Stranger Things, Sex Education, Big Little Lies* as well as *Occupied, Mr. Robot, Happy Valley* and *Fleabag*.

Use discount code **WSTSBK10** at checkout to receive an extra **10% OFF** our online courses at www.screenplayunlimited.com/online-courses/

To access free resources — including an interactive story tool, bonus content and samplers of our books — please register at www.screenplayunlimited.com/register

Made in the USA
Las Vegas, NV
12 April 2024